POWDER WARS

Graham Johnson has been a *Sunday Mirror* journalist since 1996 and the paper's Investigations Editor since 1999. He has covered a wide range of stories, including drug dealing in Britain, people smuggling in Europe, child slavery in India and Pakistan, and war in the Balkans. He currently lives in London.

POWDER WARS

GRAHAM JOHNSON

THE SUPERGRASS WHO BROUGHT DOWN
BRITAIN'S BIGGEST DRUG DEALERS

MAINSTREAM
PUBLISHING

EDINBURGH AND LONDON

For Emma, Sonny and Raya

Reprinted 2007
This edition, 2005

Copyright © Graham Johnson, 2004
All rights reserved
The moral right of the author has been asserted

First published in Great Britain in 2004 by
MAINSTREAM PUBLISHING COMPANY (EDINBURGH) LTD
7 Albany Street
Edinburgh EH1 3UG

ISBN 978 1 84018 925 4

Reprinted 2004 (twice), 2005

A catalogue record for this book is available from the British Library

Typeset in Bembo and Gill Sans

Printed in Great Britain by
Cox & Wyman Ltd

Contents

1. The Early Days   7
2. The Oslo   21
3. The Hole in the Wall Gang   29
4. Expansion   38
5. Den for Meets   50
6. The Scrapman's Gang   63
7. Caesar's Palace   81
8. Cortina Crew   89
9. John Haase   99
10. Straight-goer   113
11. The Informant   125
12. Curtis Warren   133
13. The First Consignment   140
14. The Key   147
15. The Bust   153
16. The Trial   159
17. The Intervening Years   165

18. Haase Backgrounder   171
19. Freed   177
20. The Great Escape   191
21. Big Brother Security   200
22. The In   208
23. Round-the-Clock Rackets   214
24. Protection and Extortion   221
25. Drugs   230
26. Gun Deal   235
27. The Case   243
28. The Deal   253
29. The End   260
Epilogue: Life in Hiding   263

I

The Early Days

Paul Grimes was born on 26 May 1950 in a post-war prefab on a Liverpool street that had been flattened by Hitler's bombers ten years earlier. At the age of ten, he was introduced to organised crime by his grandmother, Harriet Mellor. Fresh faced but streetwise, Paul was recruited as a decoy into a notorious firm of professional shoplifters run by his grandma.

Foul-mouthed Harriet was a 16-stone gang boss who drank Scotch neat and was known on the street as 'The Fagin'. She sat at the head of three prominent Liverpool crime families: the Grimes, the Mellors and the Moorcrofts. Amongst their inter-married members were some of the most notorious and prolific gangsters in Britain.

Billy Grimwood was a rising star on the national crime scene and a close associate of the London-based Kray twins and their clubland enforcer Johnny Nash. He was a criminal all-rounder: armed robber, hijacker, protection racketeer, killer, warehouse raider and safe-cracker.

Grimwood had married into Harriet's clan after falling for her daughter Joan, an expert 'carrier outer' in the family's shoplifting crew. Ambitious and smart, Grimwood soon became Harriet's underboss. The fearlessly violent six-footer had graduated from petty crime (in 1954 he was jailed for stealing a £90 tape-recorder from an office) to hard-core safe-blower and nightclub impresario.

In June 1960, the same month in which his nephew, Paul Grimes, was being introduced to the family business on a shoplifting spree, the 29-year-old Grimwood was sentenced to three years in jail for hiding three ounces of gelignite in the coal-bunker of his two-up, two-down terraced house. The sticks of explosive were leftovers from the gang's most recent safe-blowing operations. However, for Grimwood, doing time was no big deal. Being sent to jail was a holiday, especially from his wife, who regularly laced his evening meals with rat poison in the hope that he would die. Long-suffering Joan rightly suspected her husband was a serial adulterer.

In Liverpool's Walton Prison, Grimwood was already a living legend. Amongst the cons it was widely believed that he was more powerful than the governor. Grimwood controlled the allocation of the best cells and privileged jobs. During his sentence he smuggled in a television set (stolen from Liverpool docks) and opened up a gangsters' cocktail bar in a basement cell. He fixed it for cons like armed robber and contract killer Charlie Seiga to join him in his exclusively luxurious I wing. In his book *Killer*, Charlie Seiga recalled:

> I had only been there a few days when a con swaggered into my cell as though he owned the place: 'Get your gear packed, you're coming with me.'
>
> He then introduced himself as Billy Grimwood. I was taken over to I wing. I could see at once that Billy Grimwood had everything under control; all the cream of the top villains were there. I was introduced to a lot of the cons and offered a drink of anything I wanted. I couldn't believe how it was on I wing – it was like a little nightclub. Most of the cons were selected by Billy. Our cells were left mostly unlocked and we had a big TV. Remember this was 1963.

Billy Grimwood was a real hard-case. He never trained like most cons do; he was just a naturally fit person. When fighting, he was so fast no one stood a chance with him, but he was dead fair in his ways. I have seen men who have tried to take him out, but they never could. He was the hardest fella I had ever come across at the time.

When he wasn't in jail, the sharp-suited Grimwood acted as a mentor to Paul, grooming his nephew for life as a one-man crimewave. In later life, Paul would repay the honour by acting as his minder and bodyguard.

Grimwood's safe-cracking team consisted of Paul Grimes' father, Harold, and his uncles, Ronnie and Ritchie Mellor. Harold Grimes had married Harriet's second daughter Doreen and, by default, into a life of villainy. He regularly escaped the clutches of the police investigating the growing trend of high-value safe burglaries by jumping ship onto a whaler bound for the North Atlantic, sometimes for two years at a time. Clad in rain-lashed oilskins and a sou'wester, he laid low, safe in the knowledge that the long arm of the law did not stretch as far as the fog-saturated ice caps of the Arctic.

Billy Grimwood and Harold Grimes made criminal history in 1969 when they stole £140,000 by tunnelling inside a Liverpool city-centre bank. Grimwood and Grimes were the first British criminals to use thermal lances to burrow through a strong-room door. The infamous 'Water Street Job' was masterminded by Grimwood and underworld hombre Tommy 'Tacker' Comerford, who would later go on, according to Customs and Excise, to become Britain's first ever large-scale drug baron.

Though the gang spent two days over the August bank holiday tunnelling into the bank from a nearby bakery, Grimwood and Grimes insisted that they only be brought in for the pièce de résistance near the end of the job – the burning through the metal doors. They were probably the only criminals in Britain able to operate the burners effectively and their bargaining power paid off. Grimwood and Grimes were the only two members of the gang to evade capture.

Although Grimwood was pulled in for a grilling, he did not fold under questioning. Comerford received ten years in jail for his part in the heist, which sparked a wave of copycat raids in the capital and elsewhere. The judge commented: 'This was top-level, professional organised crime, carried out with the most modern sophisticated equipment and with all the planning and precision of a commando raid.' Scores as lucrative as the Water Street Job did not happen every day.

On routine safe-cracking raids, the backbone of the gang was Ritchie and Ronnie Mellor, who, despite being Harriet's beloved sons, ceded day-to-day operational control to Grimwood. Former boxer Ritchie Mellor was known in the underworld as 'Dick the Stick' on account of his dexterity at opening doors and windows with a short crowbar he concealed up his sleeve.

Dick the Stick would later perfect his breaking-and-entering skills as leader of the 'Hole in the Wall' gang – a fast-moving gang of warehouse raiders he set up with nephew Paul Grimes. Again, on the instructions of Grandma Harriet, Dick mentored Paul and recruited him regularly into his criminal enterprises.

His brother Ronnie Mellor was a psychotic shooter-merchant and compulsive commercial burglar. He was thoroughly untrustworthy and was held in contempt, though not to his face, by many of his underworld peers. One former safe-cracker partner recalled: 'If honour and trust were the measure of a man, there would be difficulty finding Ronnie Mellor under a microscope.' Utterly faithless, Ronnie was caught burgling his best pal's house after he had suggested the man go out for a drink.

Despite his shortcomings, Ronnie's wanton brutality had allowed him to gain control and run his own 'team' independently of the family for a while. He appointed his son, also named Ronnie, as his right-hand man. 'Young' Ronnie Mellor – dubbed 'Johnny

POWDER WARS

One Eye' by gang members because of a debilitating cataract in his left eye – grew up with Paul Grimes and was able to pass on his extensive knowledge of crime. He taught him the value of savage violence as a tool for doing business and later invited Paul to be an accomplice on an underworld hit.

In 1990, Ronnie was jailed for ten years after masterminding a £135,000 cocaine importation from Amsterdam. On his release, he moved into kidnapping and 'taxing' drug dealers. He was later jailed for three years.

The Moorcroft family married into Harriet's firm following the union of a capacious thief and home-breaker called 'Big' Christy Moorcroft and her third daughter Roseline, a shoplifter. Their son, 'Young' Christy Moorcroft, followed in their footsteps and was a criminal associate of his cousin Paul Grimes.

Finally, there was Snowball, a younger member of the family, less equipped to deal with violence, but who nevertheless grew up to be a professional thief, armed robber and drug dealer. Of them all, Snowball was closest to Paul Grimes and predictably the pair enjoyed a long-lasting partnership-in-crime.

As for brothers, sisters, in-laws, cousins – all were mixed up in the rackets in some way: whether it was fencing stolen jewellery, card-marking a safe full of cash ready for the taking or stashing a lorry load of swag 'zapped' from Liverpool's booming docks. They may not have been an Italian crime family but Harriet's crew was nevertheless a self-contained, highly organised crime gang turning over tens of thousands of pounds a year at a time when the average wage was £10 a week and the average post-war worker relied on hire purchase to buy a Hoover.

It was an ideal breeding ground for a wannabe gangster. By the age of 12, Paul Grimes was a veteran of some 20 organised shoplifting sprees, meticulously masterminded by his grandmother Harriet. Paul was learning fast that crime paid if the criminal committing it paid special attention to the planning, preparation and execution of the crime in hand.

PAUL: She was not like a normal grandmother, Harriet, in all fairness. She ran her shoplifting routine like a professional team, as ruthlessly as any of the safe-cracking and armed robbery gangs that were all the go at the time. She had a bit of a dig on her and all, too. So no one stepped out of line. If you did, you got whacked. No back answers.

She took me out grafting when I was ten. She made me wear short pants. I wasn't on my own. It was a family outing: Harriet, her three daughters Joan, Roseline and my mam Doreen came along and their friend called Carli. Was a pure firm, nonetheless. They were dressed up to the nines: hats, fox furs, the pure works. Each of them had a specific role on the team. It wasn't like the smackheads and that out grafting these days. It was more like a military operation. For instance, Roseline was just there to memorise the faces of the floorwalkers – they were the store detectives. She took it pretty seriously. Remembered what they wore, so if the floorwalkers appeared in the aisles, Harriet's mob were straight onto them.

I noticed that Harriet even found out when the floorwalkers sloped off for a sly ciggie. As they skived, she went to work clearing the shop out. If they went to the toilet, they'd come back to major crime scene.

My grandma was a 'wrapper'. That just meant being able to compress several items of clothing into a ball very quickly. But there was a bit of an art to it, in all fairness.

On this first outing, we went into a department store called T.J. Hughes. I paid close attention to what was going on.

She swiped four woollen suits off've a rail and wrapped them into a tight ball. Roseline bagged them into a big, glossy paper bag and left it on the floor by a rail. Later, when we were off the scene, my Auntie Joan, who was Billy Grimwood's wife, picked it up and carried it out. That was her job – a carrier-outer. To her, it was no different than working in a factory.

After that it was tight over to the kiddies' clothes section. To ordinary folks we just looked like a respectable family out

POWDER WARS

shopping for the day. Then I learned how to be a distraction. Being a little kid, I was perfect – all the shop assistants fussed around me. Harriet made me try on school uniforms while they cleaned it out. That was my introduction into organised crime.

Following his apprenticeship as a shoplifter, Paul was taught how the men of the family went about their business as blaggers, safe-crackers and commercial burglars. He was given a ringside seat at their monthly planning meetings around a flimsy Formica table in the prefab's cramped kitchen.

Jostling for space and hunched over the crude drawings laid out before them, the chain-smoking gangsters sat awkwardly on spindly dining-chairs and discussed the details of crimes about to be commited. Often the topics included such things as getaway routes, the amount of gelignite to be deployed if they were blowing a safe or the drop-off point for the fences on completion of the job, if there was anything aside cash involved.

Paul soaked it up. He was impressed. Grimwood was a striking figure. When the conversation got heavy, like when his father Harold revealed how Grimwood had killed a rival gangster and buried him on a nearby wasteground, his uncles would tell him to 'fuck off' for a while. But mostly it was routine business, like the systematic robbing of Liverpool docks.

To Grimwood's crew, having Liverpool docks on their doorstep was like having a free cash machine at the end of the street. It was a constant source of plunder. A wide-open, eight-mile-long warehouse stuffed with treasures beyond their wildest dreams. Lorry loads of whisky, mountains of coffee, transporters piled high with new cars, holds full of fresh produce, clothes, televisions, leather shoes, canned foods, fertiliser, electrical goods – you name it, Britain's ration-starved, consumer-hungry black market couldn't get enough of it.

The icing on the cake was that waterfront robberies were

largely risk free. The docks, in the local parlance, were totally 'boxed off' – the workers who ran them were on the take and 'onside'. Dockers, lorry drivers and security guards were mostly friends and family into making a few quid by putting up tasty work, turning a blind eye and 'rolling over' on put-up raids.

Grimwood robbed the docks blind. And when the money ran out he robbed them some more. As fast as he could clean them out, ships from the four corners of the Empire and the factories of Northern England filled them up again. Seemingly, the warehouses never ran dry. It was a dream enterprise and it was big business.

In the oak-panelled cabin boardrooms of the marine insurers, from the Liver Building to Lloyds of London, eyebrows were being raised at the horrific attrition rate; not that the plunder was a new phenomenon. The organised ransacking of stores had started ten to fifteen years before during the Second World War, when the US Army had been forced to create special cadres to stop the raiders stealing army cigarettes and looting bombed warehouses. But by the 1950s the problem was putting the economic viability of Liverpool's port at risk.

To beat the raiders, exporters like Timpson's shoes began splitting up their cargoes – left feet in one ship, right on another, so that the hijackers were left with lorryloads of stolen but unsellable single-foot shoes. In a desperate bid to stop the haemorrhaging, the electrical goods company Remington removed the magnetic motors from their top-of-the range razors and stored them in separate warehouses, miles apart from their plastic cases. But the raiders simply slipped the cargo handlers bigger bribes to pinpoint the exact locations of the various components, so that they could be robbed piecemeal and reassembled later.

Finally, in the mid-'60s, faced with huge losses from theft, the Port Authority of Liverpool invested millions of pounds into containerisation – the transport of cargo in relatively secure steel containers. But the mobs simply switched from robbing the

　　　　　　　　　　　　　　　POWDER WARS

fenced-in dock areas to the hundreds of less-secure holding warehouses that funnelled unpackaged goods into them, scattered all over the north-west. It was no surprise that the Grimes family prefab became an Aladdin's Cave of stolen goods.

PAUL: There were racks of new American suits in the wardrobes and crates of single malt Scotch off've the docks, three-deep up the walls. When televisions came out there were blocks of them up to the roof. You had to climb over them to get out the door. It got so chocca that we were forced to move into our grandma's house. There was no room for us to sleep; the place was so rammed tight with swag.

Grimwood was the top boy. He was a blagger. Ronnie was a grafter, into warehouses and factories and that. Grimwood wore a tuxedo, even if he was going down to the local boozer for a quick pint. He never let his guard down; he was a perfectionist when it came to clothes. He used to stand over his wife while she ironed his white shirts. If it wasn't done right, he'd throw it back in her face and call her a piece of shit.

Even then, at that young age, I thought it was a bit out of order. But it's one of them, isn't it? What can you do, when you're just a kiddie? But on the street everyone loved him. The dockers loved him because he always boxed them off if he had a good touch off've one of their tips. The card-markers loved him because he always used to sort them out. And the villains loved him because he stopped other villains from robbing their money. He was like a peacemaker for the underworld.

But if you fucked up, Billy could be a very violent guy. I don't know how many people he bashed up during his life, but I remember my dad and the crew talking in the kitchen about him – pure hushed tones and all that – about killing a villain who had done his head in over something or other. Pure double-clicked the poor cunt. End of. Buried him on the kiddies' playground up the road.

They sat round the kitchen table setting up jobs, saying: 'What do we need?' Everyone had their own tools. Grimwood always had the jelly [gelignite]. To explain the tools and the vans they used they pretended that they were a firm of steeplejacks, on the way to knock down a chimley [chimney] and that. That was their cover.

To make it look legit, every now and again they were forced to put in tenders for legit demolition jobs. One time they actually won a contract – to pull down Liverpool's overhead railway. Shocked they were. It was a big contract. It was in the papers that they'd won it. Billy was on a downer about it. It meant that his gang might actually have to do some proper work for a change. They tried very hard to *lose* that contract, believe you me.

There was villains coming and going all day and night. Talking about how they'd had this lorry off or how they'd broken into such and such a warehouse. Some of them were pretty heavy people. Pure players of the day. May have only been in our kennel, but in criminal terms they were sitting at the top of the tree where the fairies lived. If you were running with Billy's crew, then you'd made it. There were hijackers who'd just had off a lorry load of ciggies, someone who touched lucky on a warehouse full of canned salmon or meat. All that carry on.

I looked. I listened. Was only one topic of conversation, to be fair. Crime. Even for the kiddies. But I didn't learn a lot, to tell you truth. A lot of it was in my genes already. By the time we got to bed, police would be round, kicking in the doors. You'd be asleep in bed; the next thing the door would go in, the busies were turning the place over looking for this and that.

If my dad was on the run, my ma had to graft all the time to keep us afloat. In the day she shoplifted. In the evenings she would be at home fencing the gear and, of a night, she went out. She ran a few *shibeens*. They were illegal nightclubs, which were all the go at the time. She was a very busy woman at the time.

———————

POWDER WARS

Paul's schooling in the dark arts was made easier after his normal education was abandoned at an early age. Born with the debilitating bone disease osteomyelitis, he had been in and out of hospital for leg operations since he could walk. Harriet and the family simply saw the down time as an opportunity for him to learn how to be a gangster.

Despite his disability, Paul was a natural fighter with a stocky build and an abnormal tolerance for pain. He quickly became the 'cock' of his Mount Vernon neighbourhood. He noticed, like Grimwood, that fear was an effective instrument for managing the ragged unpredictability of street life. There was also the respect premium that accompanied his willingness to do business with bare knuckles, foregoing cutters, lead pipes and pickaxe handles – the fashionable weapons of choice at the time.

At the age of ten, on 26 August 1960, Paul was arrested for the first time for 'schoolhouse breaking and stealing', and a second charge of intent to steal. He was fined £2 at Liverpool Juvenile Courts. It was the first of 38 convictions Paul would clock up during his criminal career, including 25 for theft, 4 for firearms offences and, incredibly, taking into account his lifestyle, only 1 for violence.

One month before his 11th birthday, Paul picked up his first probation order, for two years, after burgling an office. At 12 he was sent to a remand home for 28 days for a string of offences including shopbreaking and stealing, house burglary, theft from a motor vehicle and larceny.

Shortly afterwards, Paul was arrested for stealing vanloads of newspapers and organising crews of lads to sell them on street corners. Then he joined a team of teenage jewel thieves and commercial burglars that targeted posh houses, tobacconists and warehouses.

The average score was between £350 and £500 a time and the gang were pulling off three to four jobs a week. It was big money. To show it, Paul dressed in smart clothes. He should have been watching The Beatles in the Cavern Club like a normal teenager. But as night fell, his gang would go to work, cutting holes through shop ceilings with his dad's safe-cracking tools, crudely disabling alarms and 'copping' [grabbing] for the till, and the stock if there was time.

Still only 12, Paul was caught, convicted of burglary and sent to approved school for the first time.

At 13, Paul was convicted of burglary once more. He was caught red-handed after falling through the floor of a tobacconist's shop and severing a gas pipe that triggered an alarm. He was sentenced to 12 months at St George's Approved School.

On his release he was convicted of warehouse breaking and sentenced to another year at St Joseph's Approved School in Nantwich, Cheshire. In an unusual act of familial compassion, grandmother Harriet travelled from Liverpool by public transport to visit him. She realised that she had created a monster and to Paul's astonishment urged him to go straight when he got out. This was no big deal. Paul was indifferent to it all. He wasn't passionate about crime; he just did it because that was the way he'd been taught to get through the day. Some kids grew up wanting to be gangsters. Some got a buzz out of it. But to Paul Grimes it was just stuff, it was just business. Mixing with villains young or old, there was an odd detachment about him: impressed by nothing or no one, but cool as ice on the job, and never folding under questioning. That made him ambivalent to Harriet's request, not really caring whether he carried on getting up to no good or went straight.

For the remainder of his sentence Paul just sat back and enjoyed the relaxed atmosphere of the reform home, nurtured by the Christian brothers who were in charge. On his release, Paul was fixed up with a job selling meat from a handcart. Then he landed a job at the Adelphi Hotel in Liverpool. He loved the work and was beginning to enjoy his cosy, hassle-free life as a straight-goer. But it was short lived.

One day two managers inquired whether he was part of the

POWDER WARS

infamous gangster family with the same name. Paul responded with violence – knocking them out with his fists and walking off the job. Paul claims that on the way home, as he walked down a dark entry, he was ambushed by a vanload of policemen. He says he was given a going-over with their truncheons and, as he lay bleeding in the central gutter, the was kicked in the face.

Paul was convinced the attack was a set up, claiming that the hotel managers were known to have good connections with the local police. But most surprising of all, when he was taken back to the main Bridewell station, Paul found himself charged with attempting to break into a lock-up. He was being fitted up, to boot. In January 1967, Paul was sent to a short-sharp-shock detention centre for three months.

PAUL: It was a pure sinker when I got there. I was looking forward to doing my time with the Christian Brothers again. Bit of a relax in the countryside and what have you. Throwing bricks at the cows. But borstal was a different matter altogether from approved schools, where I had been before. It was all about violence. There was a daddy and all that carry-on.

The rule was that you got battered on the first morning by him. Pure not going to happen that, by the way, I thought. Big lad, to be fair, the daddy was. From Stoke and all that. But not going to happen, all the same, thank you very much.

Comes morning, I was waiting for his good self, the daddy. But they did nothing to me. Instead they picked on two coloured fellas who I'd arrived with. Was a bit of a go around with them, the usual caper. Bullying and all. I stood there watching, to sort of protect the black lads. But not being very arsed about the whole skenario, to be honest. Waited for it to finish. Patiently, if the truth be known. Said fuck all. Then I gets hold of this daddy and sticks his head down the toilet. Is right, Daddy, I thought. You have been made to look a pure cunt now. In front of your little team and all. So I trust that will be the end of these games. For good measure, I battered one of his mates. Not totally goodo but just sound enough to let them know that there was a real gangster in town now. Ended up all right in there then after that.

Couple of screws didn't like what I'd done to their cock. He was their hero and all. Kept order. Maintained the status quo and so on. But you can't please everybody, can you? I ended up being left alone then. Got on the weights and all that.

2

The Oslo

At 17, Paul stepped up a rung on the crime ladder: he moved into the nightclub scene. He was hungry for independence, desperate to forge his own criminal destiny away from the shadows of the family. Paul was also keen to shed his teenage tearaway image. Organised graft may have been pulling in hundreds of pounds a week, but the scallywag in him could not resist the lure of small-time yobbery.

He had become addicted to joyriding, a newly fashionable crime amongst teenagers that mirrored the rise in mass car ownership. Paul justified its pettiness by targeting expensive cars and selling off the accessories he found inside – a boot full of golf clubs here, a van load of tools there. But nightclubs were a different ballgame altogether. They could be a passport into organised crime proper, a rite of passage into the big time – if he played his cards right.

By a twist of fate, an opportunity soon presented itself. Two up-and-coming gangster families, that had joined forces in a bid to challenge the old order, were putting the squeeze on a profitable seafarers' club on Liverpool's Dock Road. The Oslo was far from premier league in nightclub terms – it was situated 'off the strip' just outside the city centre in the largely rundown but industrialised waterfront area. The clientele were rough and rowdy, mainly vodka-swilling sailors from northern and eastern Europe, fresh in from the Baltic and the Black Sea. The female punters were no better, mainly prostitutes and *Letter to Brezhnev*-style good-time girls looking for a cheap night out in exchange for liaisons back aboard ship.

But for all its downsides, the Oslo nightclub was a cash cow – a money-spinning goldmine packed to the rafters seven nights a week with currency-rich sailors desperate to blow their wages on a good time. The punters may not have been A-list, but they were prepared to pay in excess of £20 for a bottle of vodka which at the time normally cost only £6. In the Wild West atmosphere, the owners were guaranteed to shift spirits by the crate load all night long, all day long.

Furthermore, from a criminal's perspective, the Oslo was wide open. It was a clean enterprise owned by legitimate businessmen. No gangsters were involved. Tucked away among the waterside warehouses and seamen's missions, the venue had largely escaped the attention of the city's villains, who didn't even go in there for a drink. Why bother? There was little posing potential to be had in front of a crew of drunken Russian deckhands. And if gangsters did visit the Oslo, it was definitely off limits as a 'den for meets', where business could be discussed openly. Unusually, the licensee wasn't even paying protection money. And the door, the club's security, was largely hood-free, run by 'ordinary, working fellers' moonlighting on the side to make a bit of extra cash. One was a mechanic for Mercedes Benz, the other was a taxi driver. In short, the Oslo was a gangster's dream.

Paul Grimes began drinking in the Oslo in the 1960s. He was captivated by the club's edginess: the beer-and-short soaked carpets, the scantily clad women reeking of cheap perfume and exotic duty-free cigarettes and the explosive mixture of battle-hardened bar-room brawlers ready to go off at any moment. For a young hood it was paradise. He felt older and respected.

Women were impressed by his sharp suits and seemingly

endless thick roll of fivers and tenners. Paul revelled in the fact that he looked like a million dollars stood next to sailors from places where the height of fashion was a Red Army demob suit or a pair of oil-stained blue overalls. The teenager was pulling a different woman every night. Paul felt at home in the Oslo. It suited his rough-and-ready tastes. He had never quite fitted in to the candlelit cabaret club scene that was all the rage at the time. The icing on the cake was that there weren't any rival gangsters to challenge his hard-man autonomy in the Oslo. But that was soon to change.

The Ungi and Fitzgibbons families hailed from a nearby dockside district called Dingle. The Ungis were descended from Filipino sailors and the Fitzgibbons from Irish immigrants. But in the melting pot of Liverpool's slums they had formed a strategic alliance based on close familial and marital ties and driven by a desire to be the number one mob in South Liverpool.

Over the next 30 years they would outgrow their own parochial ambitions and develop into a national syndicate with international links, attracting the interests of Britain's top serious-crime policemen and intelligence agencies. On the face of it, to the outside world some of the members remained no more than petty, unpredictable criminals with a penchant for street-gutter violence.

In 1969, 18-year-old Tony Martin Ungi was sentenced to borstal for killing 16-year-old drinker John Bradley at the All Fours Club in Liverpool. Ungi slashed the main artery in his victim's neck with two broken pint glasses. Twenty years later 23-year-old Colin Ungi was jailed for five years after blowing the head off his best friend, Nathan Jones, with a sawn-off shotgun as they played around whilst smoking cannabis.

The family history was littered with scores of such incidents, most of which went unreported. But such bouts of inexplicable violence formed their power base. On the streets, they were feared. This fear was systematically exploited to racketeer. By the mid-'90s their hunger for power had landed the Ungis at the centre of one of the bloodiest gangland feuds in British criminal history.

On 1 May 1995, the then family leader David Ungi, a 36-year-old father of three, was mown down in a hail of automatic gunfire as he drove his 'super low-key' VW Passat through the streets of Toxteth. The bullet-proof jacket he routinely wore – even to pop down to the local 24-hour garage to buy a pint of milk – offered him little protection. Ungi's death was the result of a long-running feud with a cocaine-smuggling gang run by a crack-addicted multi-millionaire drug baron called Johnny Phillips.

Phillips was the Number Two in an international smuggling cartel run by Curtis Warren, a Toxteth scally who had risen to become Britain's biggest ever drugs dealer. After switching headquarters from Liverpool to Holland in the early '90s, Warren had charged the 35-year-old bodybuilder to oversee the British arm of his drugs operation.

Warren, known on the street as Cocky Watchman, immediately threw his weight behind Phillips' war with the Ungis. From his Sassenheim mansion Dutch police phone taps caught Warren plotting attacks on the Ungi family HQ near Park Road in Liverpool.

'It is very easy for me to throw 20 kilos of Semtex into Park Road,' said Warren ominously. 'If they touch my brother then I would throw 50 kilos of Semtex into their mother's house.'

The enormity of the threat coupled with the notoriety of its source proved to law-enforcement agencies and to the underworld how seriously the Ungi mob was being taken.

The street war between the Phillips and the Ungis raged on. Sixteen months after David Ungi was killed, Phillips mysteriously died of a heart attack in a ransacked, bloodstained safe house on Merseyside. Rumours abounded that a secretive underworld hit squad known as 'the Cleaners' – who specialise in assassinations made to look like accidents – had been contracted to do the job.

Ungi's hit sparked a tidal wave of revenge killings, gun incidents and mini-riots, followed by a string of over-the-top East End-style underworld funerals. David Ungi's was attended by 600 mourners. The cortège was a long procession of 31 black limousines followed by 30 private cars, including a flatbed truck laden with floral tributes spelling out the word 'Davey' in yellow carnations. The arrangement was crowned with a dove, and a photograph of the late businessman formed the centrepiece. Up to 1,000 people lined the streets to watch three hearses, two packed with flowers and the third carrying the coffin, and another floral tribute in the shape of a boxing ring, enter Our Lady of Mount Carmel Catholic Church, ironically close to where Ungi had met his death. The route was secured with a fleet of police armed-response vehicles, snipers and officers equipped with Heckler and Kosh guns. A private security team, run by a notoriously shadowy 'security consultant' called Kenny Rainford, kept order with a small army of doormen.

The increased security was not an overreaction. Jailed gang boss John Haase, a long-running rival of the Ungi family and ex-business partner of Paul Grimes, had reportedly been planning a hand-grenade attack on the funeral. Despite being behind bars on remand for an £18 million heroin ring, Haase had allegedly instructed his lieutenants to purchase the bombs. To his anger they refused to carry out the attack because they felt it was disrespectful to blow up a dead man and his mourning family. Haase later denied the plot, claiming that the rumour had started after a car boot full of grenades and Semtex had been found near the Ungis' Black George's pub HQ and were wrongly linked to him.

In the run-up to the big day, tension was heightened after several senior members of the family were arrested. David Ungi's two younger brothers, Brian and Colin, were arrested in connection with a revenge shooting on a rival gang boss and on the eve of the funeral, in an operation to smash a national drugs ring, police arrested Ungi's uncle Brian Fitzgibbons, 47, and charged him with conspiracy to produce and supply Ecstasy. It was not disputed by any side that David Ungi was clearly one fatality in a long-running gang war.

However, the immediate sequence of events which led to his death were far less dramatic. They revolved around a low-level dispute between the gangs over the rights to use a local pub which the Ungis had unofficially taken over one year earlier. It was a classic Ungi tactic. Move in on a nightclub or a pub, take the premises over and turn it into a power base from which to direct operations. Ironically, it was the same *modus operandi* which had brought them into conflict with Paul Grimes 30 years earlier.

PAUL: The Oslo was a rough house, full of hell-raising seafarer types, and brasses and all of that to-do. There was a lot violence all the time. But it didn't matter. I fucking loved it in there.

You could stench the atmosphere. A pure cocktail of sex and roughness. I was made up because I was knees deep with a different pay-per-view girl every night. I was 17.

But as well as the good times there was always business to be taken care of. One Sunday night I was in there having a drink. Suddenly, I hears the wife of the owner scream, blood curdling and all, too. So I jumps up and has a peep into the porchway. Norman the doorman was getting purely filled in by a team of local gangsters.

I noticed that they were well dressed, this little firm. But only young lads, they were − 18, 19, 20. Bit older than me, to be fair, but was still kiddies all the same.

I didn't like the fact that there was six onto one so I jumps into the mix and dishes out a few small, controlled digs. There was no room for serious contact. So I gives them a few slaps. Then threw them out one by one.

Then the owner pops over for a word, looking a bit chocca about all this. He informs me that the team I've just seen off are this Ungi crew, which, he says, are a bad firm. The owner said that what they liked to do was go into a club and make it look like they controlled the place so they could do what they wanted. Then they just take it over. No back answers.

The owner said that this little firm had already wrecked the place twice and was always purely trying to get in and do more business. His head was a bit wrecked over it all.

In fairness, this place was pure wide open for the likes of these people to do what they wanted. I knew where he was going with all this, by the way. Billy Grimwood had been investing into nightclubs for a while and I was au fait with doors and all of that.

What the owner wanted was someone who could control this kind of thing. In short, to take over the door. Get paid, I thought. Don't mind if I do, thank you very much.

The wages weren't great. But they weren't an insult, either. £20-a-night to start with going up to a £50, if I kept the gangsters out. This was the late '60s and a feller in Fords at Halewood would have to drill a lot of fucking bolts onto a lot of fucking Anglias to earn his £20 every week.

There was also fiddles to be milked on a job like this. For example there was what I could make on the door myself. Used to charge normal punters £1 and £2 for the seafarers. I had the sense to charge big groups of people coming in, say, £20–£10 would go to me, £10 to the management. Small time, I know. But it all adds up. And I also got a little taxi firm going. No licences or none of that. Just a little illegal one ferrying carloads of sailors and brass back to their ships at a fiver and tenner a throw. I'd just been banned from driving for two years for robbing a car – but it made no odds. Sometimes, if there was no one else to drive the jalopies, I would run them myself. All the ships had bars on them. So I'd just sit off in the bar all night, waiting to take them back or whatever. Drinking free booze while the sailors got up to no good with Liverpool's finest.

One night one of the seamen passed round a joint. That was the first time I'd come across drugs. It was just pot. A lot of the lads weren't into it 'cos of the hippies and that. I thought it was sound, all the same.

But getting back to business the real benefits to running a door were more strategic. It got me straight into a classier kind of robbing, a tastier bracket of work altogether, if you will. Being on the door meant that there was a lot of better work being put my way. Bigger jobs, more money. It's as simple as that.

3

The Hole in the Wall Gang

In the late '60s Paul was invited to join his uncles' infamous Hole in the Wall gang. The six-strong mob, run by brothers Ritchie and Ronnie Mellor, were daring commercial burglars who robbed warehouses containing valuable commodities. They were dubbed the Hole in the Wall gang by police because of their trademark method of entry – to literally smash their way through the reinforced walls of bonded warehouses using drills and oxy-acetylene burners.

Although their method was relatively unsophisticated, each member of the team was a specialist and the planning was thorough. It paid off. The gang's hit rate was mind-boggling. At their height, the Hole in the Wall gang were breaking into three warehouses a week all over the North-west. The newly built motorways were opening up virgin territory further afield all the time. Each bit of 'work' netted Paul on average between £5,000 and £10,000 – staggering earnings for a young buck.

The booty was varied – whisky, brandy, cigarettes, cloth, industrial machinery, coffee, tea, meat, hi-fi equipment, tyres, canned food. The swag list read like a freighter's inventory, which it most often was. There was no rhyme or reason to what was stolen. As long as the Mellors could line up a fence to sell the load quickly, within hours of the raid, it was fair game. If not, if the fences could not cough up the readies instantly, often before the break of dawn deadline, the lorry loads of swag were simply dumped at the side of the road. They were written off by the gang and left to rot or be discovered and it was on to the next one.

The gang's motto was 'slash and burn'. Plenty more fish in the sea. The North-west of England was the warehouse of the world, stuffed to the brim with new and exciting goods during this post-war manufacturing boom. There was no point haggling over a wagon full of freshly stolen goods – the trail of evidence was too hot. Get Rid Quick was the order of the day.

Sometimes the jobs were to order. Other times they were inside jobs. The Mellors had a small army of 'card-markers' on the firm. These were tipsters and spies, all over the docks and the city's industrial estates, who would secretly pass on information about the comings and goings of merchandise in return for a piece of the action. Crucially, the card-markers would appraise the gang of security and the chances of being caught before the jobs went ahead.

The risks were generally low, mainly due to the non-existence of modern CCTV and the low standards of alarm systems. Some warehouse employees were paid to 'roll over' – cooperate with the gang while the goods they were supposed to be guarding were stolen from under their noses, often in broad daylight.

The gang's early success was briefly marred by the incarceration of their boss of bosses, Billy Grimwood, in December 1970. Grimwood was jailed for seven years for shooting his business partner David Chand in London and threatening to open fire on the police officers who gave chase.

Grimwood and Chand co-owned a drinking club in Liverpool but had gone down to London to discuss some business with the Kray twins. After the meet, they played snooker in one of the twins' billiards halls in Great Windmill Street. Grimwood wanted to celebrate the success of the meeting by high-rolling it in the capital's casinos. Chand on the other hand

POWDER WARS

urged him to show restraint with their money. Grimwood shot him in the leg and dumped him in a nearby hospital. The police gave chase, but Grimwood threatened them with his loaded revolver, warning one of the startled officers: 'Touch me, and there's one up the spout for you.' It was a serious case and the sentence reflected it.

PAUL: I was doing all right for myself in the late '60s. I don't mind admitting that. I had loads of ventures on the go – all bringing in a tidy amount of dough, but I was obsessed by making money. I was hungry for it. More than hungry. I was fucking desperate, in all honesty. It burned me.

That cunt Scarface had nothing on me. There was no way I was going to let it come to me. I grafted like a cunt from the minute I woke up to the minute my head touched the pillow. Prolific work rate, I had. I didn't care what it was, legit or skewwiff. If it made a raise, I was on it, all over it like a fucking deranged animal. I was into all kind. The door on the Oslo. Had a little illegal cab firm on the go.

I'd buy nice cars for cash, like a brand new Chrysler or what have you. Do a bit of posing in it for a few days. I had a new 1600 Capri when they first came out. Then I'd see the fucking thing parked up and think, 'What the fuck did I buy that for, making me no money.' Then I'd batter it to death on cabs.

Greedy twat, I was. Do anything to make a raise. I even sold fruit off've a handcart. So one minute I'd be getting paid decent bags for a nice bit of work I'd carried off, know where I'm going? The next I'd be getting pennies for a pound of apples off an old biddy, helping them across the road and that. But that's the way we seen ourselves, to be honest. As working-class fellows who were going out and taking a bit of extra for the good things in life. Bit Robin Hood, I know. Half a bit Kray-style propaganda, knowmean? But it was fucking true, la.

We all had our little going concerns on the sly. Billy

Grimwood was into the clubs and the pubs. Me dad had a little steeplejack business – when he wasn't fucking harpooning whales off've the coast of Newfoundland, that is. Ritchie and Ronnie were into a bit of tarmacing and demolition. It made them a few shillings in between devilment, to be fair. Nothing too over-the-top, but it kept the busies and probation officers right off've their cases. Anyone making enquiries as to the source of their half-all-right incomes would have to take a view on it. They'd have to say: 'There goes a so-many-grand-a-year man who runs a moderately successful small business. He employs half-a-dozen fellows in his construction enterprise and is, on the face of it, a legitimate business.'

Little did they fucking know, by the way. But none of us really brought it ontop for ourselves on the flash front. We were sound like that. Low-key, we were. Super low-key, knowmean?

I'd got into robbing wagons. Just on my tod or with a couple of people who frequented the Oslo. Meat wagons, furniture vans, that sort of caper. The odd bit of hijacking. But mostly they were parked up and we'd just have them off. Sell the vehicle. Sell the contents. Get paid.

It weren't major wages. But it was allday, know where I'm going? That got me interested in the haulage industry. So I then decides to invest into a legitimate lorry business. It was only a small going concern but it was the thing to be into, in those days, with all the new motorways and what have you. I was doing all right with straight-goer contracts. I built it up steadily. Bought a BMC flat-back ten tonner. Few other bits and bobs. But it wasn't long before I was getting into some jarg stuff as well. From time to time my uncle Ritchie asked me if I could lend him a lorry: 'Of course. Goes without saying.' Did not ask any questions. He'd bring it back the next day and say 'Put that in your backbin' and he'd slip me a drink. Nothing trifling, by the way. Sometimes it was two grand, sometimes maybe even three or four. A fair old drink for a night's graft. Specially when I wasn't even there.

He'd say: 'Don't worry about it. We had a good touch on the

docks.' Meaning they'd had a load of Scotch or brandy off or what have you. Sometimes the lorry wouldn't come back for two weeks. But I wasn't arsed because it just meant more wages for me. After three or four of them, I told Ritchie that I wanted to get more involved, to drive on the next mission. Not for kicks, but because I purely knew that they'd have to pay me more if I actually went on the job, know where I'm going? As I says, I was a greedy twat. There's no other way of describing it.

So one day my uncle Ritchie phones me up and tells me to pop down for a meeting. When I got there, there was himself and another feller, whose grid I recognised as that of a bit of a player around town. Bit of a face, this feller was. The lad was one of the Bennett family, a North End gang with a pretty staunch reputation for the old ultra-violence. Fucking nuts some of them were, those Bennetts. Proper psychos. Did not terrify myself, but you couldn't mess about with them. So, 'cos he's there I knows this is gonna be a half-tasty bit of work, whatever it might be.

My uncle tells me that he'd been working with this feller for years. And that at that moment in time he was now in possession of a set of keys to a bonded warehouse full to the brim of top-end Scotch. All's I have to do is drive down there with my wagon and load up with ten tons of it. Is right. Let's go. I couldn't wait. What I've been waiting for, in all fairness. And that's exactly what I did. Drove my ten tonner into this bonded warehouse on the docks. Passed the busies manning the gates. Passed the security guards. Passed the dockers. All boxed off, by the way. And straight inside. Loaded up, sheeted up and got off. It was that easy. Obscene, in fairness.

Afterwards, I dropped about forty pallets of it at a lock-up in Kirkby and got weighed in seven grand for my very few troubles. Get paid or what? Is that not a perfect crime? It was my first really big pay day. Fucking fortune in those days, by the way, and I was made up. Totally buzzing. Thought I was a big, mad gangster. And it pure whetted my appetite for some more.

I'd been looking for some steady work for a while. A trade,

something to get totally into. A lot of villains were getting into the safe-blowing and that. Safes was all the rage at the time, like hoola-hoops of the underworld. Crime is like that, to be fair. There are trends and fads which come and go. Like one person tries something and everyone else has to get on the bandwagon and get into it. Villains, like everyone else, are attracted to bandwagons.

For instance, you'll get a team who are into counterfeiting or cat-burgling or whatever, and they'll learn that another particular firm are doing very well out of safe-blowing. So they'll jump on that bandwagon. They'll be right on it as though they're fucking Alias Smith and Jones. So the next time the good firm goes through the roof of a picture house to blow the safe on a Sunday night, there's a queue of fucking chancers lined up in front of them. Scaffolders or what have you, playing at it.

I've met a lot of phoneys like that. Loads of them. Dreamers who think they're international jewel thieves because they've got a black polo neck and a balaclava or whatever. As I've always said, that's why the prisons are overloaded, with cunts like these bringing it ontop for all and sundry. But that's the way it goes, isn't it? Free enterprise and all of that.

But the point is, economically it's fallacy of composition. There's not enough to go around. Fuck that, fuck the safes, I thought. I was a merchant of calculated risks, an informed speculator, an adventure capitalist, and as far as I figured, safes was a purely saturated and mature market. But what about the other options?

There was armed robbery, of course. A lot of villains were getting into the old blagging at that time. Banks. PO'eys [Post Offices]. Wages vans, etc. It was fair to say that the late '60s/early '70s were the golden years for armed robbery. Is a fact, by the way. But it wasn't a trade that yours truly was fond of. Never liked pointing guns in the faces of civilians, to be fair. And I'm not being all Kray twins about it, saying that we was a better class of villains and all of that baloney. We was scoundrels, no two ways, but terrifying office birds and that always left me a bit thingy.

Of course, there were some hard-core firms who did things right, minimum collateral damage and all of that. But on the other hand there were also a lot of spray way merchants [indiscriminate gun users] who were getting involved as well. Pure hotheads, know where I'm going? These types of people did not think nothing of shooting the driver of a security van or whatever, who was only doing his job, at the end of the day.

I mean, I'm all for perforating the ornate plaster for effect, to focus folk's minds and that. No worse than bomby night that, in my mind. But some of these FNGs were pure Mai Lai merchants, know where I'm going? Birds, kiddies, the lot. Kill 'em all, let God sort them out. Did not give a fuck who or what they shot at. Did not like that side of it one bit. So on the numerous occasions I was invited to go in on a blag I politely turned them down. And some of them firms looking to recruit my good self were pure hard hitters, by the way. Did not take a knock back too kindly, they didn't.

The Hole in the Wall gang was more suited to me. OK, so the money from each bit of work wasn't as good as say blowing a safe or robbing a bank. Those lads might be looking at 20s, 30s, 50s from a nice job. But we weren't taking the same risks as them, were we? Neither were we looking at those same figures converted into time, if we got collared, were we? And you've also got to consider that those big jobs don't come along every day. Whereas we were robbing warehouses three times a week and we were guaranteed a payday each time, which you were most definitely not with other types of crime. There is no worse blues than to have a safe off to find out there's fuck all in it. Pure sinker, la. I know because I've done it. Or even worse, la, is when you've got it in your grasp, but you can't open the cunt. Frustrating isn't in it.

No such obstacles in the warehouse game. If you see a bonded warehouse, you can bet your bottom dollar that it's going to be fucking chocca with millions of squids worth of ciggies and booze. Ripe for the having off. No messing around. We may not have been top dogs in the criminal hierarchy, which exists by the way depending on which caper you're into, but the Hole in the Wall gang was a safe investment at the end of the day. Safe as houses, it was

Pure McDonald's franchise, it were in all fairness. Stack 'em high, sell 'em cheap. All day, every day, knocking off and knocking out your standard no-frills products, Fordism and gangsterism in perfect harmony. And as far as I figured, villainy wasn't about blowing bags on a Chinese and champagne all round for your cronies, and eulogising yourself that you're a Great Train Robber and that. It was about getting paid. Even if it meant getting your mittens dirty and being overlooked in the status department.

We was robbing whisky off the docks week in week out. Each load was about 30 to 35 grand so it was averaging out at about 5 grand a hit per person. There were seven fellers involved. I wouldn't get the money straight away; it took a few weeks to filter through. But that was sound.

People like Billy Grimwood were using the whisky to set themselves up in clubs and pubs. Ten tons of spirits was a hell of a lot of stuff. Then some of the dockers started lining jobs up of their own accord, circumventing the card-markers and the usual other gang masters, and ringing them into Ritchie direct. Is right. More wages for them.

This ring-in work were a bit less sophisticated. But equally as profitable. For example, there was one where there was regular and large deliveries of brandy into one of the big bondeds down on the wharf. The dockers would organise it so that out of every forty pallets that come in on the ship, one would go west, and be stored in a little corner they had tucked away for such things. So much would go into the bonded, so much would go somewhere else – to us. When they had accrued 10 or 15 tonnes of this snide brandy, which would be very quick because of the huge throughput, they would give Ritchie a ring and he would send me down with a wagon to load it up. The dockers loaded it onto the wagon themselves. Forklift trucks and all, too. Easy peasy. Allday. Get paid.

Graft like this, we just seen as our tax. So much duty to the Government, so much to the local warlords, like our good selves. Been going on for centuries in all the ports, in all the world. Just at that particular moment in history, our little crew were lucky to take over the stewardship of that most excellent maritime tradition, and the wedge was enriching our coffers, until it was time for someone else to have his turn.

At about that time the port authority introduced containerisation to flummox the likes of YT and their crews. But we were still able to get into them, these containers. It was just a bit more hassle. Dick the Stick could open all doors. You'd just have to stand next to him to see it and believe it. He was so fast and good with this little crowbar he had.

4

Expansion

To beat the menace of containerisation, the Hole in the Wall gang set their sights further afield. They simply waited for the cargoes to leave the docks before stealing them.

———————

PAUL: After they brought in containerisation and made the docks like a fortress, we thought, 'Why the fuck bother? Why not wait for it to leave the docks and go into the holding depots and factories and that outside the port?' Hardly fucking Meyer Lansky, I know. Just a bit of common sense, to be fair. But it paid off. The first one we did was a warehouse on the East Lancs Road. It was like a huge distribution depot where freshly imported commodities would be loaded onto wagons. There was so much going on that there were half-loaded wagons all over the place, waiting for the next shipment to come in, so that they could be filled up and fucked off to wherever they were going. It was chaos. I didn't even bother bringing one of my own wagons. I thought, 'I'll just drive one of theirs away.'

I was pretty good at starting them without the keys, being by then a haulage contractor myself. Easy peasy. So we just walked on there in broad daylight with overalls and donkey jackets on and that, as though we were warehousemen, and went from wagon to wagon looking for the best loads to have off.

Coffee was always a banker. High-value, low-weight and the fences could liquidise into readies within hours. A pure cash converter, it was. It's the same today with the smackheads, robbing it from the Kwickie and Netto and that. Smaller scale, I know, but same principle. That and razor blades. The horrible cunts.

So we comes across this huge heavy-goods half-full of top grade Columbian coffee. The wagon next to it had thousands of tins of corned beef in it. Being logistically efficient and that, it pained us to leave with a half-load so we thought, 'Have the Fray Bentos as well.' The market-stall folk love stuff like robbed tins – it flies out. Hand-baled that into the coffee wagon and got off. Dick the Stick did the lock on the gate and we were off. I drove it about eight miles down the East Lancs to a pub called the Oak.

We always set up the fence beforehand on jobs like this. This time it was a feller called Bobby McGorrigan who was handling it. Bobby was a sound feller. Allday, he was. Trust him with anything. He could get rid of anything and he'd pay you out cash there and then if you wanted. Not that we was short, or nothing, but he wasn't like some of these fences who were worse payers than ICI, knowmean? Ninety days and all that corporate carry on. Fuck that. Bobby was staunch. He was basically a straight-goer who had gone to jail on some small-time charge. He used to be a cab driver and he'd use his cab to ferry shoplifters around town, but in jail he'd met a little family firm called the Hughes. After jail he started investing their money into nightclubs and car showrooms and that. He was a money man. A washer. Made them good dough, he did. Then he went from strength to strength, rising up the criminal ladder until he ended up being a top fence. I got to know him because I used to do a bit of work for the Hughes as well.

Bobby, who was a big fat bastard who we called Bob the Dog, later ripped his brother off on a big deal to enable him to buy his own garage. This same brother, Bobby's brother, was waiting at this pub to drive the wagon full of coffee and tinned ham from there. Got my five grand and got off. End of story. Remember it was the late '60s and that was a lot of dough for a young fellow.

A few days later we hit another warehouse just outside Wigan. Again it was coffee and whatever else was in there. This was a two-wagon job. A card-marker had told us that the firm left two or so wagons there in the depot overnight, so we planned just to load them up and get off. Is right, logistically and that. We were extra looking forward to these pre-Chrimbo touches because the wages were straight into our Xmas backbins, knowmean? Kiddies' presents, Chrimbo bevvies and all of that. I was feeling the pinch a bit. I mean, the lads need an extra bit of tank at that time of year, don't they, no matter who they are? So we were lining up as much work as we could, sometimes back to back

We got there about eight o'clock at night and set up an OP in a field opposite, waiting for the workers to clock off and that. It was snowing and I was freezing just lying in the snow waiting for them to leave. After we seen the last feller go, we went over the fence. We were going to put a hole in the wall to gain entry, but we found a wall made out of tin, corrugated sheets and that, so we just took them off. Bonus. Got two of the forklifts going and loaded one wagon up with coffee and the second with meatballs.

Two of us were drivers. My forklift had no brakes on, so it took longer than expected and we had to graft all night to fill these lorries up. Sweating like mules and that, even though the air was icy cold. I had the meatballs. My drop off was on the M62 motorway under a bridge. It was only half built at the time. It was officially opened by the Queen in 1971. It would have been a whole lot earlier if it wasn't for YT, but that is another story. McGorry's brother was there. Handed over the keys, usual script. I got in a waiting car and got off. Got indoors and straight to the land of nod, dreaming of the eight bags of sand, which I'd figured were coming to me from that little caper, easy.

The next day Ritchie met us to divvy up the dough. But he had a pure face on him, la. Says that McGorry wouldn't take the meatballs. Pure knocked them back. Apologies sent and that, but pure could not get rid for the life of him. That was the riff anyways. Fussy twat, I was thinking, those meatballs are fucking gorgeous as well. Heinz they were. Fucking lovely on toast and all, too. Was half plotting whether it was worth it to get them back and punt them round the markets myself before Chrimbo. But, in all fairness, I had a lot on my plate already, so I didn't think I had time

Ritchie hands us over two grand. Bad one, la. Two bags – a pure waste of, knowmean? But the thing with Ritchie was you couldn't trust the cunt. Sometimes if we got ten grand a piece for a bit of work, he'd say he'd only be weighed in two grand each and he'd make up a little fairytale like this to cover the difference. Even to his own brother Ronnie. No one trusted Ritchie. But that was the nature of the criminally minded, la. So there was no point in getting a cob on about it. We just sent Ronnie back to the drop-off point to check that Ritchie wasn't telling lies, and that he hadn't shaded them off to another fence on the sly. Ronnie reported back stating that the meatballs were still there, sitting at the side of the M62. We could have got them back. But who cares? We just put it down to experience and went onto the next job as quickly as possible. Onwards and upwards, la. That was our motto. That kind of thing happened quite a bit, but in every industry there is always wastage and spillage to be accounted for and ours was no different, so why worry?

We learned our lesson from that. From now on it was gonna be market-led targeting. The fences were screaming out for coffee. So that's what we gave them. For instance, one time we got into a distribution depot and there was a fleet of wagons partly loaded up to be taken out the next day. Some had coffee in them. Others were half-loaded with hi-fi equipment in them, which was new out at the time and very expensive. There was no argument about what to take. The coffee. End of. We took all the hi-fi equipment out using a pallet-loader and filled the wagons with coffee. That's what the fence ordered. That's what he got. I remember that I personally got between £2K and £3K for each consignment on that one and there was a fair few.

Then we found out about this new factory unit, which manufactured branded coffee, all bagged and tinned. Allday or what? I borrowed this huge, fuck-off furniture van off've a mate of mine so that we'd get maximum volume, knowmean? But was this place a no-gooder or what? Swear the place was cursed. To get into it we had to break into the warehouse next door, which was a steelmongers, which made wrought-iron gates and all that. Then we put a hole in an adjoining wall which got us into the coffee place.

The first time we hit it, we were rumbled by a guard, so we had to dust double quick. In fairness, it was the size of the van, which had brought it ontop, attracted a little too much attention and we had to leave it behind. Pure fucking downer, that was, because I had to weigh the feller in who'd lent the van to us.

Few weeks later, went in again. Dick the Stick opens the main door, but there's an inner security wall inside. No probs. Put a hole in the wall. But it's like the Bank of England, la. Pure fucking castle walls, knowmean? A foot thick and all of that. So we're twatting fuck out of this wall with our tools and one of the lads smashes his hand with a hammer. Farcical or what? But it's near hanging off. The poor lad was in bulk, in all fairness. He was no mummy's boy by any stretch but soon he's in bits. You could tell the pain was bad, but we're like that: 'Stop moaning will you. You're going to bring it ontop for all of us.' But in fairness the wound is bad. Half thought he might need an amputation. So we had to take a view there and then and abandon ship once again and take him home.

A couple of weeks later we went back again. It was getting personal, this coffee place now. Got in. Loaded the wagons up. Thank fuck for that. But still no joy – we couldn't drive them out because the big warehouse doors had these special locks on the inside. Huge Chubbs, they were, which even Dick the Stick was having trouble with. Had to bring the engineering gear in, the burners and that, to cut them off. We were doing all this in the dark, by the way. But after a couple of hours the locks were off and we were in business.

There were several lorry loads. Pure Italian job, it was. But even then we couldn't fit all the coffee in. One of lads noticed that there was a BMC van tucked away in this warehouse, obviously owned by this firm, with its livery on the side and that. So we put the last five tons of coffee in there and whatever else we could lash in. Then we decided that we would drive our lorries to the drop-off point and that I would come back for this last van with the five tons in it. Dick the Stick had already lined up the fence. So we were under pressure to make the meet and hand over the bulk of what we had.

The fence, by the way, was a very rich businessman called Arthur who owned a string of butchers and supermarkets all over the country. He was legit so he'd be getting very jumpy if we were late with the drop off. He was looking forward to this robbed coffee keeping his shelves stocked up for a long time to come.

By the time I got back to the warehouse to pick up the last van it was about five in the morning. There's no cunt on the roads still, but I'm thinking that it won't be long before working fellers will be on their way and that. I'm regretting not taking the van there and then last night, in fairness, instead of leaving it. But I start her up and get off, and in no time I'm bombing down the East Lancs making good progress thinking this is allday. But suddenly this car goes past with a couple of workies in it.

I have to stop at the lights and next minute, in my rear-view mirror, I noticed that one of these pikies is running towards me, gesticulating and all that. Instinctively, I know that obviously these fellers work in this coffee firm and they've clocked that I've had their van off. They're obviously double alert after so many attempted break-ins of recent and they're on my case. The only thing was to jump out. There's no way I'm chancing a *Streets of San Francisco*-style car chase through the suburbs with these have-a-go types, especially loaded down with five tons of Mellow Birds in the back. So I say's fuck it. Cuts my losses. Jumped out and got on my toes over the fields. It was about five-to-eight-grand load lost, but it would give the others a chance to get clean away.

It was all in a night's work, as far as I was concerned. There were plenty more successes than no-gooders. For a good couple of years I was doing pure wages – week in, week out – often more than five to ten grand a week. You've got to remember that the average weekly wage was about £30 a week then, so it was happy days.

Sometimes we'd just drive a wagon through a wall like a battering ram. One time we did this at a warehouse storing tens of thousands of pounds worth of salmon. We used the work's wagon we'd found on the premises. But during the getaway the brakes totally went when I was doing about 70 mph. Bottle went, to be truthful, but there was no way I was going to let go this little fortune I was carrying. So I stuck with it all the way to the drop-off point. Round roundabouts, through red lights. The full fucking sitcom skenario. It was touch and go and that, but I managed to deliver the load and get the money for it.

A few days later Ritchie rang me: 'Birds' clothes. Pricey gear, it is. Frocks and all that. There's two wagon loads just leaving the docks and they'll be parked up for the night in a depot down south. Get your wagon ready for Friday night.'

At that time I was getting very into being a young businessman. Was making maximum use of my assets in my haulage business. Very proud of it I was, and all, too. In the day they were doing legit deliveries for proper firms all over the place and of a night and at weekends they were commandeered for hole in the walling. No logistician in the business was as efficient as my good self. Pure Sir John Harvey Jones, I was, know where I'm going? It was busy. I was having to get more drivers and lads in to work for me. Sometimes, it was that chocca, it was touch and go whether I'd have a wagon available for doing a warehouse. I'd got our Snowball working for me. He was one of the family. But he was a pure black sheep, knowmean? Even in a family of black sheep, the cunt could not be trusted. At all.

A few days before we were going to do the women's clothes job I was getting calls from my legitimate customers saying that stuff was not getting delivered or it was constantly late. I didn't mind anyone having their own sidelines and that, but he was taking the piss. When he got back to yard I told him to sort hisself out otherwise I'd fuck him off.

'And make sure that ten tonner is back by Friday afternoon,' I double warned him, for good measure.

Comes Friday, he's not back. I makes a few calls and the lads tell me that he's been hanging around with this South End villain called Dave Dicko. Dave – or Dick the Trick as we called him – dabbled a bit with the warehouses and that. He had his own wagons, but it was obvious that he was paying Snowball to use mine in robberies and that. I knew that because they'd pinched some of my burning gear as well, so it was obvious they were breaking into warehouses and that.

Like me he had his own haulage firm and an engineering business. He went on to become a very big gangster, in all fairness in the end. Snowball had been card-marking Dave Dicko on warehouse jobs that he should have been ringing-in to us. Only fair and that. So it was triple fucking betrayal in my book. They were using my wagons and my burning gear to rob places which my good self should have been robbing. Liberty or what? Not only that but his non-appearance with the lorry fucked up the bit of work re. the tarts' clothes. Could not get hold of another wagon for the life of me. Am £5,000 down and Richie is going spare, la. Calling me all the cunts, he is.

Fuming, I gets in the jalopy and goes out looking for Dave Dicko. I found out that the cunt still lived with his mum and dad in a tenement block off've Scotland Road. Gets there, knocks on the door, he answers, I drags him onto the piss-smelling landing and batters him there and then. Am kicking fuck out of his head and ramming my boot into his bollocks. Cunt is writhing around in agony. Picks him up by the hair, drags him over to the metal railings and starts twatting his head and teeth on the metal crossbar. Blood everywhere, in all fairness. Not only that but I'm half thinking his ma is watching all this from their kitchen window.

I'd already battered Dicko once before, a few years earlier. Was how we met in fact. So I'm still booting fuck out of him when Snowball comes running out of Dicko's ma's kennel. But I'm thinking there's no way Snowball is going to jog in. He's a shithouse, knowmean? But while my back is turned he gets me right on the crown with his fist, the sneaky cunt, and I go down. Stars and all that. I'm half conscious.

A few seconds later I'm coming round and I feel that they've picked me up and are carrying me across the landing. Don't know where this is going in fairness, but do not have the means to fight back. I can feel myself being manhandled across the iron crossbar at the top of the wall over which is a four- or five-storey drop. Suddenly I can see the ground. I'm half hanging over the edge. I'm dead, no two ways. If they throw me off at this height. Pure pulverised, I am, no two ways.

But I could sense they were struggling. Dave Dicko was a near-dead man walking after his thrashing, wobbling and blabbering all over the show. So I kicks out wildly. Grabs the fucking railing and would not let go for the life of me. Snowball was punching and biting me. Kicking my hands. Doing everything to make me let go, la. Digging his nails in. Pure birds' stuff. But pure willing he was, to throw me off. After all I'd done for the little cunt, as well. But would I let go? Would I fuck. Don't know how, but by my own physical strength I edged my way back to safety. Pure contorted my way over the railing, grabbed Snowball who was now realising the balance of power was shifting, and punched him.

I battered them both. They were both covered in blood. I gave them one hell of a beating. Snowball never robbed one of my lorries again and Dave Dicko never stepped out of line.

After a few years with the Hole in the Wall gang it started to dry up. So I started to plan my outro. We started losing money. I remember it began after we'd planned to do this tyre warehouse, which had thousands of big wagon wheels inside and all that. These were fetching big money at the time and I had good connections in the haulage industry to fence them through. We did the business and I made about eight grand off my end, which was about a grand-an-hour in my estimation. The lads who we sold them to were screaming out for more. So we lined another tyre warehouse up in St Helens, but when we got there it was too belled up. Alarms were becoming fashionable then and this one was a shocker so we aborted the mission. But by this time the lads were getting greedy. They didn't want to go home empty handed, cut their losses and that. So Dick the Stick backed the wagon into a warehouse depot on an industrial estate nearby and opened the doors. It was a slaughterhouse with a huge refrigerated storage area. So we cleaned it out of the meat, steaks and all that. It was a quick hit. A chancer, but we got £1,500 each. I was slowly realising that the Hole in the Wall gang had possibly peaked. That kind of tank was no good to me, in all fairness.

The next job was a huge cigarette warehouse in Speke, Liverpool. If it came off, this was big time, worth tens of grands to us, so we had a team of seven men looking at it. We'd done these before and it had always been a military operation. In. Out. Get paid. But the card-marker who'd put it up had got his gen wrong. When we met outside the warehouse they were all arguing, saying: 'He said it wasn't alarmed but it fucking is and that.' Pure scene, knowmean? Amateurs. Bringing it ontop for all and sundry. The next thing a busie car drives past. I clock them in the mirror and was thinking it all looks a bit skewwiff this, know where I'm going? So I turned to Ronnie and said: 'I'm fucking going.'

A few days later Ronnie rings me up and offers another one. It was a Crown Paints warehouse. It was a simple hole in the wall job. But as soon as Ritchie puts his head through the hole there's alarms going off everywhere. Even though he'd assured me that it had been disabled. There were busies and guards all over the show. I managed to run down this road, then along a railway line and up an embankment and get back to the van. I realised that Ritchie was getting sloppy. No two ways. After that, I didn't want to know any more.

———————

During his time with the Hole in the Wall gang Paul had decided to set down some roots. He got married to a local girl called Christine from a respectable family in 1971. A short while later on 1 July 1971 she gave birth to their first son, Jason.

———————

PAUL: We were always getting nicked for this and that. But it always seemed to be minor things, which no one cared about. We just got on with doing the time. It was second nature. It was a nice break from all the madness.

When I was 21 I got sent to borstal for robbing a car. It was for something daft, which I couldn't even remember doing. I done it for a laugh with the lads. I was still only young. The only problem about being inside is that you couldn't earn. The Hole in the Wall were at their height and making a lot of dough. And here I was in a fucking borstal with a load of fucking vandals and bike robbers and that. Serves me right for being a tit, in all fairness.

On home leave I married Christine. I was half-doing it because I knew getting married might get me out of borstal quicker, go down well with the authorities and all that. It did. I got out. But I didn't bother going home much. It was straight out onto the street to start earning again.

———————

CHRISTINE: When I first met Paul I didn't know he was a villain. He had two jobs. He seemed respectable. I noticed that people were frightened of him, but I thought nothing of it. I just thought he was well respected. He had a nickname – he was known as Oscar in the pubs and clubs. So when people would be going on about how bad this Oscar was and being terrified of him I didn't fully understand. It was as though they were talking about someone else.

He went to borstal for car theft. He just brushed it off as though that was normal. Even then I didn't know he was a gangster because it seemed such a small thing. I married him when he came back on home leave. My mum went crazy at the time. Mine was a respectable family. We all had normal jobs. It was only after we got married that I realised the price I had paid.

He was a villain. A big villain. He was robbing warehouses and factories all the time. Stealing wagons with Ritchie, his uncle. He was always committing crime. I couldn't believe it. It was non-stop. Paul would disappear for about ten days at a time and when he returned, if his dinner was not on the table, he'd be off again.

That was my life with Paul Grimes. I was a fool.

5

Den for Meets

Meanwhile, back at the Oslo, an orgy of gang violence had erupted. Paul was gradually consolidating his power base. His ambition was to make the club his personal headquarters, a 24-hour-a-day operational centre for organised crime. The plan was simple: to make the Oslo open season for gangsters, allowing him to oversee and control all of their various graft and thus entitling him to a slice of all the best action that went through there.

But paving the way to power was violent and bloody work. There was no structure to the Liverpool gangs. They were disorganised, fiercely independent and totally fluid in membership. Many of the top faces were little more than latter-day guns for hire, who would join a gang to carry out an armed robbery or a warehouse raid, and then move onto their competitors once the 'work' had been executed. There was no hierarchy or manor to protect. The pecking order was purely based on crime-driven revenues. Financially, many of the gangsters were wealthier than their counterparts in London and Manchester. Organisationally, it was a recipe for disaster. There were constant gang wars, internecine feuds, shootings, stabbings, murders . . . it was total chaos.

Loyalty was based on who was paying the 'wages' at any instant. Astonishingly, the one keystone, the only constant that kept the whole house of cards from imploding on itself, was the code of silence, or the gangland code as it was known to doormen and club owners. No one talked to the police, no matter what. Against this backdrop, Paul launched his bid for power and began his struggle to carve out a profitable niche.

PAUL: Before I took over the door, the Oslo nightclub was pretty innocent. It was stuck in a time warp. It was full of Norwegians and Germans who just wanted to get drunk and get laid. Sometimes they'd refuse to pay £25 for a bottle of vodka. They knew they were being ripped. Which is fair enough, but it's one of them. I'd have to do them in anyways. I was taking my wages out of the place and the right to charge drunken seafarers £25 for a bottle of vodka was that of the management. That's how they made their bonuses. As long as I ensured it kept coming, it was happy days all round. Mind you, I half used to think about taking the place over lock, stock. But in truth, I could not be arsed with the hassle.

On my second week a huge German seaman just refused point blank to hand over his dough to the barman. There was no messing round in these situations – it was rule by rod of fear, literally. I hit him over the head with a baseball bat. Had a good run up as well, to be fair. But the baton just snapped like a chopstick over his skull and he was just left standing there. He picked me up and threw me across the room. But that was all civilian stuff. Silly stuff. I was too busy plotting and scheming to be bothered by sailors kicking off and that.

It wasn't long before I started letting in all the bad lads. I turned the Oslo into a den for meets, where the lads could come and sit down and have a meeting about this and that, without having to worry about the busies and none of that. There were a few places like that around town. Useful places, where the boys could come and do business. For instance there was the Jokers Club on Edge Lane near Littlewoods. It was 24 hours on the trot. There were card schools in there and all the gangsters would go there to discuss work. Not to have a good time and show off and that, but to organise things, to get all their ducks in a row before doing something.

There was another place called the Lucky Club. It was a seamen's club and if you were English you needed a letter from God to get in. But that was the point, Billy Grimwood could go in there and put together a blag and no one would understand nothing. The seaman would be halfway across the Atlantic by the next day. No witnesses to meetings, no surveillance, fuck all. So that was my template for the Oslo, know where I'm going? That's what I desired most.

For security I brought in my best mate Mick Cairns on the doors. I met him when I was 17, fighting on a ferry as it happens. He had hands like shovels. He could hangle violence. One night some gangsters chopped him up with a sword, hacked right down his spine and cut his back to ribbons. It would have killed most men, but he survived. He was also a good earner as well and if he had a good score, he'd kick some back to me – just good manners and that.

Not long after he started in the Oslo he came in with a huge haul of jewellery. He got £26K in cash there and then. He couldn't fit it all in a bag so we put it in a pillowcase. I told him to buy a house with it. A nice semi-detached was only about £2,000 then, so I figured he could have bought a mansion. The soft cunt spent it within a couple of weeks. Mainly on his family, to be fair, but he did like his drink too, Mick did.

We used to do little one-offs on our own. Stealing wagons and that, on the side. We served a bit of time in Walton for having a lorry load of sewing-machines off, but as well as muscle you needed to be Kofi Annan to keep everyone happy in the underworld. It was very diplomatical. There was a lot strife.

I noticed that one crew were coming in quite a lot. Tommy Cabana, Georgie Lawton and Poppy Hayes. They used to rob together; they were a crew. They were armed robbers, but they used to do snatches as well and other things. A few sneaks here and there. So after they started coming in the Oslo I'd go out robbing with them as well. They'd put me onto things, put some work my way. A bit of tribute, if you will. That's the way it worked.

Cabana was their car man, their getaway driver. Lawton was a big feller who could hangle himself. He had a big neck, looked a bit like Arnie, in all fairness. Poppy had been driven near-insane by too much bird too young, staying in his cell for five stretches and refusing to come out, all of that. But they were fucking hard work, these fellers, totally uncontrollable. In fairness, some of it was half comical.

One night Poppy ran in the Oslo with nothing on and ran round. I told him to leave it out. The sailors did not want to see that kind of carry-on, thinking it was a fruit bar and that. He looked half-cake, knowmean? Running around with his cock out and that. But he kept on coming in on his own and standing around and talking to people with fuck all on. The lads were chocca with it, to be fair. They'd be planning to go over the wall on some big caper or whatever and he'd be standing there bollocko in the meeting. I could never understand that kind of behaviour. But then they would do mad things, fucking stupid things, which would cause untold, and bring the heat on – literally.

They came into the Oslo looking for a bloke called Charley Crow. They were edgy and maniacal, knowmean? I got onto it straight away, knowing there was going to be grief and to be honest I was looking for an easy night. Ritchie had called to say there was a Hole in the Wall job on and he wanted to come down and have a word. There were a few other bits and bobs that needed sorting. Suddenly Poppy Hayes gets hold of Charley and sets him on fire, there and then, in the bar. Poured lighter fuel on him and put a flame to it. Whoosh! Could not believe it, la.

The lad who I had on the door, Mick, ran over and was trying to put the flames out with his bare hands. Poppy and them were just laughing and wanting to do it again. Mick was like: 'What did you do that for, you silly cunts?' But then all three of them turned on Mick, and tried to set him on fire, trying to properly human torch him with the lighter fluid and that. Could not believe what was going on myself, but luckily I was able to put it out with my hands and jacket and that. By that time I was fuming, la. Again literally. Had had enough by then. With Ritchie coming down and that. Did not pure need it, knowmean? I waded into these three clowns and it kicked off big time. There was a bit of a go-around in the bar, but me and Mick battered all three of them and threw them out.

Later that night it kicked off again. They waited for us to finish and tried to ambush us. This tit-for-tat thing went on for months. Boring to be honest, but what could you do with dickheads like these? They wouldn't let it go. If they seen me they attacked me on sight. Like Kato, la, off've the *Pink Panther* and that. No messing, there was always a big to-do in the middle of the street; they just wouldn't let it go.

Two weeks later I was coming back from a Hole in the Wall job with my wagon full of swag. Sees Georgie Lawton driving his big American car round, sees red instantly, and tries to reverse over it. Then I jumped out and kicked fuck out of him. I hit him in the body with a metal bar, swinging at him with everything. Then when he went down I booted fuck out of his head. Smashed his skull. Left him for near-dead. But didn't kill him.

That happened a lot with villains. One day you'd be doing a bit of work together and the next you would be fighting. Way it goes. It was bad for business, in my book, but fellers like these lived and breathed violence. They were unpredictable. Even the big firms.

We were doing a lot of business with the Bennett family on the docks. Making a lot of money, to be fair. But one part of their family decided to go to war with the doormen in town, trying to take over and that. Their tactic was simple: drive-by shootings. Just drive by in a car and shoot up the door. No back answers. They were psychopaths. Then on the side, one of them declares his own one-man war against us at the Oslo and a few other clubs. Just because one of them knocked him back one night. A few days later he shot up the door at the Oslo. He was a fitness fanatic who trained like he was in the SAS. He used to run down the Dock Road with a haversack on full of bricks. He pulled up in a car on his own, wound the window down and pinged a few off. It was time to get armed. If this one tried it again I wanted to slot him there and then at the wheel of his jalopy.

After the shootings, I got myself a gun for self-protection. I settled for a .38, a silver one with pearl hangles [handles]. Better it was. Nice and small, but flash enough to be noticed. Which is important, by the way. Saves you having to use it half the time, knowmean, if folk know you've got one.

When I got back to the Oslo, I put the gun on top of a little shelf above the door. It was one of those high doors of an old bank. All kind seemed to be coming in the Oslo. Later that day Paul Conteh popped in. One of his associates apparently knew 'Alan', a new guy who was working for me. Paul was John Conteh's older brother. John Conteh was the world light-heavyweight boxing champion at the time. Paul was a robber. He and his gang used to sit and plan robberies.

The Fitzgibbons family were coming back in. Even though I'd had murder with them I'd met a couple of them in prison on remand for something or other and we'd made up, but they were always kicking fuck out of people in there for no reason. I could never understand that.

On the first night they were allowed back in I found them kicking fuck out of someone on the door. I dragged one of these Fitzys into the toilet along with the feller they were twatting and stood between them. I couldn't work this Fitzy out. He talked with an American accent. You do get a lot of eccentrics in the underworld, in all fairness, but you'd get that in those days especially. People would go to the States on the boats or what have you and come back thinking they're Steve McQueen, knowmean?

So he'd started talking in an American accent. I told him:

'You're not a yank. You're just one of us, you little tosser. Remember I used to protect you when you were on remand. I don't want any messing about in my club.'

Afterwards Mick's like that: 'Bad one, la. Do you know who that is? You're going to bring it ontop talking gangster to that lot.'

'Mick,' I said. 'Forget about them beauties now. There's a proper gangster in town now, knowmean?'

Mick's still looking a bit half thingy though. Arse had gone, to be fair.

To keep things under control I put Alan on the door. He was a bit of a hard-hitter, but I didn't mind all his behaviour as long as it didn't interfere with business, knowmean? At least he provided somewhere for the boys to sit and talk and not be interrupted.

Paul Conteh's firm were planning a big job in the Oslo. There was four of them; Paul, two brothers George and John Brown and Michael Maloney. They were all from Kirkby. I didn't rate them much, in all fairness. They were typical of the new breed of robbers coming up, chancers, if you will, but they were half-all-right fellers and they used to sit in the corner and play cards whilst scheming on their big job. No hassle, knowmean?

It was going to be a bit of a mini Great Train Robbery. The plan was that they were going to rob a mail train chocca with registered goodies from London at a remote railway station on Bodmin Moor in Cornwall. They'd got the idea after John had lived with the postman in Cornwall for a few weeks. And for about three months they sat in Oslo planning it.

Good plan and that, lads. But not going to happen for youse clowns. I only let them sit in the Oslo 'cos Alan asked me. I also warned him to tell his mates to give the work to someone who could hangle it, but they wouldn't listen and one day in July they set off for Cornwall. About two days later I heard they'd been nicked by a roadblock. The pricks had got pissed before the job and held up the wrong train.

Dickheads or what? Paul got three years and the others got fours and fives. I told Alan to stop letting in beauts like that, but by then he had started to think he was bit of a boy and that hisself, which he half was, to be fair. He gave Mick Cairns, the other lad on the door, a good hiding, to show him who's boss. To be fair, Mick had had a few drinks at the time and was easy to take advantage of. I was too busy out grafting to put Alan under manners for it, which I should have, mind you. But to tell you the truth, it's fucking murder getting on top of these office politics all the time. It'd take up most of your working day to solve just a few of these fucking playground disputes. So I told Mick to let it go.

'It doesn't make you any dough, all this palaver, does it? Let's get on with business,' I said to him.

The door was a bit tense for a few days after that, to be fair. Then to clear the air Mick and Alan decided to have a straightener, but in the khazi of all places. 'Bit daft that,' I thought. Mick got his leg caught in a pipe. Alan held him down and took a running jump onto his knee. Just snapped in half like a lolly ice stick. Then he pummelled fuck out his grid. Looked like a dead body, in fairness, Mick did, afterwards. Could not let that go, at all, by the way.

I gets the call informing me of this incident while I was in a meeting with Billy Grimwood. I'd been on the missing list for a few days – away on business with the Hole in the Wall crew. I'd just got back and Billy was filling me in on another bit of business. A big crew from London wanted to 'invest' a lot of dough into a large slice of Liverpool nightlife. So Billy was putting together a meeting between a handful of the city's nightclub owners and this London firm's top boy, a feller called Johnny Nash, who was heading north on the rattler.

There was a strong possibility of a go-around, so me and Billy were sorting out the security arrangements, so as to offer maximum protection for this Londoner. Not that Johnny Nash needed it. Johnny was huge in London at the time, super-heavyweight, if you will and he could hangle himself. Billy just wanted to make sure that all went smoothly, knowmean? No hassle off've beauts and that.

So I could have done without all of this squabbling doormen carry-on, but I knew I had to do Alan in good and proper for his troubles and I figured that I could drive down to the Oslo, twat Alan, and get back to Billy in time to finalise the arrangements. Mick turns up. He's out of ozzie already and ten hours into a bender, his head wrecked with all this. I bought him a bottle of Bacardi to keep him happy.

Then I phones the Oslo and orders the lads to keep Alan there, jumps in the jalopy and goes the Oslo. The lads are saying that Alan's going nowhere; he's settled in for the night and is too busy holding court and telling everyone how great he is. As I pulled into the car park I was half-thinking of running and smashing Alan's head on the bar, straight away, no back answers, but I thought I'll see what the beaut's got to say first.

When I arrived Alan got right on his high horse, thinking he was it. As though it's his fucking boozer, by the way. Half-taking me for a cunt, he was, to be fair. So it's bang, bang. Punches fuck out of Alan and gets him on the floor, ready to break his legs, but Mick intervenes – he wasn't into that. So I tells Alan I want a straightener outside pronto, a one-on-one right now. We only made it to the doorway before it kicked off. Both of us strip off to the waist, pure WWF and get it on. A few digs and he's in bits, to be fair. Like a lot of these so-called hard men, he couldn't pull a punch. He was too fat. He was one fat cunt, in all fairness. I purely knocked fuck out of him without breaking sweat. He goes down, just as the busies arrive on cue, so I grabs my shirt and gets off back to see Billy. End of.

So the meeting with the cockney is set up for the next day. Billy meets him off the train at Lime Street. He's all right Johnny Nash. Allday he is. Looks the business, like all of these cockney gangster types always do. Loads of gangster greetings and all that carry on. Goes a bit Chaz out of *Performance* on us, to be fair, which I'm buzzing off, by the way. He has us laughing straightway, though.

He tells us that to get out London he had to change cars three times and switch trains. It's that ontop for him, in all fairness. The busies are trying to crucify him and following him all over the show. So it makes it double difficult to travel. But there's a serious underlying point to all this as well – if it's that hard for Nash to move around then it makes these meetings extra flippin' important, knowmean?

We walk over to the Big House, a boozer opposite the station. All of the Liverpool club owners are sat round a big table in a circle. Pure mini-Appalachian, knowmean? Behind each owner was their teams, sat off, keeping an eye out and that. A lot of them were carrying. Could just tell. They were a bit thingy with us. I noticed Tommy Comerford was there. He was a heavyweight armed robber juiced into the nightclub scene like no one's business, but he's quite funny with it, a good laugh and that, so he's putting everyone at ease with his banter and that. I sat right behind Billy. I didn't need a shooter. I knew most of these mushes and they knew there'd be untold if they made a show of Billy in front of his posh London mates and that.

Billy and the main boys started talking. The gist of the meeting was that this London crowd were offering top dollar for the four biggest clubs in Liverpool. They were going to take over, give Billy a slice and do them up. New bars, new decor, new windows – the lot and they wanted a sit down with the local gaultiers and that to make sure there'd be no noses out of joint, knowmean? Good manners, in all fairness. Very civilised, our southern friends are, to be fair.

Johnny lived up to his nickname, 'The Peacemaker', by brokering a good deal for them. Billy was to help himself to two separate clubs as a sweetener for him, to make sure that the deal went through. There was no way anyone could refuse. Nash controlled the West End in London. Liverpool was small fry to him, in fairness. Nash had a massive protection racket going in the Smoke. All the big West End clubs coughed up and the dough was split three ways – between him, the Kray twins and Freddy Foreman. I remember Billy telling me that the alliance nearly went tits up after the Krays caned that Jack 'The Hat' McVitie, because he was related to Johnny's top boy. But I could never be arsed with gangster gossip and I just took Johnny as I found him – which was dead fair.

There was few grumbles from these Liverpool club owners. Obviously, some of them would have liked to have cherry-picked these premium venues for themselves and of course, a few more newly refurbished tarted-up clubs about the town makes more competition for them and makes their paint jobs and that obsolete. So it's a bit of a sickener for them, in all honesty, but the deal had been sanctioned from way high up, so there's fuck all they can do. Rubber stamped. End of. Meeting closed. Ding ding. Let's get knees-upping.

We're having a good craic, to be fair. All of the boys are there. Loads of birds and that. Everything's allday. At about one o'clock we go to a club and Billy introduces one of the boys to Nash. Suddenly this feller goes to Billy: 'What are you introducing me to him for, the cockney cunt?'

Bit outers, to be fair, I thought. Rude and that. But they don't like people poking their noses in up north, as the line goes, so it's bound to happen sometimes. This feller shouting the odds was a bit of a scallywag, in all fairness, and he didn't like the fact that these cockneys were throwing their weight around on his manor. But times were changing, weren't they? I was ready to knock him out, in fairness, but Nash steps up to him and gives it the 'I like a bit of a cavort' routine and pulls out a pistol. An automatic it was. Nice it was as well. Like mine, la, 'cept mine had pearl hangles.

'Do you know who I am?' Nash says. The scallywag's arse has gone a bit to be fair by now, with the shooter and that. He done one from the club sharpish. About an hour later the doorman come over and says that the scallywag is outside with a sawn-off wanting a fucking showdown with the Cockney or something. High noon or what, la. Quite fancied a bit of gun-slinging entertainment to round the night off, to be fair, but we just told the doorman to fuck him off in the hope that he'd cool off and come to his senses.

No way, la, would this cunt listen. Next minute, the big window in the club shatters. Bang! Bang! Bang! He's pumping rounds into the club pure Michael Ryan-style. Windows are going in left right and centre. Like a film, la. Pure *Wild Bunch*, knowmean? Ricochets off the plaster, the works. To be truthful, I'm buzzing, but there's pure mass hysteria, especially with the birds, and that. You can smell the cordite. The cunt's still going, thinking he's James Cagney, and that. Reload! Bang! Bang! Reload! All hands are going for their armaments, but there's no point, he's got them pinned down.

Billy's like that to Nash, buzzing with him: 'Don't worry, Johnny. Your investment is safe with us. Safe as houses, Liverpool is.'

Johnny goes with it, to be fair: 'Do any of you scaairce cunts know where I buy some bullet-proof glass? That's the first thing on my shopping list for my new clubs.'

We're all in bulk at this, to be fair. There's a busie siren in the background. The scally stops shooting up the club and gets off. We dusted ourselves down and got off to another club. The scally with the sawn-off got nicked, by the way. His name was Syd Tollett. Eight years he got himself, for blowing the windows in. Could never understand that type of behaviour.

After Nash went back to London and that, it was Billy's responsibility to make sure that the Cockneys got their parcel of dough every month. It got taken down on the last Sunday of every month – no back answers, no excuses, get paid or get off to South America and don't come back. Pure grands there was in there. Me and Billy got our due, goes without saying, for making sure it had a smooth trip, etc. Making sure it didn't leave the train unauthorisedly at any other point than Euston, knowmean? Sometimes Billy would take it down himself, so he could go on the piss and hit the casinos and that, which he just loved doing, by the way.

Nash came up four times in total after that. The script was always the same. He'd come into the Oslo to see me. I'd take him around all the Liverpool clubs and then we'd head back the Oslo at two o'clock. Billy would turn up and him and Nash would talk business all night.

6

The Scrapman's Gang

Paul's next big scam was a lucrative construction racket. He masterminded the large-scale theft and resale of thousands of tonnes of building materials, scrap metal and mechanical plant from all over the UK. It was big business and until that time a largely unknown crime. The post-war building boom was in full swing. Billions of pounds were being poured into the construction industry – high-rise flats, new towns, new hospitals, motorways, pedestrianised town centres, industrial estates, even new railways – all manner of projects were going up at breakneck speed, with seemingly scant regard for the protection of assets.

Paul was quick to recognise a gap in the market. On-site security was relatively poor, and as far as competition from other criminal gangs was concerned, it was untouched, wide-open virgin territory. 'Get paid,' he thought, as he surveyed the miles and miles of valuable but unguarded materials that lined the work-in-progress M62 motorway, the subject of his early 'market research'.

For the job, Paul brought together the Scrapman's Gang, a small band of criminals, like himself, with good contacts in the haulage and scrap trades. He had a fleet of trucks at his disposal and he bought a scrap metal business as cover. The Scrapman's

Gang's first targets were the under-construction motorways. As fast as the contractors could lay the miles and miles of steel-erected reinforcements for the roads and bridges, the gang were able to rip them up and spirit them away.

Night after night they returned, often to the same section of road, to steal the mesh structures that had been put in place that day or to remove the huge bails of freshly delivered steel rods that lay at the side of the foundation ditches. The gang moved on to stealing bulk loads of steel girders from industrially sized construction sites and then onto dismantling whole steel-framed buildings piece by piece using powerful oxy-acetylene burners, cranes and mechanical pulleys.

Many of the buildings were brand-new factory and warehouse complexes covering several acres and worth millions of pounds. In a fraction of the time they took to erect, they were pulled down or left standing supported only by a dangerously minimal structure, carefully left in place like a giant optical illusion to allow the gang to make a clean getaway.

PAUL: After the Hole in the Wall gang I took a year off from what I called full-time work – the organised robbing of warehouses night after night. Wearing me down, la, it was, to be truthful. Was also getting a bit para with the busies and that too with the lads getting a bit slovenly of late.

'Quit while you're ahead,' that's what I always said. This was going to be my gap year, if you will. A time to chill out and ponder about the future. I looked forward to these little furloughs, in all fairness. It got me thinking that I might have preferred my life more if I'd gone straight. In fact, I used to imagine how sound it would be just to have an ordinary job, like everyone else.

To be honest, I used to fantasise about it. About getting up and going to a factory and that. Weird, I know, but it used to give me a warm feeling. It goes without saying that I had well enough

POWDER WARS

dough stashed away from all the devilment to keep me going for a long, long time during a crime-free period. There was also the Oslo, which was ticking over just nice. It was throwing up half-decent bits of work every so often – one-offs and that, to be fair. Also, under the good husbandry and stewardship of my good self and the wife, my legit businesses were beginning to reap in some half-decent wages as well. Nothing mad, but wages is wages at the end of the day.

Taking long holidays here and there was something I've often done throughout my criminal career. Get a good score and go straight for six months. It was something all of us did: Billy, Ritchie, Ronnie, even my auld feller and that. Even if me dad got £20,000 out of a safe, he'd be out tarmacing or whatever the following week or doing the demolition or whatever. Keeping things looking normal to the outside world.

It did us good, these straight-goer breaks, because more often than not it was a chance to get into some other legit business. Was also a good opportunity to get the busies off've our backs and all, too. We were always under surveillance for something or other and the busies were always TO'ing [turning over] my kennel looking for swag.

As if, by the way. By that time we had a good network of lock-ups and safe houses and that, even our own little warehouses well out the way and that. Those early morning calls were most unnecessary in my view. In all of their relentless searches, the busies could never get nothing. Frustrated to fuck, they were. To wind me up they'd confiscate my cars saying that they could forensic them or what have you. Just harassment and that, but no use whingeing about it. The police couldn't prove nothing, but they were definitely getting wise to the Hole in the Wall and being a straight-goer for a while meant that they had to take you off their target list. They couldn't justify putting a van on your plot if you weren't committing crime. But no matter how comforting time out was, it was never long before the urge to get up to no good came back.

Towards the end of the year, myself, Ronnie and Ritchie met up to plan what we were going to do. Ronnie wanted to get back into the warehouses, but Ritchie told us about these top card-markers he'd been getting into. Card-marking is basically safe-cracking and commercial burglaries in which we were getting our cards marked about hidden cash and jewels and so on. But Ritchie's card-markers were triple-platinum, knowmean? Only interested in big hits and they weren't timewasters, so they said.

'Nice one,' I said to him. 'This could be a nice way of easing ourselves back into gainful employment.'

On the first one, the card-marker told us about a millionaire businessman who was skanking the tax big time. He was putting all his money, including the slotted tax, into diamonds. He figured that one day he might get an early morning call off the Revenue and his master plan was to just pure offski with the jewels, knowmean? Spain, Kenya, wherever. But he didn't figure on being taxed by us first.

The card-marker told us that there was about £50,000 to £100,000's worth of these jewels in one safe alone, in a house off Prescott Road in Liverpool. The card-marker also told us when the family went out, their comings and goings and so on and loads of details about the security. Little sketches and all that carry-on. 'Bonus,' I thought, 'this is going to be a pure walkover.' I was half kicking myself for taking a year out when crime was this easy peasy. Lazy twat at times, though, I am.

He said that every Sunday night the whole family would fuck off to the pictures or something. After the de-brief with the card-marker, we decided to put the house under surveillance. So the next day I went down and clocked the regs of their cars and the layout of the house and that. 'Good,' I thought as I watched it from my car. There was a fenced-in courtyard where they parked their cars. That was a pure godsend. We would need that to park our van in so we could lift the safe into it, get it off the plot and blow it in an underground tunnel later.

When I got back, me and Ritchie met up at me mam's and he revealed the plan round the kitchen table. He said: 'This is the way it is. The card-marker has told me the exact make of the safe and I've been to a safe shop to check it out. It's light enough to carry. I know because me and the salesman in the shop fucking carried one.'

There was a bit of an argument about the fact that we should blow the safe in the house. We decided not to for three reasons:

1. I wasn't really into using jelly and didn't like explosives in general.

2. The house was in a quiet residential area, it was very old and it was stuffed full of antiques and that. The explosion might have caused untold noise, knowmean, windows, the lot, going in and brought it ontop straight away.

3. We would have been covered head to toe in dust. When you blow a safe the ballast in the back goes everywhere, putting the evidence all over you. There's half a chance that in a quiet residential area that'll get noticed and if you get stopped by the busies you're fucked.

Ritchie concluded: 'So we go in through the windows and carry it to the van and fuck off.'

Simple as. End of. Every Sunday for a month we continued to watch the gaff.

There was a pub opposite and every Sunday I'd stand in the doorway with a pint and watch the family drive out of the house. It was a brand new Jag driven by the dad or the son. We sussed out that if they didn't come back by 8.30 at night they'd be out till about 10.30. Give or take various factors that gave us an hour to do the job. It was all set for the following week. Everything was going allday, but on Friday morning I woke up to find the busies had towed my jalopy away. The usual caper –

said they wanted it as evidence for something or other. In fairness, they were just giving it to me.

Bad one, la. I was too busy to be without mon danny today, especially before going to work. I had fucking loads of running about to do over the weekend. Ritchie wanted me to have a last look at the gaff. Christine wanted me to run her into town. Billy wanted me to pick him up and run him to this sit-down with some lads from Manchester. There was only one thing to do – the Fisherman.

The Fisherman was a bent busie who used to come in the Oslo. We called him the Fisherman because that's what he loved to do – go fishing and that. He was all right for a busie, just sat there at the bar talking about pike and the Liverpool–Leeds canal and that, ignoring the vast amount of organised crime that was going on around him. Fair play to him. His drink was free and we took care of him, so he did us favours in return.

I looked at the paper. 'Fuck,' I thought, 'it's Friday. He'll be halfway to fucking Bala Lake, by now, with his rod and can of Party 7,' knowmean? They love all that, busies. I phoned the Oslo and told one of the lads to get a message to him at the busie station. Luckily, we'd caught him just before he was going off duty. They told me that he'd pop down the Oslo later to sort it. Is right. That night all's I had to do was tell him the make and model. The next day he got it back for me. Back on track.

On Sunday we got into position. The family in the Jag left at about six-thirty in the evening and didn't come back at eight-thirty. Game on. One by one we went over the back wall. Dick the Stick got busy opening the various doors and windows. Need not have bothered, in all fairness. The back door was unlocked. I just walked straight in and gave them the fright of their lives, as they were all crawling around like cat-burglars.

Between the four of us we picked up the safe, but it was fucking heavy. It wasn't the safe-lite model that this card-marker had said it was. We pulled, pushed, dragged the fucker across the ground floor and down a flight of steps into the garden. Fuck's sake – there was a tow truck blocking us from driving our van into the courtyard. The gates wouldn't even open. No way, la. We'd have to drag the safe right across this fucking rolling estate, acres it fucking seemed, and hoist it over the garden wall into an alleyway.

Time was not on our side, in all fairness. It took 30 minutes of pure *World's Strongest Man*-style feats of heroism for the four of us to get it to the garden wall. We're well over budget on this one by now. The *Countdown* clock was just getting to the bit where the musical finale starts, but one last Geoff Capes impersonation, safe over wall, and we were at least £50,000 richer.

Literally, it was balancing on the top of the wall when we heard the noise – the unmistakable sound of the Jag coming down the driveway. Crunching gravel it was, but it sounded like thunder to me. Finished, we were. F-U-C-K-E-D. I spelled out in my head. Finished. Let the safe go, crashing into the alleyway. We all did the offski over the wall into the night. We had to leave the safe next to the back gate.

We didn't get collared but we were totally fucking sinkered anyways. No one could believe it. We'd been inches away from getting the safe away, no two ways. Fucking seconds, knowmean? Total gutter. Kites on us said it all, but there was only one thing to do: find the card-marker and give him a good thrashing, which we did, by the way. Apportioning blame in those situations was always a good way of relieving the stress of a no-gooder.

We gave him a few slaps but the card-marker saved himself from a pure pummelling by offering up another job there and then. Penance, it was. It was a big Volvo garage with a cash-rich safe. We hit it a short while later. Walkover. Had the safe off, got £800 quid each out of it. Wasn't too good wages, in fairness, but it was better than fuck all.

After that I fucked the safe-cracking off and decided to move into being a sneak thief. I got into it through one of my doormen called Bobby Chalendor. I brought him in to replace

Alan. One night he said: 'Do you fancy doing a bit of work? I know a butcher who drives round with £7,000 takings in his boot.'

I got a set of pass keys off one of the lads in the Oslo. These were a bunch of keys which would fit most cars. Car locks were piss poor in those days. Bobby said: 'This butcher owns a string of shops and every Saturday he collects all the takings and drives home.'

So the following Saturday night we followed this butcher coming out of his shop. Sure enough, he throws a bag in the boot. We carry on trailing him and he stops at a pub to go in for a bevvy. I goes over, pops the boot and has the bag off. Very heavy, mind you. Sure enough, there was six, seven large in it. Get paid. I kept £5,000 and Bobby had the remnants. It was the beginning of a beautiful relationship.

It turns out that Bobby knew a card-marker who worked in the meat trade who knew all these big butchers, who drove around with huge fucking bags in the car, thinking it was allday. We did about four or five of them sneaks before the source dried up, but they were all good payers. So good in fact that we decided we'd do our own card-marking. Find where these big shopkeepers lived, put them under surveillance, and work back from there.

The first one was another big butcher. We could work out how much there'd be in takings from how many shops they had. We took turns to watch him for a month. He had a load of shops and this feller also owned a few market stalls and a wholesaler. He was doing very well. Every Saturday it was the same deal. Collect his winnings from all five or six shops around North Liverpool, other vans would turn up as well to drop off money to him and then he'd drive home, but on the way he'd stop off for a bevvy at this pub in Bootle. Get paid.

I sent Bobby to follow him into the pub and see what he did and for how long. While he was in there one of us went over and tested the key. It was a nice, expensive car, but we could open the boot with a Cortina key easy peasy. That was just a dry run. The next Saturday we followed him to the boozer and while Bobby was stood next to him at the bar we twirled his boot. Bobby was a cheeky twat; by this time he had got right into him. He was even telling the butcher jokes and talking about the match and that. There was £8,500 in there, mostly in notes. I left most of the coins.

We began tailing shopkeepers all the time and having them off. High reward. Low risk. We were getting rich again, but you can only do that for so long before it comes ontop. It's one of them, the law of averages and that. After about nine months solid of it, I began looking around for something bigger, a proper venture. Soon I found it – scrap metal.

Through my haulage business I'd often been paid to deliver scrap and I could not believe, for the life of me, the value of it. It was a pure case of where there's muck there is most defo brass. Not only that, the streets were literally paved with it. I'd noticed from spending a lot of time in the cab of a lorry that there was a lot of steel lying around on the new motorways and roads that were being built. Get paid.

One night I got a ten tonner and drove it to a new motorway that was being built. We stole all of the reinforced steel that we could see and drove off. It was in the middle of nowhere. Just a field with tonnes and tonnes of unguarded gear on it. We weighed it in as scrap at a mate of mine's yard in Widnes. I got £500. It was that easy. I knew I was onto something.

The next time I went out to recce another good spot on the same motorway. I had a look at it, saw what the situation was and had another ten tonnes away. I then started to run it like an operation. Twice a week the lads would go out. After putting a load of steel into the ground, the contractors would build a little fence around it. That was all the security. We'd just take it down. We had a few scares but it was making us a lot of money. I was making a few contacts in the building game. They were giving me a better price for the steel than the scrap. More money. Get paid.

Then I met this timber merchant who told me that he made a fortune cutting up old railway sleepers and selling them to the coal mines for shoring up. Say no more. I drove onto a siding and loaded as many sleepers as I could. We found out where the railwaymen were doing repairs or putting in a new line and just go and have them off. These new lines were double-bubble. We'd steal the tracks and the sleepers. Miles and miles of it. Just fucking disappear, literally overnight. The lads would tell people they were workies and just drive the lorry down onto the tracks. It was money for old rope. Easy peasy. The security was hopeless.

It wasn't high stakes. It wasn't big time. But it was good money. I bought my own scrapyard then. My mate Mick Cairns told me that he was making a few quid taking the scrap of this old disused dog track. I said to him: 'Why take little bits when you can have away bigger bits? Girders and that. The whole fucking place if need be.'

Using the wagons we took between three and four tonnes a day. On top of that, there were hundreds of four-by-four girders. I'd found a builders' merchant who'd pay me £60 each for them. Meanwhile, the council were trying to sell the tender to demolish this place, hoping to make a raise of the scrap value themselves. Within weeks we'd done it for them. Felt sorry for the poor cunt who'd won the contract, turning up on the first day to find an empty space.

That was it then. Any empty building was fair game. I invested in state-of-the-art burning gear. We'd go in and cut all the girders out, rip the floor off. Take the metal sheets out of the wall. Was obscene, in fairness. Some of them were brand-new buildings, recently erected at great expense, waiting to be sold or rented out. Within days they would be reduced to a hollow shell, swaying in the wind. Massive fucking warehouses and factory units. The local council had no option but to condemn them. They were fucking dangerous.

No one asked any questions. We looked like a proper contractor. We looked better than fucking McAlpine – wagons, plant, radios, hard hats, the works. But one day we're taking down a warehouse in Kirkby piece by piece. It had only just been built – there weren't even any doors on it. They hadn't had time to finish it before we were fucking ripping it to bits. I was supervising the operation. I looked around and suddenly there is a busie watching me through one of these non-existent doors. All the lads did a runner, even the wagon and the van with the burners. The busie was on his own so I just gave myself up knowing that the wagon would have time to drive out of another gate.

I got nicked. They tried to do me for burglary. My brief was good. He told them that they couldn't because there was no doors on the factory. No breaking and entering. The busies went back to the site and found one door and they marched back into court, very smugly indeed. Kites on them, la. You'd have thought they had just found Lord Lucan, knowmean? But even then the judge wouldn't have it, door or no fucking door. He just fucked them off and told the busies not to be silly.

Then they tried to do me for robbing scrap. The busies knew I was behind a big racket, the Mr Big and all that. Deep down they knew I was turning over a nice few quid from this scam, but they couldn't prove it and if they mentioned it in court they would've looked like pricks. But the judge threw it out of Crown Court because none of it could be put down to me. He said it was a waste of time. They were fucked and he knew it.

After that the business got a bit out of hand, knowmean? We began to get people ringing us up card-marking us, where there were new building sites and that. Cocky watchmen, wagon drivers, even workies who were desperate for an early dart 'cos they wanted to go the match. Having the site screwed was their perfect outro. A good excuse to down tools and spend the afternoon on the piss. All hands were phoning them in: 'There's a load of girders due in to such-and-such a site at four bells or whatever.'

We'd be waiting for them. No sooner than they had been

lifted off've the delivery truck, we have them off. Me and Mick Cairns would go down, if no one else was around, on these on-specs. I lifted the girders onto the wagon with my own hands. Once you've got the bed of steel on the wagon, with a layer of girders, and it was steel on steel from then on, it was allday sliding them on. Get off. Get paid.

I was making a hell of a lot of dough. Each lorry load was a grand. It was a 24/7 operation. I'd just be getting my head down. It was four in the morning. I'd been on the door that night and the phone goes. One night it was Snowball, one of the lads, who was also a relative of mine: 'I've got a forklift truck on the back of the wagon. We've just had it off and I want to stash it in your yard.'

No sweat. Drove down to my scrappy, burned the paint off, resprayed it and resold it. There was a big market in robbed plant – JCBs, cement mixers, cranes – you name it. Mainly because a lot of these big building firms and plant-hire companies were basically tight bastards and loved getting jarg gear on the cheap.

Then we had four huge drain cleaners away. Those are those big lorries like the wagons which the council use to sweep the streets, but the thing with gear like that is that it's super specialist, knowmean? There's only so many buyers in the market for industrially sized drain cleaners. You know that they're going to end up on some fucking borough council in Northumbria or somewhere, so you can't charge the earth, knowmean? 'Cos someone is going to have to replate them and all that carry-on, before they are sold on to the fucking Grimsby Council Clerk of the Works, with me? So I only got £1,500 out of that. Stack 'em high, sell 'em cheap. End of.

Another good earner was robbed lorries. Big ten tonners, low loaders, big vans and that kind of thing. I got the idea after a few of my mates, who were hijackers, started to bring in the lorries they'd highwayed off from somewhere, for me to cut up, so as to destroy the evidence. They were always brand new. Shame it was, la, but we'd just cut them up piece by piece with the burners, sell the metal for scrap and engine for spare parts. It'd take two or three days to dice a wagon into little bits. We'd make about £1,000 off've each wagon if we were lucky.

But then a lot of people started asking us to do it. Pure snowballed, it did. Mates in the haulage industry for insurance, traders who couldn't sell a vehicle, anyone did it for every reason. We had that many we had to rent a big, covered yard at the back of a garage owned by a friend of the family. And we got a production line going using a few lads and that. Then we developed a system whereby we didn't have to destroy the whole wagon. We just cut the big boxes off've the back and sell the front bit separately. It was a good system. We sold them to farmers in Wales who would never get nicked with them driving them around on their land and that.

It got so that the hijackers wouldn't even sell the load before they give the lorry to us. I'd just stand there with a clipboard backing the lorries in, making a note of the contents. Davey Knox turned up with a huge lorry full of cloth. He copped for a load of very expensive silk from China. I cut the rolls of silk and cotton up and sold them to a fence. Then I cut the back of the lorry up and sold the cab to another feller. Paid Davey in cash. One stop service, it was. The lads were made up.

Mick Cairns turned up with a refrigerated lorry full of New Zealand lamb. Sold the meat to a big butcher we knew and cut the lorry up. Everyone was happy. The best week we had we cut three wagons up, one after the other. Then I asked Snowball to start going out to rob them himself to feed the production line we'd set up. He had about five off, one after the other. We was making good punt out of it to be fair. Then we went a step further.

We knew where we could cop for several brand new Volvo wagon cabs. Known as tractors in the trade they are. They're the lorries that are at the front of articulated lorries. They were sitting in the yard of a wagon firm on the Dock Road. Had them priced up. The total haul was worth £140,000, if you were buying them new out of the showroom. Easy peasy, it was. Over the wall, broke the lock on the gates and drove them out, in a little convoy. Got them into my yard and battered the phones to get a buyer.

Rang round the haulage moguls I knew, but they were like that: 'No way, Paul. They're too ontop being brand spankers and that. Every Volvo north of Birmingham is getting a tug already. They're looking for them.'

I knew I had to get rid of them quickly. Otherwise I'd have to cut them up with the burners and get the scrap value. Which was a sickener, by the way, with these being premium artics and that. I was in the yard when I got a call off Billy Grimwood. He told me he was in the Crow's Nest, one of the boozers in town he'd took over, and this fence was saying that he could get rid of the Volvo wagons.

Went down to see this feller. He was giving it loads, saying that he knew a big haulage firm in London who would take them off us for £40,000. This feller seemed too keen, knowmean? As though he was trying to impress me and Billy with this big mad London deal, but the meter was on, la, I was under pressure. It was only a matter of time before the busies would turn the yard over so I had to show some commitment.

The feller said that we'd have to drive them down to London there and then. So that night I drove one and Snowball drove another. A-roads and all of that, to keep a low profile. Got one of the lads to follow us down in the car to make sure we was all right and that. But when we get there there were no cockneys to meet us. This feller says he'll have to run round to get the buyers to come and see us.

I was like that: 'For fucks sake.' So we parked them in this nice, quiet street well out of the way, and went to get our heads down at a mate of ours. I fucking hated crashing like this in London. Roughing it. Waking up with a hangover on someone's floor, like as though I was going to Wembley or whatever. I felt grim and lost. I just wanted to do the deal and get off.

Twenty-four hours later still no show. I went back to have a vidi at the tractors to make sure they're all right, and lo and fucking behold, the busies have got onto them. Pure under surveillance, they were. Just a little car with two plain-clothes busies well up this suburban road, but I was onto them straight away. We'd also got one of the lads to keep an eye on them. He said that there'd been people sniffing around them the night before. Either the fence had set us up or his London pals were turning him over. Either way, la, I was extremely bored by all this. Telling you, la, but I said fuck all. There was no point.

The next day me, Snowball and the fence got in the car. I told Snowball to get on the M1 and get back to Liverpool. Snowball was driving. I was in the front passenger seat. It was a Nissan Sunny – Japanese cars had just started taking off over here and that. It was small and super low-key. The fence was in the back seat. In fairness, he didn't look guilty. He just kept going on that he was sorry and all, too, about his fucking around and that.

As soon as we got on the motorway I turned round and just laid into the cunt. Proper fucking punching him, I were. Proper haymakers and digs and that. Just holding his head so he couldn't move and twatting his face repeatedly and without no mercy. He was fucking screaming and crying. His legs were hitting the roof, leaving indentures in the polystyrene roof lining. Crying for his mum, he was, this prick. He knew he was going to die, in fairness, was fighting for his life.

I was like that: 'You cheeky cunt. You not only lose me £40,000 and grass me up, but now you're putting marks on the roof of my car. You cunt.'

I'm furious with the prick by now. Proper lost it, I did. Snowball now joined in. He was doing 70 mph. I remember thinking, these Sunnys are sound, la. Nifty and that. He had his right hand on the wheel, but was lashing out at this feller with his left arm. Pulling his hair and that and ragging his nose. Next thing I say: 'Open the fucking door to the middle lane.'

Snowball's like that: 'Fuck that. You'll kill the cunt.'

I'm like: 'Just do it, will you, you prick.'

I'd had enough of this fellow in the back now. Blubbering and that. There's no way he'd be staying in the car for the next three hours and that, all the way back home, but I can see Snowball's half thingy about it. And next minute he's like: 'I can't reach the hangle and that.'

I'm thinking, 'It's only a fucking small car, you shithouse. You're not even trying there.' So I opens the back passenger door on my side. By this time, I've got one leg over the front seats and I'm half in the back. There are families, driving past and that. Teams of Indians in minibuses and that, on the motorway, like you used to get. All astonished at this caper going on in the car and I'm just carrying on wellying him hard up the arse.

Kicked him out onto the hard shoulder, I did. Watched him out the back window, la. In bulk, he was. Rolling over dead fast, but his arms and legs smashing on the ground even faster. Flailing, they were, uncontrollably. Pure fucking splattered goodo, he was. We were doing 70 mph, by the way. Laughing, I was, in all honesty. Hysterically. There was loads of cars behind. Everyone saw what was going on. It was ontop to death, but I could not give a fuck in all fairness. Afterwards we just carried on fucking going as though nothing had happened. I was reading the paper and that.

When I got back I had murder with Grimwood. Could not let this little escapade go, in all fairness. Was the first time I stood up to him properly. I was half fucking going to do him as well. He could have brought my whole operation ontop and got me serious time. For all I knew it might have been a set-up from the word go. For all I know the busies might have been onto me for a while and knew about all the other jobs and this was the grand finale. The sting, to get the evidence first hand. I knew I could take Billy in a one-on-one and I was going to do it then.

I was looking at him. He'd come down to my yard for the steward's and all that, being all 'I can't believe it' and all that baloney, but he looked half pathetic, in all honesty. For the first time I noticed that he looked old. All the time he'd served over the years was taking its toll. His suits didn't look that great any more. He'd passed his sell-by, in all fairness. Times were a changin' and there was no room no more for these Kray clones. Trading off their tales of derring-do and their daft overcoats and that. Their idiosyncrasies and all. Modern villainy was about grafting hard and getting on your bike.

Billy was getting sloppy, to be truthful. He was too used to waiting for things to come to him and now that it was drying up, he was taking chances on pricks like the fence, to make the numbers up. Was drinking a bit too much for my liking and all and he was surrounding himself with gangster ghouls, phoneys and yes men. Gobshites, the lot of them.

As he was jabbering on I was half-thinking of just twatting him there and then, to shut the cunt up. I spied a nice iron bar about six foot away if he proved to be a bit more tasty than his demeanour of late had suggested. But deep down I knew doing him in would just cause untold. Pure beefs, it'd lead to, no two ways. Not only back home, mind you, but in London and that, where he still had a few be-suited community leaders on his side. They used to meet up at their big mad gangster funerals and that. He loved all that palaver, Billy. Years later he went to the Krays' funeral where Johnny Nash was pallbearer. In truth, in the end, I could not be arsed doing Billy in. Just left it, I did. I said to him: 'You are full of shit. Stay out of my fucking yard.' And with that, I fucked him off.

Business carried on as usual after that. Builders used to ring us up: 'I need a caravan for a site. Can you get us one?'

'Of course, no sweat.'

I robbed a couple of these big fuck-off caravans they used as offices and digs for the workies and that. Could not believe it, la. Sold one for £3,000 – that was nearly enough for a house at the time. So I told Snowball to have off as many as he could. When we couldn't get the big ones off the sites, he'd rob normal size ones from outside of people's houses. Cunt's trick, I know, but as

I says, we had no regard for nothing at the time, in all honesty.

Snowball would suss it out on someone's path and that and just tow it away in the middle of the night. I'd get a call at four in the morning, open up the yard and he'd drive it in. The next day we'd change all the locks, burn the numbers off and tow them down to Plymouth. We had a contact down there who'd put it in the local paper and get rid. Mostly we'd get grands here and there, but sometimes for a good one we'd get £2,500. Was good bunce, in all fairness, considering it was just caravans and that. It was all money in your backbin, knowmean?

The Scrapman's Gang was making good money. It had been good to all those involved: nice houses were being bought, cars, exotic holidays, golf clubs – all that carry on. We were also spending a lot on going out – pissing grands and grands up the wall. Got into being bits of playboys and that. The kiddies around town if you will. Ten-day benders were not uncommon – especially if we'd had a good touch. I didn't go home for weeks. Was out shagging all kind, I was. Getting totally slaughtered.

At about this time I thought it was a good idea to knock it on the head for a while. Were starting to attract a bit of attention, in all fairness. Busies were sniffing round the yard and that. It was time for a bit of a long break, to be truthful – from the robbing at least.

7

Caesar's Palace

Meanwhile, back on the doors Paul was embroiled in an endless round of gangster violence as the battle for control of Liverpool's bloody and brutal clubland raged on. It was 1976. Change was in the air. Disco was invading the dance floors. Punk rock was kicking off. Chicken-in-the-basket cabaret was fighting to hold its own. In Liverpool, a new and exciting youth trend was taking root.

Fuelled by Liverpool Football Club's success in Europe, fans had taken to wearing expensive training shoes 'zapped' from exotic sports shops in Italy, Switzerland and Germany. The scally or football casual was born, the bane of door teams across the land. That year there was also a heatwave. Society was restless. Like a fresh wound, an unnerving undercurrent of panic meandered through the nation's collective psyche.

Old institutions were being affronted, insulted and torn down. The underworld was not insulated from this cultural upheaval. New gangs were growing stronger, tearing up the rule book and challenging the old order. As Paul gently expanded his own influence on the nightclub scene he was locked into a war of attrition, fighting on two fronts with old enemies and the young bucks alike.

The Oslo moved from the rundown Dock Road area to a more prestigious and lucrative town-centre location. Paul took over the door on several other clubs including one called the Beachcomber, and when a new three-tier dance-floor-on-every-level club called Caesar's Palace opened, it wasn't long before Paul had muscled in on the action. Business was good, but it came at a price.

———————————

PAUL: The punks were sound, in all fairness. No trouble from them at all. Their clobber was truly outlandish, knowmean? Mad kecks, kilts and all of that. Some of the lads couldn't get over them, knowmean? We was wearing flares and shiny bomber jackets and all of that so we thought we were the greatest thing ever.

A lot of folk thought the punks were hell-bent on trouble, just 'cos of what they wore – razor blades on their heads and so on – but the way I seen it, the punks just came in my clubs for a good time, not for meddling with fellers like my good self and the lads, so it was sound, as far as I was concerned. Did not half-mind some of their tunes, mind you, too. The Sex Pistols and The Clash and all of that. Used to loiter around the top floor when those tunes came on, to be truthful, just to have a sneaky listen.

In the mid '70s a new club came to prominence in Liverpool. Caesar's Palace was a bit sleeker than the other clubs, a bit aspirational, if you will. It was a new club for a new era, with Mrs Thatcher coming into play and all that carry-on. It was half the super club of its day, . There were three floors, each with its own entrance.

On the ground floor there was a gay disco run by a flamboyant queg called Sadie. He was known as the Queen Bee and the bar became known as the Queen's Club. Not that I'm cake myself, but they were an all right crowd. No gip, no nothing. Is right, the quegs.

On the middle floor there was the actual Caesar's Palace

nightclub, for your discerning '70s groovers, knowmean? And on the top floor was the Swinging Apple where all the punks went. Also there was a little bar called Caesar's in the upstairs, in like a little living-room bit. Needless to say, and it does go without saying by now, in total fairness, my good self was taxing all three floors of Caesar's Palace, without prejudice, to death. Full stop.

I got my foot in the door at first by offering the owners a bit more security. I used to go in there and chat with the owners and sort out any problems with some of the gangsters who were coming in. Anyone leaning on them. Come and see your Uncle Paul, knowmean? And I would lean on them back and the problem would normally disappear. Then I formally took over the door, and as well as the gangsters, I had to deal with the normal punters running amok as well.

As well as the punks I noticed that a few of the younger lads coming in had started to dress a bit different. Especially off've a Saturday night, after the match. They caught my eye this crew, with their distinctive dress. More often than not they wore green Peter Storm cagoules and tight kecks and that. Some of them looked half cake with their big, mad floppy wedges and so on. And I used to buzz off them and ask them if they were here to go in the gay bar, just to wind them up. But they were nasty bastards, this crowd, from Gerrard Gardens, and the Bull Ring and Scotty. Cutters, they were. Stanley knives and all of that business, so you had to watch them. Luckily enough they insisted on wearing trainers. So it was one of them when a crew of these scallies turned up, trying to blag in and that: 'Sorry, lads. Not today. No trainers. Can't help you.' And they would be knocked back.

Not that I was arsed, having to deal with these wayward youths and that. It was just that there was enough trouble in the club anyway, from villains. I was having trouble with all of the major Liverpool crime families – the Lambs, the Hughsies, etc. All on my case for dough and one thing and another. But the Ungi crew were still causing me major blues. Would this crowd let it go? Would they fuck. Even though they were just little skirmishes, glassings and that, they could escalate into big, mad gangster wars if you weren't careful, and we had too much to lose not to be careful.

One Saturday night I was on the door giving it loads to this crew of snarling urchins trying to get in: 'Not today, lads. Even if you take your Addi fucking Dassler off you are not getting in my club . . .' etc.

At about half-ten the bell goes from the second floor in the club. Joey Ungi, the well-known Liverpool up-and-coming community leader, is kicking off at the club. Did not need this one bit tonight, la, it being chocca and that and all kind of heads popping in to have a word about various bits and bobs. So I just bounces up there, gets hold of the cunt and throws him down the stairs. Out of my club. End of. I got straight back to my usual job of teasing the Ordinary-to-Chelsea types who were now very nicely rising to the occasion. Throwing bottles and that at the lads on the door. Pure pack of hyenas, this crowd were.

After I sorted the scallies out I went and had a word with the owner and asked him why the Ungis were kicking off. He told me that they were tapping him for money, straightforward protection and that. So it's a bit more serious than I originally figured. At about midnight I fucked off round the club for a mooch and that. At about half past 12 a big team of these Ungis steam into the club, do the two doormen on the door downstairs and proceed to run pure amok. Is there any need, I ask you?

They find the owner, a feller called David Tonner, and smash a pint pot into his head and do him in good style. Head's done in, literally. To be fair, it's one of those big, heavy, old-fashioned glasses and he's on the floor with a fractured skull. Serious, la. I runs down into the milieu and Joey Ungi is just standing there, it's his fucking team, knowmean? There's no back-up for me so I'm thinking that I'm just going to front it out, *Men Who Would Be Kings*-style. Hopefully force the cunts to fuck off.

One of them takes a run at me and hits me over the head with a claw hammer. Fucking killed it did, but I just stood there, blood gushing all over the show. He tried to have another go at me, but I moved a touch and connected a dig onto him. The lad panicked and threw the hammer right at my head and ran. It hit me and that purely killed as well, but at least he was disarmed and I was still standing, despite a big fuck off gash on my head.

From nowhere I get a tyre lever on my head as well. But I don't go down. Fucking angry, I was by then. I starts to grab them one by one and do them in. By myself I battered five or six of them. They had knives and bars and all manner of hardware but still they were going down – no back answers. Joey Ungi could not believe it. He's stood at the door overseeing the massacre of his top boys by yours truly on his tod and he can't get over it. Sickener, it was for him. It worked, though. Soon this team were getting on their toes. The busies were no doubt on their way. Joey Ungi is still standing there saying: 'Anyone says anything and you're fucking dead.'

Who does he think he is? *Shane* or what? I replies back: 'Go and fuck yourself, you fucking prick.'

And with that he gets off and the party's over. Not the maddest go-around of all time, but certainly one that had to be dealt with, as soon as. Had to correct their bad manners pronto, in all fairness. If I let that go, next week they'd be looking to have the door off've me, no messing around and muscle in on my action. There were also wider issues – all manner of beauts would be looking to have my good self off, if I give this crowd a walkover. No doubt the affair would be all over the fucking clubland bongos by now. No amount of fucking fishwife-gangster gossips would be relishing this little incident and its implications of my imminent downfall. So I plans to execute the only option open to me – to do them in, totally, on the morrow.

First things first. I goes the ozzie, gets my 20 stitches for the gash and gets back to the club early doors. It's ten bells, the cleaners have just arrived. I can hear the in-and-out drone of a Hoover somewhere in the bowels of the club. The place stinks of beer-soaked carpets and ciggies, but I love that smell, by the way, so it's sound. I bells one of the lads and tells him to get in sharpish to give me a sitrep. He tells me that the owner has got a fractured skull and is still in ozzie and the two doormen are in the same ozzie with bruises and all that carry-on. The owner was in a critical condition and he ended up staying in intensive care for two weeks.

I'm half-thinking of putting a call-out on these wretched Ungsters once and for all, and having be done with them, totally. But then I'm thinking that will lead to a full-blown skirmish, shooters, serious bloodletting and untold, knowmean? Put the whole caboodle in bulk, that would. That in turn would give the busies a green light to turn the likes of my good self over, which I could totally do without. I was setting up a new legit business – a waste-disposal business, tipper wagons and all of that – and I was lying low trying to keep a low profile, trying to put all my energy into that. I'd even laid off the robbing for a few months, to keep the busies purely off my case while I got all my ducks in a row.

On top of that, I couldn't afford to bring it ontop for the Billy Grimwoods and Johnny Nashs of this world. Plunging the whole nightclub underworld into a mini civil war would put their little arrangement at risk, and that income stream was purely sacred at the end of the day. Too many salaries riding on it, knowmean? Much as I'd like to do it, the consequences of mindless violence might be self-defeating. Nash would be right up on the rattler if it kicked off, demanding answers from my good self as to why there were teams of uncouth northerners fighting each other in the street and interfering with his wages. So all in all I was looking for a two-way solution here – a face-saving outro that would make me look good and not lead to all-out mayhem. Easier said than done in this game, believe you me. I got my thinking cap on. Later that night Dave Dicko floats in with a shooter. Clean. No history. No numbers. Untraceable.

'If you want, I can slip you this . . . and you can pop Joey now.

End of. No back answers. Is right kidder. You know you've got to.'

I was half tempted, to be truthful, but this one required half a think through before it came to cold-blooded doorstep shootings. Which is what it would have meant, by the way. The fucking lot of them. Then Johnny One Eye, Ronnie Mellor's son, says that events were moving apace. Breathless, he arrives at the club and says he's just had a phone call off the Ungis and they want a meeting.

At first, I told them to fuck off. The Ungis knew it was coming ontop for them. They'd sent one of their boys, a feller called McGorry, to the ozzie to check on the owner, to make sure he wasn't going to die. Clumsily, he tried to cut a deal with the owner's people there and then to smooth things over and that. The Ungis were desperate because the owner's partner, a very rich businessman who owned a mini oil refinery on the Dock Road, a total straight-goer, was putting pressure on the busies to find the attackers.

The next night the Ungis sent their top emissary, a feller called Tony Murray, who they trusted as a negotiator, to the club to have a word with me. To see how the land lies with YT. He kept following me round the club, asking if he could have a word and set up a meet and that. He just got fucked off. I was going to bash him up there and then. Plug the cunt in his temple and put his body in the Mersey just to send out a message. I had to walk away from him to stop myself from doing it. Dave Dicko talked me out of it and told Murray to leave well alone.

The next day the Ungis phoned Johnny again. For a meeting. One of their younger members of the family had been nicked for the twatting me with a hammer. His name was Ronnie Stephen Ungi. He was only 17 and they'd charged him with maliciously wounding me. After thinking about it, when they phoned back, I told Johnny One Eye to tell them 'Yeah!' to a meet.

Why not? I figured. If it's a straightener, I'm laughing – 'cos the poor kid Joey will be going down and will be going to sleep. So that's allday. If they want to shoot me, then that's allday, as well, 'cos I'll give them half a run for their money. But I was half-hoping deep down that they just wanted a chat, say sorry and that, so we could all get on with making dough again.

Of course, I'd have to make a big to-do about it for appearance's sake, verbal them to death and that, but that would solely be for public consumption, knowmean? To reassure the doubtfire fishwives just who was still on top. But that would still be classed as a truce, to be fair, seeing the enormity of the liberty that had been taken.

8

Cortina Crew

Paul was set for a showdown with his enemies. But like many of these workaday meetings, they were more anti-climax than St Valentine's Day Massacre.

PAUL: The meeting was set up to take place in a side street off've Prescott Road. They said that they'd pull up in a car and two of us would jump in the back seat and we could have a cosy gab, sat off there. The deal was that there was to be no back-up. Just two of them, one of their top boys, a gangster, let's say he's called Fred, and a sidekick, and two of us, my good self and Johnny One Eye, as well as a driver, of course.

I decided on not taking a armament. Did not need one with these beauts. Also, I wanted to try and keep it purely business. But I did tell my brother Stephen, who would be driving me, to get a big heavy motor so that he could ram them off've the street if they turned Turk. He lent a big fuck-off white Jag off've the Lambies, an outfit who, most ironically, I was having a dispute with at the time, but our Stephen was still coolio with. So he blagged it off've them, saying it was for a caper or whatever. Just right for the job, it was, of juggernauting an enemy vehicle into oblivion. Spanker and all too, by the way. Which was a shame, mind you, seeing as the only reason we didn't want to use one of our own top-of-the-range jalopies was because there was a good chance it was getting purely written off, in an ontop ball of highly evidential flames, with fried gangsters stuck to the burnt out wreckage and that.

So we drove down. It was an overcast, autumn night. Bit of wind and elecky in the air and that. We pulled up by the Fairfield pub. They pulled up in a Ford Cortina. In it was Fred and his sidekick, a pure gobshite called Tony Murray. Murray owned a garage in the South End. He thought he was a bit of a mediator, a bit of a thinking man's villain who could straighten out to-dos such as this between the savages by behaving as the voice of reason. Dickhead, he was.

Put simply he was a shithouse. Just a big shitbag who thought he was hard because he knocked around with these people. He'd started off at the bottom of the crime ladder and worked his way up, so to speak. He'd started off as a gofer for Billy Grimwood's wife Joan Mellor, who was a shoplifter, and he used to run her round and run cash and swag to and from the fences and that. He virtually moved in with her, but there was no funny business. We thought he swung both ways, a bit cake, knowmean? Didn't bother me like, but he got loads off've the lads for it. He used to stink as well. The cunt never got a bath. I mean NEVER. I remembered that our Stephen had butted him all round the place and threw him through a pub window a few months before.

Just then another Ford Cortina pulls up on the opposite side of the road, behind Fred's car, with four fellers in it. No sweat. Enemy forces and that. I says to our Stephen, who was driving the Jag: 'If that moves, ram it off the face of the earth and make sure those four fellas are going nowhere. Squash the cunts for all I care.'

He's like that, grinning and foaming, quite clearly relishing the prospect: 'Is right,' he says. 'Any devilment and it's curtains and that for the Cortina crew.'

Both me and Johnny One Eye slides into the back seat of the

other working-man's Rolls Royce with Fred in it. I says to Fred: 'What do you wanna do?'

Fred says: 'We'll have a chat and see where it goes.'

'Sound,' I says, 'but if there's any misbehaviour from your four mates in the Cortina then everyone goes, knowmean? Straight to Valhalla, with me?'

The fuckers then had the gall to turn round and say that the Cortina crew weren't with them. So there's a bit a panto banter: Yes, they are/No, they aren't, etc. Which was très boring, by the way. Meanwhile Johnny One Eye, who is itching to get down to business, pulls out a gun from nowhere. Without my knowledge, in all truthfulness, but bad news any whichways.

One Eye says: 'I don't give a fuck whether they are with youse or not. If there's any behaviour out of them, youse'll get fucking this.'

With that he brandishes the gun at Murray's grid. Goes without saying that Murray's arse completely goes. Now we'd got their undivided no-bullshit attention. Mind you, I was a bit pissed off with Johnny for pulling a stunt like that, all the same. I was looking at him, like: 'What the fuck are you doing? I'm in charge here.'

But he's lost, la. High off've the smell of blood and foaming at the mouth. These hotheads, la, they love these go-arounds. You couldn't have a business chat with a guy like that. You just didn't know where he was going. Going to a sit-down, you could end up fighting for your life. A pure hothead, One Eye was. A psychopath.

So now I had several variables to deal with. Not only did I have Fred and Murray to contend with, keeping them sweet and listening to what they've got to say, but I had to make sure that Johnny was under control. One moody move, one slight – no matter how small or mistaken – could result in a pure massacre here. Brains all over the dash and that. And he'd do it, One Eye would, no two ways. There and then. Bang! Bang! Johnny would pop them here and now and not be arsed. Pop into Fairfield for a pint afterwards, too, he would. He was a hairline trigger, this guy.

So I had to tread carefully here, diplomatically, hostage-trained speak, knowmean? Work towards bringing this palaver to a close as quickly and as smoothly as possible. But there's not much material to use here, by any stretch. It's all monosyllabic gangster behaviour and sly looks in the mirror.

Just then Fred throws me a bone, a window of opportunity, if you will. I'd come to this meeting thinking that Fred had the same worries as me: to avoid all-out war. But it seems, on balance, that he's more worried about the busies. The busies, for God's sake! He must have had something hanging over his head. Trouble with the law must have meant he'd be looking at some jug for something or other I didn't know about. Get paid, I thought.

So I plays it cool, not letting on that I don't give a fuck about plod, thus investing me with some free bargaining power, ta very much.

Fred says: 'I have heard that you're giving a statement to the busies.'

What? Me? Is this beaut brand new or what? Me, talking to the busies. About this load of bollocks. But I went with it. Pure blanker, I gave him. Giving him absolutely nothing to work with. My best poker face.

'And the owner. The bloke I twatted with the glass, he's making a statement, isn't he?' he went on.

Fred lad. Don't ever go into the negotiating business 'cos you're fucking last.

'I could well do without that,' Fred said, pathetically, in all fairness, his head half-down and that.

Now I knew where he was going. A GPS could not have given me a better route map to his wants and needs. For some reason he was shitting his Lois jeans (that's what these urchins were all wearing at the time) over the busies. He was probably looking to box me off. Give me a dropsy for not turning up and that. Crude, la, crude, to say the least. Who did he think I was? Some kind of fucking nugget. A fucking snake's rag-arse like hisself. That was it with these bucks, they had zero fucking respect. They judged everyone by their own very low dirty-rat bastard standards. But I maintained a pure dignified silence. Let the prick sweat. He was gifting me a top outro here, a pure Dayton peace plan pleasing to all parties, weren't costing me nothing and I was gonna walk away with the prick shaking my hand and telling me what a boss feller I was. Gangsters against the world and all that carry-on, knowmean? Laughing, la, I was.

'I know,' I says, holding his stare and that so he thinks I'm a serious stand-up guy who's telling the truth and really wants to waste time being here. 'The busies are all over us. They want you bad, la. They are putting pure pressure on us to throw you in.'

Lie, by the way, but so what? No way I was getting into heaven anyway. This whole fucking skenario was pure drama over substance anyway. The owner had told me earlier that there was no way he was pressing charges and all that carry on, but of course Fred did not know that. 'Well, what are you going to do about it?' he droned.

Pure showing his hand by now, he was. The fool. He had that look on his face like a feller who was asking someone not to tell his tart about an affair he was having. By the bollocks, I had him.

'Listen, I'll make it easy for you 'cos I do not have the time for this malarkey. Stay out of my club and I'll straighten the owner out. The busie thing will disappear.'

Fred's like that, near fucking exploding with excitement: 'What do you mean?' Sliding around the plazzy seats, like he's a big kid.

I said: 'I've just told you. I'm not prepared to give a statement. I'll make sure the owner doesn't. I'm giving you a walkover. As long as you leave off've the venues.'

He's like that, pure made up, as though I've just granted him his freedom. As though this was a really big deal. Strange, la, but true. We shook on it and got off. Double result there, me thinks. Number One: averted war and kept the business safe for Billy and Nash. Number Two: got the meeting over without Johnny One Eye blowing the heads of these two pricks all over the PVC seats. Was half thinking at one point of how I was going to have to crush the Cortina with the bodies in it to get rid of evidence, if it come to that. Funny what goes through your mind when you're in a situation like that. Forward planning mostly.

Overall, I couldn't believe what a big waste of time it had been. But that was it with a lot of these villains. They were always frittering time away on shit matters such as trying to persuade someone to drop the charges on some fucking trivial matter or other. That's why most of them end up skint, in my book.

A few days later Johnny One Eye tells me that Fred would like another meeting. I told him I'd see him in the Farmer's pub on Upper Breck Road. I gets there. Fred's acting like he's my new best mate. The beaut. He buys me a drink. But I fuck him off and tells him that I'll buy my own. You've got to treat this lot like birds, knowmean? Treat 'em mean and all that.

'Don't be nasty,' he says. Which half-amused me, in all fairness. Maybe I was not giving this one all he was due. Maybe, he could see through my tough-guy act and was a bit post-ironic hisself. The next thing he's thanking me for not giving evidence. As though I'm arsed, by the way. Was getting bored of this by now to tell you the truth.

So I said: 'Listen, I don't like you so let's forget all this nonsense and go our separate ways.'

He started laughing, shook me hand and said he admired me. But it wasn't a big, mad bonhomie moment. I just got off into the night.

I remember that there was a lot of incidents like these. Pure timewasters. A drain on my resources, they were. They didn't make me any dough. They didn't advance my cause. They just went with the territory. I guess it was the price of living in that world. It was like being the boss of a big company and being dragged into meetings all day, knowmean? The only thing is, when you're a gangster you don't have a PA to filter out the shit from the big decisions which will get you paid. You've got to bounce around your patch like a feudal lord, dishing out instant justice, etc., and being seen, and being king of the patch and all that carry-on.

The next crew to have a go were the Lambs. They were a pretty heavy crew. They'd got into protecting all of the Liverpool showbiz stars of the day, many of whom were completely unaware that they were dealing with the underworld – Ken Dodd, Tom O'Connor, Cilla, all the pop groups that came to town and that. Payments being made for 'security' were going straight to the Lambs. If you wanted to shoot a TV programme, a sitcom or a film, and there was a lot at the time with *The Liver Birds*, and Alan Bleasdale and *Boys from the Blackstuff,* and Willy Russell and *Blood Brothers* and *One Summer* and what have you, you'd have to pay them first or all of your camera gear would go west ASAP. They controlled all that. It was a good screw.

On top of that, they had a little fiddle on the side. They'd turn the stars over they were supposed to be protecting and sell big stories to the papers. That's how it came on top for Tom O'Connor with the prostitutes. They'd sort out a brass for his room, but also tell the *News of the World* who'd be sitting in the next hotel room. Get paid, the Lambies. But now they were looking to get into clubland as well.

One night a crew of six of them comes into Caesar's and starts snarling at the owners, making demands on them, saying that they're going to petrol bomb the club if they don't get dough. Usual stuff, but very crude if you ask me. They'd chosen that night purely because it's my night off, but I gets the call and bombs down there with Mick Cairns. I orders a pint and stands right next to them at the bar, staring and snarling back and just laughing at them. They gets the message and fuck off.

Later that night they come back with cans of petrol, swords, a metal gear lever, a rubber mallet and a foot-long metal bar. Mick and I battered all six of them. Just purely done them in just with our fists. In all fairness, Mick got chopped up with the sword across the back. They went to finish him off and slit his throat but he ran through a fire escape onto the roof and leant on the door behind him. Even after the cavort had ended, we had to smash down the door onto the roof because he wouldn't open it. He was terrified for his life. I booted each one of them down the stairs and to add to their humiliation the busies were waiting in the street to nick them.

I was like that: 'Bye, bye. Later, lads. Yes, see you later.' Just buzzing off them, we were. It was like the end of *Scooby Doo* when the villains are being bowed into the police cars and are scowling at their captors. Amateurs they were. Amateurs. All six of the beauts were charged with affray and carrying offensive weapons and for the protection bit they were charged with making threats and causing fear to the club premises. Definitely a lesson on how not to racketeer in clubland, that one. It proved to them that being a gangster is one thing, but making it on the doors is another, with me?

Meanwhile, violence was spiralling out of control all over the place. People would get crippled and coma'ed and chopped up for nothing at all. It was natural. Like driving or going to buy a sandwich. Beating someone until they went blind or brain damaged or choked on their own broken bones and teeth was a daily occurrence. No one got caught. It was just business. It meant more dough. So what? Leave them where they fell. Are they dead? Don't know. Don't care. Fuck 'em off. Get paid.

I took over the security on a string of massage parlours. Was screwing good punt out of it, to be fair. They were always getting heisted and had off or the punters would shag the girls without paying. So after the clubs I'd go and sit with the girls and use the gym and the sauna and what have you.

One of them was owned by a feller called Dick the Snip. He was a barber. One night a punter refused to pay. Gets the call. Snipper's like that to the terrified brass: 'Keep him there. We're on our way down. Suck his cock some more, just don't let him go.'

Little did this punter know that we had a good system organised, a quick-response so that I was there even before this flash little twerp had his kecks on. I only wanted to give the feller a hiding and get his dough. But Dick the Snip starts smashing his head in with a baseball bat. Furious, he was and foaming at the mouth. Ripping his hair out and kicking his teeth in. The guy is screaming for his mam. The brasses are wailing in pain just watching it.

If that wasn't enough, Ritchie Mellor, Dick the Stick, who was partners with me in this vice-security venture, runs in with a villain called Rodney Brown. Dick the Stick pulls out a big, fat butcher's knife and stabs the punter in the back and belly. He's running the blade into his body like a fucking jackhammer and slashing him in the face and neck for good measure.

I was always amazed, to be fair, in these skenarios, just how much the human body can take. Most people would have been dead, no back answers. But in one last burst for survival this feller springs to his feet and runs for the door and straight through a reinforced plate-glass window. Cut to bits, he was. I don't know how he did it. It was like fight or flight, adrenaline or something. We just stood there, mouths open. That's that. Dick the Stick is laughing like a hyena. I was indifferent, just looking at the knife, dripping with claret and that. All of us were breathless. There's blood and shite all over the place.

'I like to leave marks,' Dick the Stick says.

Funny thing happened though. I got talking to one of the brasses and she told me that she used to work on the streets until it became too dangerous. We were laughing, bearing in mind what had just happened. She said that this little team of black lads were going round terrorising the brasses and the punters and that in the red light in Toxteth. Taxing them and so on. But she says that recently the culprits been stuck down for two years now, so she was considering going back on the streets and that.

'Who are they?' I says.

'They're only a pair of scallies' she said dismissively, ' Their names are Curtis Warren and Johnny Phillips. D'y know them?'

'No. Should I?' I didn't know it yet but one of these lads, Curtis Warren, would have a very big effect on my life in the future. At that time he was just a rag-arsed scally. He went on to be yowge [huge]. I mean really *yowge* in the drugs game.

There was a lot of violence in the air. It seemed as though everywhere I went there was smashed heads and broken bones.

Trouble followed me round. For instance, the next night I was having a game of darts. Out of nowhere this feller called Willy accuses me of kopping for his bird. He's drunk. He's got me confused with another feller called Nick. But I was so wound up that he'd interrupted me darts that I dragged him outside and used his head as a human football. I just booted him until he fell into a coma and then battered his head against a car boot. I was in a trance. All's I could see was red and rage.

My mate grabbed me and goes: 'You've done him now.' I threw him on the floor and left him for dead. That's that.

9

John Haase

One night at Caesar's Palace Paul had a chance meeting with a gangster called John Haase. Haase was an armed robber who led a notorious gang of raiders dubbed the Transit mob, a name derived from their trademark use of Ford Transit vans. The gang terrorised Britain in the '70s and early '80s, targeting post offices and security vans. It was the beginning of an extraordinary friendship.

PAUL: One night a man called John Haase was trying to get in Caesar's. That night I met him for the first time, but he would go on to have a very big effect on my life over the next 20 years. I was in Caesar's doing business with the owners. There were two lads on the door downstairs and I was sorting out a problem upstairs. The bell went, signalling trouble downstairs. I thought it was probably a crew of tweed-clad scallywags trying to blag a late one after a midweek away somewhere. But the owner and the other heavies upstairs wouldn't go down, because of who this John Haase was and what he could do. Terrified, they asked me to sort it out.

When I got down there, there was a feller called Johnny Oates, one of the lads, with another smartly dressed mush, this John

Haase, giving all sorts of abuse to the girl on the door till. My two lads on the door were stood off as though this feller in the suit was some kind of untouchable bad lad or something. He was a notorious shooter merchant who would think nothing of coming back and shooting up the place, so they says.

So I asks him what the problem is. He turns to me and tells me to fuck off. Here we go, I thought. Going to have to administer some sleeping tablets to this young fellow. But I notices he's got a plaster-cast on his leg and think twice, seeing as it wouldn't quite be cricket, notorious shooter merchant or not. Obviously, he's a bit of a player so I just says to him: 'Listen I don't give a fuck who you are but you are going to have to leave now.'

With that I chases him from the club. When I turn to the lads they're like that: 'D'you know who that is? Pure bad one that, Oscar. Should have given him a walkover.'

'Not arsed,' I says. 'Who is this fella, by the way?'

'John Haase, la.'

It turns out that he's supposed to be some kind of rooting-tooting armed robber or something. Hard-core and all that. About half an hour later there's a knock on the door again. It's Johnny Oates.

'All right, Johnny, are you coming in?'

He says: 'Yeah, sorry about before and that, Oscar. But . . .'

'Yeah, no sweat, Johnny. No problem . . .'

Then I sees this Haase behind him. I says to Johnny: 'I don't give a fuck about you but he's not coming in with you.'

Johnny's like that: 'Come 'ead, Oscar, la,' etc. etc.

After a few minutes of this toing and froing and that I says to Johnny: 'Listen, if he apologises to the girl on the till and the lads on the door, then I might consider it.'

Only did it because Johny Oates' dad was mates with my auld feller and that. I can see this Haase is fuming. This is a big humiliation for him, to be fair. He's a big feller in the scheme of things, could just tell, knowmean, and this is pure doing his head in, but he says he's sorry and they go in. He wasn't in there long before he gets off again. On the way out, he gives it a big, mad 'We'll meet again'. Trying to be chilling and what have you with the big gangster veiled threat.

I'm like that: 'I hope so.'

With that he disappeared into the night.

Five months later me and Mick Cairns are having a little drink in the Fairfield. It was a nice little boozer, which we used to have little meets, no hassle and that. No one went in there. No gangsters, no doormen, no nothing, just ordinary working fellers. By that time the busies were on our case badly. Putting surveillance on us at every opportunity, nicking us for little things. So the Fairfield was a little den for meets where no one knew where we were.

But one night Mick and I go in and it's like a gangsters' convention. It's like a mini fucking Appalachian for the Scouse Mafia, knowmean? There's the Hughsie brothers, a feller called Tommy Smith, this cockney gangster (who later turned out to be a big grass; who'd been put into them by the busies), a few other notorious scallies, and lo and behold this John Haase is there, too.

Straight away me and Mick are looking at each other thinking: 'What the fuck is this? These are going to bring it right ontop for us in here.' Plus, we didn't like the cockney straight away. Definitely, skewwiff him, la, knowmean? Had him sussed straight away. We happened to be there 'cos we were planning a one-off, a bit of graft which we had come across, to tell you the truth. So we were using the Fairfield as our most secret and low-key HQ.

So we're looking over at this crew aghast. Tommy Smith spies us, cutely, not looking too happy, puts his ciggie out, looks up through the swirls of smoke and bombs over. Shakes our hands and all that gangster carry-on. I'd known Tommy for years. He was sound. Allday, he is, Tommy. He was a handsome bastard, Tommy, though he was always sullen and reserved. I liked that.

He'd been through the mill over the years and I had time for him.

At an early age he was cut up, his tendons beneath the knees were severed. Later he was shot by the busies while attempting to rob a PO'ey [Post Office] with the Hughsies. But talk about front. He sued the busies and got compo, la, after the busies were forced to reveal that they had targeted him deliberately. Cheeky or what? He married into our family later on, to a girl called Deborah, who was Joan Mellor's daughter. Dick the Stick became his driver.

So he bombs over. Straight away he knows there's been a diplomatic faux pas here. Next minute the Hughsies mosey over.

'What are youse doing down here?' I says.

'We're having a meeting,' Hughsie replies, as though it's the most natural thing in the world.

'Listen, it's not the fucking Holiday Inn conference centre. Not in here you're not. This is my patch and you're bringing it bang ontop with the busies and that.'

I didn't want them bringing waves down to our patch with the auld bill and that. It was that touchy with the busies, at the time, in all fairness. Get to hear about a little meeting involving several well-known community leaders and next minute they want to know what's going on in the boozer. So they start watching it and next thing is we're fucked. And I couldn't be doing with that at the time. As well as my one-off with Mick, I was doing a few little warehouse robberies all to myself on the sly. Is right and that.

So the Hughsies are like that: 'Did not know, la. Sorry and that. We're off, Oscar. Say no more.'

'Anyways, what are you doing with him?' I says.

I was looking over at Haase. He was dressed in a suit talking to the cockney, who was also sporting a whistle. Haase is looking over at me. I didn't like the look of the cockney at all. I knew that Haase's head was wrecked because I knew all these so-called Top Boys. Not only that, they were suckholing me and all, too.

He was gobsmacked that I knew them and that I did not give a shit about them. Little signals mean a lot. Underworld office politics and that.

When I first came in he probably thought he was intimidating me, being with these cronies and that, but it purely backfired. Trivial I know, but loaded with meaning if you know where I'm going? So on the way out he slides over, shakes my hand and apologises for the carry-on at the nightclub and this little faux pas that was going on as well.

'No sweat and that,' I says as I watch him get into a cab outside.

As I says, the Hughsies later discovered the cockney was a grass. I knew I was right and it justified me overreacting to make them fuck off from the boozer. It was a golden rule never to discuss work in front of strangers. Careless talk costs lives – ironically in this case his own. Needless to say, shortly after it was discovered that he was a grass, the cockney was zapped. The brakes on his 'motor' were cut and the steering was ragged. Very professionally, mind you, so no one would know. Pure Princess Di-style, knowmean? After a night out, he went round a roundabout near a nightclub called the Coconut Grove and crashed. By the time the busies got to him, he was dead. It had to be done that way, made to look like an accident, so the busies didn't get suspicious. After all, they'd put him onto his killers in the first place.

A few weeks later I was out with my former doorman Alan and we bumped into Haase. Haase was bevvied and we got talking. Hasse told me that he was constantly at war with the Ungis. That they were causing him untold and that. As I got to know him I began to like him. He was a shotgun merchant, an armed robber into post offices and security vans and that. Give him his due, he was a pro. Not one of these chancers. People were afraid of him. Physically he was nothing, but people were afraid of what he could do with the hardware.

At the time, I was getting more and more involved with my

legitimate businesses. The tipper wagons were turning a profit. Basically, it was shite removing. Taking away rubbish from households and business and tipping it in the countryside. Of course, we fly-tipped as much as we could so we didn't have to pay landfill and that. We tipped thousands of tonnes in the disused docks down the Southend. Cunts we were, but, in all fairness, we knew no better.

We had adverts in the Yellow Pages and all the papers. A good few wagons and a few lads working for us. Me and Mick both took £60-a-day in drawings and left the rest in to expand the business. John Haase then asked me if he could invest in the business. He said the busies were on his case and he wanted to cover his money, so people wouldn't question his illegal income. So he put some dough in the kitty. It was only £170 but it was just a token gesture. In between robbing post offices and that he'd turn up for work, as though to prove he was a regular blue-collar guy, but he'd wear a suit. Even though it was shite removing he'd wear an expensive suit and an ironed white shirt and that. He insisted on rubbing barrier cream on his hands to keep them smooth. Vain wasn't in it. Mind you, he did graft. I'll give him that.

Sometimes he'd disappear for weeks, on bits of work he was taking care of, knowmean? Or he'd been nicked. The business was sound for him as well for alibis and that. Obviously, now he was on the firm and that, I'd vouch for him when the busies came asking where he was on such-and-such a date, but one time a private detective I knew turned up and said: 'I believe you've said Haase was working for you on the day such-and-such a warehouse was robbed. Just to let you know we've got him on camera doing the job. You'll end up going inside yourself for perjury, if you are not careful.'

So I had to pass on that, knowmean? Meanwhile, his feud with the Ungis and Fitzys was hotting up good style. I'm in Caesar's one night and I gets a call from Haase asking if this Fitzy lad was in.

'He's just left now,' I says, literally watching his cab get off.

Haase picked up his trail and followed. Then he jumped the lad in question and cut him up ruthlessly with a Stanley knife. He never used his fists. Haase repeatedly slashed him across the arse. It was all because this Fitzy lad had punched Haase's bird, Vera, in Black George's pub on Park Road. Then Haase went to prison on some charge. After he got out, I gave him £300 and told him that that was his stake in the business. There was no point him being involved in my legitimate businesses. He was too ontop and I was getting some big contracts at the time, which the likes of his reputation could jeopardise.

Six weeks after he was out I gets a visit from him. It was February 1980 and it was bitterly cold. I'd just won a big contract in Bootle to clean out this huge warehouse that'd just burnt down. Get paid, it was. Pure bundles. But it was murder working near the docks at that time of year, with the freezing winds and that coming in off've the Atlantic. So I was literally on site, in my overalls and that, taking care of business. Was enjoying being a well-off legitimate businessman, in all fairness. Meeting a different class of people. Straight-goers, other businessmen like my good self. Was feeling half-good about the achievements of my good self, in all fairness.

But one day John turns up with his main hombre Bernie Aldridge, who was Vera's brother, and says that he needs me as back-up to help him sort out two Ungi brothers. Haase is fuming. He's going off've his head saying how he's going to kill the Ungis and that. Fair enough, I thought, it saves me the hassle.

Bernie was trying to calm him down a touch. He was sound, Bernie, in all fairness. I knew him from being in the jug with him. He robbed warehouses in the early days, like me. He was a likeable fella, who just liked getting drunk with the lads and that. But Haase was always treating Bernie badly. Bernie never once slighted or betrayed him, but behind his back Haase would always call him 'a piece of shit' and take him for a bit of a cunt. Order him around and that. I was a bit thingy about it, to be honest.

As far as the fight, I thought it was just gonna be a straightener with these Ungis. Just fists, iron bars and maybe the odd machete and that – no shooters, knowmean? So I grabs a couple of pickaxe hangles for good measure off've one of my wagons. But Haase is getting more and more angry. He then decides he wants to shoot everybody. He asks Johnny One Eye, who was working for me, to go and pick up a shooter from his house and to meet us in Kitchen Street, near the Dock Road.

I didn't mind this in all fairness. Haase shooting these lads and all. It'd be one less headache for me and if he was pulling the trigger, then there'd be no financial comebacks for my good self or Billy. Sound as, in my book. The Ungis had it coming to them, to be fair.

So I'm like that: 'All right. Let's do it them before they do it to us.'

Haase found out that Joey Ungi was at a mechanic's garage owned by our old friend and top gobshite Tony Murray. When we gets there he and Johnny One Eye steam inside and started smashing the place up looking for them. John was dressed like he'd just walked out of Burton's window as usual. Tweed jacket, black kecks and a nice white shirt. Of course, they're ballied up and that.

It turns out that the Ungis had well fucked off by the time we got there. So Haase and One Eye were trying to scare Murray into telling them were they'd gone. First they smash up Murray's car. Then Haase was pointing the shotgun at his head threatening to blow him away. As usual Johnny One Eye gets impatient with the talk, grabs the single shooter off've Haase and blows a hole in Murray. He was aiming to kneecap him from the back of the legs, IRA-style, but he just ended up shooting him in the back of the leg. Blood everywhere, la. Murray's in bulk. Murray's sidekick, a feller called Desmond Fox, also gets a thrashing. They smashed his kneecaps in with an iron bar because they were busy reloading. All the while I'm stood outside in my ovies with the pickaxe hangles to make sure no one gets in. Suddenly, Haase and

Johnny One Eye run out and we get off. I'm not arsed, by the way. This kind of thing, shootings and that, happened all the time.

In the car, I asked Haase why he'd flew off the hangle on this particular day, even though this feud had been going on for years.

'They'd insulted me bird,' he says.

'What? You've gone and plugged someone because they slagged off your tart.'

'Yes,' he says. 'They'd give her loads in a club in town. Had to be done, la, no back answers.'

Haase's bird was called Vera Aldridge, Bernie's sister. She was a grafter, a shoplifter, whose full-time job was to basically rob nice suits for Haase. They had a kid together. She was a good woman, sound and that, but she had a drinking problem. Often, when Haase was in the jug, she'd drop the kid off at ours and disappear for days on end, in the clubs in town and that. That was her way of coping with the stress of the lifestyle. Was not arsed myself about her letting off steam, but I did worry about her and the bin lid, to be truthful, on occasion, with the firewater and all.

Anyways, we thought no more of this shooting in the garage. It was one of them. Allday. I went back to my clearing-out contract in Bootle. Haase went back to planning his bank capers. Little did we know, la. The thing blew up out of all proportion. I mean, out of all fucking proportion. You'd have thought we'd shot the president by the way the papers were going on.

Murray was rushed to hospital and a surgeon battled to save his leg. As though the cunt was *worth* saving. The papers made it into a big soap opera as though he was hanging onto his life by a thread and that he was just a nice feller who'd come a cropper. They described him as a garage boss. The busies said it was a big, mad gangland attack which they were going to stamp out. The papers were making out it was a fucking massacre or something. Was even on *Granada Reports* and that with that cunt Tony Wilson making out Liverpool was full of savages and that. Cheeky twat, that Anthony H. Wilson.

The busies said they were determined to get the fellers who

did it. Bit over the top, in all fairness, in my book. Three days later Haase and Bernie get nicked and charged with attempted murder on Murray and GBH on Foxy. They were sent to Risley Remand Centre. They are looking at a total stretch, in all fairness. Not that Haase was arsed. He was totally unfazed by doing bird. But we felt that John was being hard done by. So we started plotting and scheming how to make this go away.

The most obvious solution was to sit down with the Ungis and get Murray paid not to turn up in court. I could have straightened it out myself without any money changing hands. They owed me one for the other business. But it wasn't my problem – I never liked being in debt to anyone, especially for someone else's devilment. Going cap in hand to them would start a chain-reaction of doing each other favours. Not today, I thought. So I didn't mention it. In the end, Billy Grimwood got it sorted.

Billy summoned Murray to a meeting. Murray goes out of respect and all that carry-on. Billy points at his leg, which is in bandages and plaster-cast and all that, and says if he turns up in court his whole body will need a fucking plaster-cast, knowmean? Plain as. Murray rolls over and tells him he ain't prepared to point the finger. Billy sweetened the poison by promising to do him a little favour he was asking about.

On the day of the court hearing in July Murray went missing, of course. The papers ran a story begging him to come forward and give evidence. They even had the prosecution barrister pleading with him in court to come back, saying that his leg would fall off within seven days if he didn't, as it had a big mad infection. Then they said he had peritonitis, which would kill him if he didn't get to a doctor fast, but Billy had made sure that he was well out of the frame. On the lam he was and not coming back until the case well and truly disappeared. The court said that if Murray didn't turn up within seven days then they'd discharge John and Bernie.

The busies are furious. They're going round the city turning people over and putting the heat on people to try and find Murray. They're saying that Haase had had him kidnapped not to turn up or that Murray was a lamist because Billy Grimwood was putting the scares on him. The bongos were in overdrive.

With this in mind, so as not to bring it ontop for Haase, Murray is wheeled out of hiding and told to give himself up to the busies the next day. He goes to his solicitor and told them that he was defo going in the box before the seven-day court extension expired. The busies are made up now. Making sure he doesn't leave their side and that and rubbing their hands saying that it's a definite ten for John.

They're like that: 'Get paid. We've been after this cunt for years. Now we've got him bang to rights.'

But on the day of the court Murray goes and has a freak accident, doesn't he? Can you believe that shit? Yes I can. Why? Because it was all done on the instructions of Billy. The car crash happened at dawn (no witnesses) as Murray was on the way to court. Unlucky or what? But instead of going into the box, he's rushed to ozzie with his shot-up legs even more mangled. Pumped full of drugs by the docs. Result: he's in no fit state physically or mentally to give evidence in a court of law. Get paid. Game over.

Don't know whether Murray knew he was going to be a crash-test dummy, but the night before the accident I was told to keep tabs on him as he went around town on the piss. He came into the Lucky Club. Me and Mick Cairns followed him in there. We kept an eye on him from the next room until he got off home.

When the busies are told in court that Murray won't be turning up they are totally sinkered by this. The papers call it a drama. The busies bomb down to the hospital and virtually try and drag him from his bed to court. But the docs are like that, telling them to fuck off dragging him back in, saying he's a fucking sick fella and how dare they and that. In the end, they have to leave it. In a last-ditch attempt to keep Haase behind bars, the most senior busies in the city pleaded with the court not to drop the case, but they're told no way, the case is discharged. Haase and Bernie walk.

Haase was getting a reputation as someone who could beat cases. After the Murray shooting, the Ungis were more low-key and let their heavies do the dirty work. One of them, a big feller called Eddie Palmer, used to come in Caesar's. In fairness, he was a bit of goer, a big feller with a menacing air about him. Evil, he was, to be truthful. Mind you, I never got no trouble off've him. When he came in, it was one of them: 'I know who you are. I know who you run with and I don't give two fucks. Give me behaviour and there'll be untold, knowmean? End of.'

He was like that: 'OK, la. No sweat and that. Just out for a quick bevvy and that.'

Talking that way was showing respect to guys like that. They liked to know where they stood. So he respected me back for it, so it was allday.

A short while later Palmer was stabbed to death in a bar-room brawl. All the gangland caper – the stabbings and the shootings, the tie-ups, etc. weren't always bad for business, to be fair. In fact, you could turn it to your advantage if you wanted, to make a raise. What it did was make my good self totally indispensable to likes of the fellers who owned the clubs. All this random savagery put the shits up them good style and they needed me to protect them from it. Hence the protection rackets. But it's a bit more subtle than that, in all fairness.

It's more like what politicians use to start a war. It's a phoney pretext. The fear factor. I used every little battle and threat to increase my influence on the club, to run the place but without actually taking over it. No way I wanted the hassle of managing a gaff like that, but I was interested in maximising the dough I could squeeze out of there. Anyways, there was no way someone like me could get a licence for a place like that. Caesar's was turning into a goldmine and I was makin' sure that I continued to make good bunce out of it.

Sometimes, after a particularly bad attack, the owners would panic and come to me and say: 'Paul, we need you to run this.'

'Sound,' I says, 'as long as I gets paid, not a problem.'

One such incident happened in 1982. The management had brought in a feller called Dennis Kelly as a doorman. But one night he flew off've the hangle and murdered one of the punters, a newsagent called Billy Osu. Billy was a bit of a bully, but all right, knowmean? It brought a lot of heat on the club. The police launched a massive manhunt. An incident like that could get you shut down, no back answers.

Only a few months before, the owner, a feller called David Tonner, had asked the busies whether he could turn Caesar's into a pub and change the licence and that. This was to cool the aggro down a bit by deterring the late-night gangster crowd. But the busies fucked him off because they wanted to keep track of comings and goings which the signing-in process did.

Dennis had some beef with this Osu. Literally, it was over some throwaway banter on the door and that. Osu had insulted Kelly or looked at him bad, but even that could get you killed in the club. That's how easy it was for a guy to get whacked. Everyone was getting killed for no reason. Kelly and his mate Austin McCormick go looking for him. They drive down to a bar in Chinatown called the Kowloon. They hit him with a hammer and a bottle and Osu was stabbed three and a half inches into his heart. Osu didn't even know he was dying because these types of fights were normal. He jumped in a cab to go home but the driver took him to A & E instead. He died there.

It would have been worse if Dennis had killed him inside Caesar's. Luckily for us he had done the deed in the Kowloon. Kelly got life and McCormick went on the run for two years, where he survived dealing drugs under false names. He was eventually caught in London. The owners thought that they might lose the club over this caper, but they asked me to step in and sort it out. Make sure there was no comebacks. Take a bigger role running the place. Of course, I did. I was also taking over the doors on a lot of pubs as well. Any excuse would do.

Me wife Chrissy got a little job in a pub to get her out of indoors. It was a rough pub full of seriously heavyweight villains. It already had a door team. The manager was up the wall trying to keep an eye on these villains, who were always running amok, as well as his staff. One Sunday when I was minding the kids she come back, crying her eyes out saying that the head barman had called her a robber and all that carry-on and sacked her. So I walked into the pub and this fat cunt was behind the bar and I said to him: 'There is only one robber in my house and that's me. Don't accuse my wife of having the till off or I'll blow your pub up.'

All of these supposedly big-time villains who were there didn't like that I walked into their gaff and shouted the odds. I could have done them all in there and then and smashed the pub up, but to tell you the truth I couldn't be arsed. It's all a load of hassle. So I told the fat cunt to get the manager and I said to him: 'If that fat cunt is here tonight I'm smashing the pub up.'

So that night I went in and the fat cunt wasn't there and neither was their door team who were too terrified to turn up. The manager asked what I would have done if the fat cunt was still there. I said that if he was here I would have done him and then I would have smashed the pub up. The manager, who was pissed off that his own team had not protected him, said: 'Nice one. You can have the door.'

So I took over the security of the pub. All the villains used to come in, like even the old-timers Poppy Hayes and all that, and they knew me and they all respected me. So from then on there was never any hassle. So I just used to pop in a couple of times a week, have a look behind the bar, get me tank and fuck off. I was getting paid from a lot of pubs like that.

10

Straight-goer

It was 1985 and Paul had reached a crossroads in his life. He was pondering the unthinkable: to be or not to be a straight-goer. That was the question. One factor above all else had sparked a crisis of conscience at the age of 35 – drugs.

Since the mid-'70s villains in Liverpool had been organising the large-scale importation and distribution of cannabis, heroin and cocaine. A fledgling cottage industry concerned with the manufacture of amphetamines and hallucinogens had also taken root. Narcotics were a natural extrapolation of the Liverpool Mafia's expertise in smuggling and trade-based crime. The usual and formidable barriers to entry that prevented most gangsters from getting into the drugs trade at the top end were leap-frogged with ease by the Liverpool villains.

They controlled a busy port, supported enviable international connections and had established a robust underworld banking system. The money-washing and cash-transfer network was smaller, but just as sophisticated as that which greased the wheels of the Italian Mafia 'clip side of the big moist' in the US. A fortunate juxtaposition of such advantages allowed the Liverpool Mafia to steal a march in the drugs trade on their rivals in London, Manchester and Scotland.

Two other factors would later prove decisive in the exponential growth of the Mersey narco-phenomenon. The first was the historical and family links between the Liverpool villains and the 'Bhoys' – the Dublin-based IRA. The Bhoys were warmly referred to by their Scouse allies as the 'Ra' (pronounced 'rar'). The second factor was the long-term development of a criminal distribution network.

Spanning the UK, this system had been in existence since the war and was more than used to handling everything from contraband to stolen goods in industrial quantities. This loose but unbreakable organisation of fences, middle-men, moneymen, drivers and couriers across the country was the envy of their land-locked rivals in other cities who traditionally feared to tread outside their 'manors'. Gangsters in London were particularly reliant on the personal fiefdoms they controlled to provide income, more often than not the singular profit centres of their discreet, illegal empires.

Year after year the Liverpool Mafia's inter-city cash-and-carry networks were refined like a machine. In the '60s by stolen warehouse swag. In the '70s by pot. In the '80s by heroin and by the time the cocaine boom of the '90s came around, it was flooded with cheap Colombian powder like a ring main, taking drugs with unprecedented efficiency and profitability to all corners of the UK. The result – it made the bosses, the gatekeepers of this system, the richest criminals in British history. The side effect: an explosion of mainstream Class A abuse and an epidemic of crack cocaine.

Paul Grimes began to notice a power shift away from the traditional gangsters towards the drug dealers in the early '80s that corresponded with the ascent of Mrs Thatcher and the Toxteth riots of 1981. By 1985 it was an unstoppable sea change. The drug dealers were now the top dogs simply because they were making the most money, always the benchmark of success and influence in the Liverpool underworld.

As Paul surveyed the new criminal landscape, unnervingly he

noticed that the big drug dealers were not necessarily new faces muscling in on the old guard's turf. They were the old guard. They were the villains whom he'd known all his life. The gangsters he'd robbed with, made money with, fought with, fought against, sheltered, ripped off, shot at, lent money to, shared cells with, got respect off and most importantly respected himself. These pioneers were embracing a goldrush, rushing forward into the international super-league of villainy and begging Paul to come with them.

Paul was hesitant. He was confused. He didn't know what to do. He noticed that the new drug dealers were quick to abandon the traditional underworld codes they had loosely lived by all of their criminal lives. Forging new alliances was the source of their power. Paul observed how the mainly white, middle-aged gangster elite was forming unprecedented links with the young, black drug dealers of Toxteth's Granby ghetto. As he weighed up the pros and cons of getting involved, he looked around him and was shocked to discover the huge number of close associates who were heavily involved with drugs.

Tommy Comerford

Paul had known Tommy Comerford since the late '60s. He was an armed robber and safe-cracker cut from the same cloth as Billy Grimwood. It was not surprising that Tommy and Billy became partners on several huge robberies. The duo had masterminded the infamous Water Street Job in 1969, a commando-style heist on a Liverpool bank ripped straight from the pages of a Hollywood plot.

After tunnelling into the strong room for two days the gang made off with a whopping £140,000. Billy was never linked to the crime officially, but Comerford was later jailed for ten years. Following his release Billy helped Comerford invest in the nightclub scene. Paul had got to know Comerford better as they sat in meetings together, particularly when Johnny Nash was in town.

Paul was convinced Comerford was staunch – an anti-drugs gangster of the old school who, like Grimwood, refused to deal heroin and cocaine. Even when Comerford was jailed for seven years for recruiting dockers in a cannabis-smuggling conspiracy, Paul refused to condemn him, arguing it was 'only pot'. It came as a huge surprise when in 1983 Comerford was arrested with half a kilo of heroin at Heathrow airport and later jailed for 14 years for masterminding what Customs officers described as Britain's first Class A drugs cartel. Paul was disgusted. He felt betrayed.

Tony Murray

Paul hated Tony Murray because he was part of the Ungi crew. He was the gangster shot by one of Haase's henchmen, and who later refused to give evidence in court. But Murray went up in Paul's esteem when in 1985 he declared war on the city's drug dealers. Murray publicly vowed to 'wipe them off the face of the earth' after his 14-year-old nephew, Jason Fitzgibbons, died of a heroin overdose.

Jason's death triggered a national outcry. Even the then PM Margaret Thatcher commented: 'Jason's death reminds us of the threat drug misuse poses to the well-being of all our young people, their families and society.'

Murray went further in a statement to the *Liverpool Echo*:

> When I find out who did it, then they are dead. I will do it with my bare hands if I have to. These people are nothing but rats. They are scum of the earth. They should be wiped off the face of the earth.

A few years later Murray was jailed for 12 years for plotting to supply £1 million worth of heroin. He was caught red-handed offering to sell one kilogram of heroin to undercover police officers and conspiring to offload a bulk consignment. Of all the Liverpool villains who abandoned their old-school principles in favour of drug dealing, Murray was the most symbolic.

Michael and Delroy Showers

The Showers brothers were unusual in the Liverpool underworld. In the '60s and '70s, they were one of the very few black families to break into the heavyweight league. Paul had charted the rise of Michael Showers from barman to Lime Street doorman to racketeer. He was evil, violent and feared.

One evening, Showers caught Paul with his on/off girlfriend Pauline Dunne when he popped into her flat unannounced. Paul was sitting on the couch in his boxer shorts, Dunne was half naked. They had just finished having sex.

PAUL: Pauline wasn't nice looking, but just a good shag. Michael used to go abroad and send her bags of marijuana. This was in the early '70s. He came upstairs and I was sitting there. He knew the script. He knew I'd been giving her one. He said something about stepping on people's toes and that. I just said to him: 'I'm staying here.' That's that, knowmean?

So he just sat down, a bit chocca about it all. In all fairness, he accepted his plight with dignity. We ended up having a natter and a coffee and that, in her pad. Then he got off. He knew what I could do. That's why we got on. That's why we could do business.

Between 1977 and 1979 Michael's brother Delroy upped the scale of the cannabis-importing business. The muscle-bound teetotaller flew to Kenya on a false passport and bribed corrupt officials to smuggle suitcases of cannabis on ships bound for Liverpool. Though disapproving, Paul did not cut his ties with the Showers because he argued that the drug was cannabis and not heroin or cocaine. Paul was also mindful of 'stepping on toes' because of Delroy's close links with south London mobster Charlie Richardson, who was in turn connected to Johnny Nash.

In 1980 Delroy was jailed for nine years for being 'the ringleader' of the smuggling operation. Meanwhile, Michael was carving out a political career as a self-styled spokesman for the riot-torn Toxteth ghetto. Astonishingly, he was given a £16,000-a-year job by Liverpool City Council and appeared on BBC's *Question Time* and *Panorama*. Of course, he was still racketeering at a rate of knots, but Paul respected his efforts to establish himself as an old-school 'community leader'.

It came as a great shock when Michael was jailed for 20 years for smuggling 12 kilos of heroin into Britain from Afghanistan.

The Banker

The Banker is one of Britain's biggest drug barons, but cannot be named for legal reasons because he has never been caught. The Banker was so secretive about his cannabis, heroin and cocaine smuggling that Paul and Billy Grimwood did not know that he had dirtied his hands. To Paul and Billy, The Banker was just another successful warehouse raider and hijacker. Billy had known him since he was a corrupt docker who made enough money to invest in a string of small businesses.

PAUL: I never liked him, but he did jobs with Billy. They'd do warehouses and armed robberies together. The Banker was also a doorman on the She club, which was Billy's favourite hangout. One time him and Billy went on the missing list after doing a robbery. The Banker had left his van outside Billy Grimwood's. So I robbed it. I was only about 18. The Banker gave a statement against me and I ended up getting six months in jail. I wasn't arsed about that, but I was when I found out he went on to become one of the richest drug dealers in Britain. It knocked me for six. I thought he was a stand-up guy who wouldn't touch the junk.

The Others

As Paul looked around him he realised dozens of his lifelong associates had sold out to drugs.

PAUL: They'd all started to get into it. Even my partners. Even Johnny One Eye. Could not believe it, la, when he started flying it in direct from the Dam without a care in the world.

He kept his scheme a secret from me because he knew how I felt about drugs. Would've pure smashed his blocko off if I'd've known. Eventually he was jailed for ten years for organising a parcel worth £135,000 which came into Liverpool and Harwich. It was like a kick in the teeth for me, to be fair, when I found out one of my own was dabbling.

Then there was Glyn Inkerman. He asked me to take over his scrapyard in Wavertree so he could concentrate on running a car-ringing scam in a hidden shed at the back. Fair enough and that. Goes without saying that I was robbing them blind of £500 a week on top of what I was charging them legit to manage their business. But later Glyn got nicked for dealing in the heavy stuff. Again, I was gobsmacked.

Another mate called Charlie swore blind to me that he wasn't doing the nasty, but later I found out that burglars had screwed his flat and took a telly with two ki's of yayo [cocaine] hidden in the back. That's where he used to hide his stash, in the back of his Trinitron. But he never banked on a couple of smackheads screwing his flat and having the telly off. They probably sold it for £50 not knowing there was 60 grand's worth of tackle in the back of it. Charlie came to me because he wanted someone to find those responsible and get it back. No way.

The list goes on – Leslie Shields, Brian Barrett – all what you would normally call, at a push, ordinary decent criminals who got mixed up with the gear.

The city's underworld was soon split in two. The drug dealers and those that were against drugs and didn't believe in it. They had kids, like me, who were growing up and all that and they didn't want the likes of that shit on the streets. They were terrified in case their kids got involved with drugs. It was all over the papers – 'Generation in Peril' and all that.

It was purely down to morals. The drug dealers said that our distatse was down to jealousy, but we were making plenty of money so that didn't come into it. My main motivation was that these scumbags were killing people. They were making lots of dough, but they were killing innocent people as well. End of. For the first time in my life I was actually facing up to the fact that there were victims of crime. Wrecked my head it did, for a while, in fairness.

A lot of the big villains who I knew were anti-drugs also looked down on drug dealers as something that the blacks done. They were in pure denial, but they were very shocked when it turned out that it was whites what was doing it as well and what's more, it was their own – their families, mates, partners, brothers, sons. They all had blood on their hands.

I didn't go totally fucking crusader about it either. Was not Roland off've *Grange Hill* and that, dancing about with a T-shirt on and that. Was a realist at the end of the day. After all, I had a draw myself – regularly. Having a smoke and winding down to a bit of *Dark Side of* now and again was my way of getting through the day in an oft high-pressure environment. But for me, there was a big difference between cannabis and Class As. Know it's a bit thingy, but it's true, la.

I wasn't arsed about the little dealers knocking out a bit of speed to their mates. The difference between them and this new crowd was the sheer *scale*, know where I'm going? This new lot just wanted to get *everyone* bang into it on a fucking industrial scale. I watched them. One minute you had a nice auld neighbourhood somewhere where everyone knew each other and that. The next minute it was *Escape From New York* 'cos these cunts had flooded the place with brown. Everyone running about screwing each other's houses to get money together for a

£5 bag. All kinds of bits of birds on the game and that. These new gangsters would have been made up if everywhere was reduced to smoking ruins, so they could run amok selling their pollo [cocaine] unhindered.

A lot of the big gangsters who were anti-drugs just started keeping quiet about it, not wanting to ruffle any feathers. They never had the bottle to tell the dealers that they didn't like what they were doing. Some of us even had a meeting. They were that fucking worried about the dealers finding out it was in total secret and they whispered their concerns like old women. I said that I was prepared to make a stand. To shoot some of these cunts if necessary. But they just ummed and arrhhed and said: 'We admire your stance and that but . . .' And they didn't know where to look.

These were big names. Hard hitters who had killed and maimed in pursuit of wealth with their own hands, but they were behaving like pathetic kids who purely did not know what to do. They gave up the fight before it even started. After that, drugs just became acceptable.

Paul was disgusted. In a life-changing decision, he then decided to plan his escape from a life of crime. Financially he could afford to abandon the thieving and the clubs. For a 35-year-old villain he was in an enviable position, even though he was torn between two lives. Several new acquisitions had been added to a web of legitimate business interests: a stone-cleaning company, a second scrapyard, a car-breaking business and a skip-hire firm.

Paul had invested his illegal earnings well. Each of his enterprises was generating healthy profits, especially his new metals business in Greenland Road, Dingle, under the watchful eye of his wife Chrissy. Realistically, Paul knew he could live more than comfortably for the rest of his life on what they made. In addition, there was a stack of cash stashed away for a rainy day. Only Paul knew where it was.

Following their divorce, his ex-wife estimated the hoard to be several hundred thousand pounds. Underworld sources swore blind he was sitting on several million plus. Only Paul knew.

––––––––––––

PAUL: One day I just woke up and decided to stop being a gangster. It seemed that everything and everyone around me was being tainted by drugs and I wanted no part of it. So I stopped everything – the robbing, the warehouses, the doors, the protection. Walked away. All of it got binned in one fell swoop. I just started going into my office in my yard and being a businessman. Cut all ties. Of course, I still dabbled. I got a lot of fiddles up and running so I didn't have to totally rely on the generosity of the free market. Be fair!

I immediately boxed off a load of lads who worked for the GPO who laid the cables for the phones and that. They also used to pick up the big old cables out of the ground. So much would go back to the GPO, so much would be weighed into me. The cables were solid copper with like a thick lead sleeve. Melted down they were worth a small fortune. So I had a big furnace built especially which would melt the lead off leaving the wire. I made between £250 and £500 a week off that. It was a good screw. Chrissy, my wife, was getting good punt out of it and it went on for years.

Then I had a deal with these lads who worked in Fords [Ford car company] at Halewood. Every week they stole and smuggled these big blocks of copper, tonnes and tonnes of it, out of the factory. It made me a lot of dough. Then I started crushing cars for people who wanted to get the insurance. I used to do it for a gang who specialised in insurance fraud, so they put all their work my way. The cars were always Mercs or Rolls, mostly new, owned by businessmen who were having problems. It was a good earner.

I was making money legit, but not legit, if you know what I mean, but compared to robbing warehouses it felt like I was helping old ladies across the road. I even started doing charity work. Sponsoring people to jump out of aeroplanes and that. Mind you, I still had all the lads coming in to try to tempt me back into getting up to no good, but it was just drugs, drugs, drugs with them.

One day John Haase came in with Bernie Aldridge. They had 20 kilos of cannabis. They were desperately trying to break into the drugs market for the first time. Haase didn't even know how to sell it so he thought with my connections I'd be able to get a buyer. They'd already squeezed all the oil out of it. They offered me a £1,000-a-kilo commission. I told them I wasn't interested, but they even left behind a kilo sample to try to tempt me. I looked at it. Even though it was crap stuff I knew I could have sold it with one phone call, but there was simply no question, 20K or not.

My stone-cleaning business went through the roof. I couldn't keep up with demand. I even bought a portable phone. I was one of the very first people to have one. I had to go to Manchester to buy it. It was a car phone but I could take it out of the Jag and carry it around with me.

One day I gets a call from the young lad who worked for me in the yard. Tells me a feller had been in demanding dough otherwise he'd burn the scrapyard down. A protection racket. Could you believe that shit? I had to laugh at the irony of it. Asking me of all people to *pay* protection and that. Clearly this clown had not done his homework and had no idea who owned this particular piece of real estate.

He was only a kid, 20 or so. A half-caste lad from Toxteth, which was only down the road. Liked his style and that but I really had no time for this type of messing so I just told the lad to tell him there was no money and to fuck off, hoping that he would just do one so I could get on with my business and that. So the lad gets off the phone and goes and tells this young scally that he's getting fuck all. Give him his due the scallywag will not take no for an answer. Says he'll be back at four o'clock to collect dough or else. 'Or else,' if you will! So I tells the lad not to worry and that. I jumps in the Jag and bombs back to the yard. I hid in one of the back offices and waits for the 'heavies' to come back.

Dead on four this young lad moseys into the office. My lad tells him that there's no money forthcoming. The scally says that's too bad and that. At that point I emerge from the shadows. The lad flinches, but in fairness he stood his ground.

'I want money for the yard. Otherwise it will come ontop for you.'

'You're getting fuck all here, mate,' I replies. 'The only protection in this yard is from me. I am the dog.'

'Put it this way,' the impudent rapscallion says, 'your yard will not be here tomorrow. That is a fact.'

'Won't it now?' I says.

I grabbed hold of him round the neck, punched fuck out of him, kicked fuck out of him and bounced him all round the yard until he lost consciousness with pain. Then I dragged him up to the main gate and dumped him in the street outside. Totally done in. I told the lad to call an ambulance for him. He went to hospital. I later found out that the lad was a bag-snatcher who was just trying his hand at being a gangster. Is right and that but not with my good self. His name was Curtis Warren. Later he would go on to be the biggest gangster this country had ever bred in 2,000 years of criminal history.

As I watched the ambulance men peel him off've the floor I had a funny feeling that our paths would cross again. I was not wrong. I also noticed in the corner of my eye that there was a surveillance car parked across the road. Two fellers who looked like busies sat off next to an ice cream van. 'I wonder who that might be?' I asked my good self.

11

The Informant

In 1990 Paul Grimes' personal crusade against Liverpool's drug barons took on an unfathomable and dangerous twist. He turned informant. It was the bravest and unlikeliest decision of his life. Cooperating with the law went against everything Paul believed in. His straight-going stretch of late had done little to temper his deeply rooted hatred of the police and all they stood for.

For the last 25 years he had waged unrelenting and uncompromising total war against the authorities he believed were out to stop him from making a living as a career criminal. When he got pinched, he conducted himself like a prisoner of war. Like the majority of old-school hoods, he said nothing, not even his name, or fed them such a blizzard of unhelpful bullshit guaranteed to secure a lengthy sentence whether guilty or not. Ratting on even the most despised crooks was frowned upon. Grimes had never cooperated with the police in any shape or form. He lived by the old code. Omerta, no back answers. The police and their agents were his sworn enemies. On the many occasions he was offered the chance to bribe a bent copper to drop a case, Paul had always steadfastly refused; he couldn't live with the thought of police officers, corrupt or otherwise, spending his money.

Of course, there had been the Fisherman and the odd 'dropsy' to the local bobby to look the other way or straighten out a particularly unhelpful witness, but that was par for the course, especially in the nightclub game. Paul had always religiously steered clear of the systematic corruption of senior police officers, which other villains had used to stay ahead of the game. For him, having a copper on the books was akin to grassing. He believed the exchange of information always ended up being two-way. So when on a summer's day in 1990 Paul picked up the phone to begin 'grassing' on the villains he had known all his life, it was a momentous act. The motivation behind it was simple – his family.

Jason Grimes had always held a special place in his father's heart. He was, after all, Paul's first-born son. But more than that, Paul had always seen in him the potential to make something of his life in a way that he could not have. Jason was honest, clever and hardworking and had no intention of following his father's footsteps into a life of crime. He was a happy, stable child who never brought trouble to his father's doorstep. At school he excelled academically and was popular with both pupils and teachers. Jason loved sport and won an amateur schoolboy championship in his teens. He rose at six o'clock in the morning, six days a week, hail, rain or snow, to earn pocket-money on a two-hour milk round before getting ready for school.

In short, Jason was a dream son who Paul and his mother Christine were very proud of. Of course, like most teenagers, there were times when Jason went off the rails. At 14, Paul caught him smoking cannabis in his bedroom. He gave him such an earful that he hoped it was enough to steer him away from further excursions into the twilight world of drug abuse.

Paul had high hopes for Jason. He encouraged him to join the Royal Navy and was delighted when his brother-in-law, an ex-sailor, took him on regular visits to Plymouth to see the fleet. At 17, Jason signed up and passed out with flying colours. To celebrate, Paul bought him his first car, a Ford Escort, wrapped it in ribbons and presented it to him at the gates of the naval base in Plymouth. When Jason hinted that he would have preferred a four-by-four,

Paul had a Suzuki Jeep delivered two weeks later. Nothing was too much for his beloved son.

One year later Jason was a registered heroin addict who was being hunted by the police across Britain for a string of habit-feeding ram raids, wage snatches and shoplifting sprees. The 19-year-old junkie had dropped out of the navy and was shacked up in a bed-sit with a heroin-using former girlfriend.

PAUL: I was crushed. Nothing had ever sledge-hammered me so hard. I felt dead. I just used to sit there for hours staring into space thinking: 'Where did it all go wrong? What has happened to my son?'

When he dropped out of the navy, no one could believe it. We even went to see his commanding officer who said he was the best in his class, but he could offer us no explanation. When I found out he was using the other gear, it was like being told I had cancer. Part of me died. But another side of me welled with anger. I could not believe that my own flesh and blood had got mixed up with drugs, something which I had always fought. It was ironic to the point of cruelty. I blamed myself. This was payback for my sins, for sure. Crime karma come back to haunt me. I had inflicted loss and pain on society all of my life and now this was society getting paid in return. That's how it got me thinking. Head was wrecked with it all, telling you, la.

More than anything I couldn't believe how quickly he descended into a drug addiction. A smackhead who would do anything for drugs. He turned into a robber just like his auld feller. He started following cash vans around and having them off. Because Plymouth hadn't caught up with Liverpool in the robbing, security was much more lax. His speciality was snatching the takings from the vans that went round to collect the money from slot machines.

Could not believe it. I tried to help him. I brought him back to Liverpool and gave him a job in my stone-cleaning business.

But as soon as I would leave the particular job I'd put him on he would disappear, looking for drugs. We ended up having a fight in the middle of Molyneaux Street. Then I wouldn't see him for months. I was helpless. I was angry. The drug dealers were killing my son and there was nothing I could do.

One day I went to the bookies in Park Road. There were Mercs and BMs and RS Cosies parked outside. These were owned by the drug dealers who just sat off in the bookies all day placing £500 and £1,000 bets on the dogs. Although they were the new generation of drug dealers I knew them all. I knew their auld fellers, their brothers. I had shared cells with them. One of them had a plazzy bag with £30,000 in it stashed inside his zipped-up tracky top. Just dipping into it he was, taking out £500 at a time and betting on the dogs. He didn't even write out his bets. He just shouted the trap number to the girl behind the bullet-proof screen. Some of them were snarling at me. But I just burned holes in them with my eyes. I could have massacred them there and then, with my own bare hands. These were the men who were killing my son. But I had my own plans. They'd have to wait.

A few weeks later Paul's scrapyard was raided by Customs and Excise. Instinctively, he knew they weren't looking for contraband. It was too businesslike. Just a short, bearded officer taking notes and a few investigators asking questions and sniffing around. On the first visit, Paul managed to convince them that he wasn't who they thought he was and that he didn't own the business. They went away. Two hours later his shaken accountant phoned: 'Are you sitting down? They don't care who owns the yard. They want £170,000 off you in unpaid VAT.'

Paul put two and two together. They must have had him under surveillance for a while. The surveillance cars he'd sussed on the day he had beaten up Curtis Warren were most obviously in hindsight Customs.

PAUL: £170,000? Off've me? As if, la. As if I was going to hand over170 grand to these folks.

I had the dough all right, goes without saying and that, but as if in a million fucking years they were going to get their hands on it. Not going to happen, is it, knowmean? When they came to the yard I was like: 'No I'm not here. Doesn't work here. Sorry, can't help you, see you later.'

Then I went to this meeting at Customs' HQ on the Dock Road. There was the small feller with the beard. We'll call him Dominic Smith [not his real name]. There was also a big cunt, six feet tall, with a nose all over the place. They started giving it good cop, bad cop routine. I told this big fucking feller that if he didn't shut his fucking mouth I'd straighten his fucking nose for him. Then I declared the meeting over. The accountant was having a fucking heart attack.

A lot of businessmen are intimidated by the Customs and Excise. They come with the health warning that they are 'more powerful than the police'. But what they didn't understand is that guys like me weren't arsed about them. I told them straight: 'If I have to give you a cheque for £170,000 then I'm on a plane out of here – with the fucking cheque. And what can you do, put me in jail? No one is going to win this argument.'

Then I got to thinking. I could purely use this situation to my advantage. I'd already been toying with the idea of approaching the busies with a deal. Of ratting on a few 'community leaders' and that. So I got to thinking of cutting a deal with the Customs instead of the police and killing two birds with one stone. Get them off've my case for the VAT they said I owed them and grassing up a few hard hitters into the bargain. So I had another meeting, this time with just Dominic Smith and that. I still told him that I didn't owe them the VAT and that if they wanted it they'd have to go and get it off've my customers. At the end of the meeting I said: 'Drugs are becoming rife now. If I hear something I'll let you know.'

He understood what I meant. So I left it at that.

At first I didn't really know whether I could trust them. So I figured that I would test them with a few smaller fish. At the time, as well as drugs, my other big beef was with the proliferation of firearms. All hands were now using guns to do armed robberies. High on coke they were, shooting up innocent people. I took a very dim view of this. It came as no surprise to my good self that this new breed of trigger-happy shooter merchants were often drug dealers as well.

The script was that they were often doing their bloodthirsty armed raids to raise dough to fund bigger and bigger drug deals. That's the way it went. So I decided that this type of crime would be my tester with the Customs. I'd got wind of one such job, which was just about to go off. It was being planned by my old oppo, Snowball. After I'd retired, he'd got mixed up in other stuff. I couldn't believe it, la, one of my own into that! But that's the way it was going then.

Snowball used to confide in me. He told me that he was working for a family who were connected to the drug dealers. They had a demolition firm and they'd made him a foreman and driver. At the time this firm got a contract to gut one of the warehouses at Littlewoods Pools and make it bigger. It was next to the warehouse that Littlewoods delivered all the cash from the pools' collectors. Every week hundreds of thousands of pounds went through this little hatch and all that separated it from Snowball and his team was a sliding door.

They planned to heist the room with shooters and have the money off. Snowball even invited me down to Littlewoods to ask me my appraisal of the job. It was easy enough, but I realised that shooters were involved and that these were the type of fellers who'd have a snort beforehand and would damage every cunt within a three-mile radius as a result. As far as I was concerned there were two types of armed robber and these were the worst kind. I told Dom Smith of their plans. He told the busies. The busies told Littlewoods and they managed to block the robbery before it went off. They simply secured the big panel door and beefed up security. Snowball and his team soon realised they couldn't do it.

That was my first grass. That was it. A few weeks later Littlewoods invited me down. Their head of security thanked me and they give me £250 as a reward. It was a weird feeling, being one of the good guys, but I kind of enjoyed it and weirdly enough I did actually think I'd done the community a service. Snowball didn't even know he'd been grassed on. One day he just said: 'Remember that thing we were looking at. Forget about it.'

Then he added: 'Anyway we've got another one going off. It's bigger and better.'

That night we went for a pint. Snowball couldn't help spilling the beans to me about this other armed robbery he was planning. He told me that they'd been gutting an army base in Wales. They'd come across a hand-held rocket launcher and robbed it. The plan was to use it on a post office van. They weren't going to fire it, just use it to scare the drivers. They'd already got a little team together. I realised that Snowball was doing a lot of armed robberies.

A few days later Snowball said that he'd got a getaway car, a two-litre Cortina Ghia, and he asked me to hide it in my yard. As soon as he dropped it off I phoned Smithy and told him. The busies came round and got the car and then nicked Snowball and the owners of the demolition firm. To keep my cover the Customs arranged for me to get arrested as well.

Even the busies didn't know I was the informant. At the station they gave me a hard time. They were playing good cop/bad cop and I was screaming all kinds of abuse at them making sure that if Snowball and his team were in the other cells they'd hear me. After about an hour of this charade I mentioned the name of a sergeant that I'd been given by Customs. It was like a signal and the busies eased off. After that, they knew the score and it was allday.

I still had to make a statement for appearances' sake, not one that admitted that I was a grass, but one that said I was just a scrap dealer who had been asked to hide a car for a few days. In the end, they all got time for it. For me it was only the beginning of fighting the criminals that I didn't approve of. Now I turned my sights on bigger targets.

12

Curtis Warren

Paul set himself a simple task. From now on his aim was to infiltrate the Mr Bigs behind Liverpool's rapidly growing cocaine and heroin cartels. Why? Because they were the specific narcotics that were killing his son.

In 1990, when Paul was thinking about how he might penetrate the Liverpool drug rings, he did not know exactly who his targets would be. Though he didn't know it yet, it turned out that he was setting out on a journey that would end with the capture of two of Britain's biggest drug dealers: Curtis Warren and John Haase. Curtis Warren would go down in history as the 'richest and most successful British criminal who has ever been caught'.

He was primarily a cocaine dealer. Up until that point Paul and Warren's paths had only crossed twice by two weird twists of fate. Warren had first come to Paul's attention when a prostitute he was guarding in a brothel under his protection told him how a couple of 18-year-old Toxteth scallies, one of whom turned out to be Curtis Warren, had set up their own racket, blackmailing streetwalkers and their punters.

Then a few years later Paul came face to face with Warren when he walked into his scrapyard and demanded protection money. The confrontation ended quickly and Warren was rushed to hospital after being 'made to lie down and go to sleep' (left bleeding and unconscious) in the cobbled street outside the gates of Paul's premises. Paul, an old hand at the extortion game, had been unamused and unimpressed by the young buck's 'performance'.

After targeting Warren, Paul turned his attention to his old hombre John Haase. To his disgust, Haase had followed the now well-trodden route map from armed robbery to drug baron with spectacular results. Like most of the Liverpool Mafia that went before and after him, he was jettisoned at the touch of a portable phone into a stratospheric world of mass cash and wildly disproportionate, pan-continental power: power which would bring him into the bosom (and equally into conflict) with the highest lawmakers and politicians in the land. But to fully explain Paul's transformation into a supergrass it is necessary to first understand how his first big drugs target, Curtis Warren, rose from a rooting-tooting scallywag to become Interpol's Target One.

Curtis Francis Warren was born on 31 May 1963 into a working-class, immigrant family at a fading former merchant's townhouse in Upper Parliament Street, Toxteth, Liverpool. His father, Curtis Aloysius Warren, a mixed-race seaman from South America, had jumped ship in Liverpool from the Norwegian merchant navy in the 1950s and married local girl Sylvia Chantre, also of Latin descent, in 1960. Warren was part of the second generation of dockside settlers who would accelerate Toxteth's decline from a largely peaceful but exotically lively melting pot into a riot-torn, crime-ridden, no-go ghetto with international drug links within the space of 20 years.

Two centuries earlier the wealthy merchants of Toxteth had controlled 80 per cent of the world's slave trade. Ironically, Warren would make Toxteth the hub of an equally distasteful global trade network once again. For a period in the 1980s and

1990s, the 'merchants' of Toxteth controlled a similarly high proportion of the cocaine entering Britain.

Warren's criminal record began at the age of twelve when he was placed under a two-year supervision order for joyriding by Liverpool Juvenile Court. At 13, the serial truant was sentenced by the magistrates' court to a day's detention for burglary. His gangland apprenticeship coincided with a massive explosion of youth crime in Liverpool, a legacy which has hung over the city's reputation like a black cloud until the present day. Warren was truly a leading light in the city's first generation of 'scallies'.

Over the next two years he was caught for theft, stealing cars on four occasions, robbery, offensive behaviour and going equipped. After three months in a detention centre he came straight out and was fined for assaulting two policemen. At 16 Warren mugged a 78-year-old lady on the steps of Liverpool's Catholic Cathedral along with two other accomplices. His victim fell badly, suffering horrific, headline-grabbing injuries. After magistrates dealt with a second separate assault on the police, Warren was sent to borstal for 11 months.

Warren's teenage crime spree had been played out against a background of structural change in Liverpool. Since the mid-'70s unemployment had been rising. Under PM Margaret Thatcher it rocketed to the highest rates in the country. One-fifth of UK manufacturing capacity was wiped out in a shock recession. This had devastating knock-on effects for the struggling port and even more so for ethnically diverse, docks-dependent Toxteth.

Liverpool's sea trade fell off the scale and in an attempt to salvage the residue the docks were relocating from the south end to the north end of the city. Unemployment shot up to a staggering 80 per cent. To add insult to injury, a new phenomenon was thrown into this potentially explosive mix: a breakdown in police community relations. Residents of Toxteth were complaining of racially motivated police heavy-handedness, aggravated by the widely despised suss laws which gave them arbitrary stop-and-search powers.

On 3 July 1981, structural change gave way to tectonic upheaval. Toxteth erupted into rioting, following hot on the heels of earlier disturbances in Brixton, south London. Warren, who had been released from borstal earlier that year, was back in the thick of it. The civil unrest would result in CS gas being deployed on the mainland for the first time and although a string of copycat riots flared up across Britain, none would come close to the scale and savagery of Toxteth. There were 244 arrests and 700 out of 4,000 police officers who held the thin blue line were injured.

Toxteth's criminal fraternity were quick to take advantage of the chaos. From the smoking ruins, they were able to forge a community in their own image, a base from which to wreak havoc on the rest of the world. Liverpool 8 became a de facto police no-go area. The seething population effectively cut itself off from the rest of the city, which in turn had cut itself off from the rest of the country in a wave of militant-inspired revolt. Suspicious and angry, Toxteth turned in on itself, fiercely protecting its own at all costs, even if they were criminals. A haven for lawlessness soon established itself. A perfect breeding ground enabling the exponential growth of street criminals into gangsters in double-quick time.

Drug dealing, ram raiding and muggings were seen as legitimate earners. A self-sufficient black economy boomed, employing whole families and streets from grandmothers to children. Even the chief community leader and council appointee Michael Showers was an international heroin dealer and racketeer.

At 19 Warren was sentenced to his first spell in a 'proper jug' after he was convicted of blackmailing a prostitute and a punter in a crude backstreet extortion racket. His accomplice was Johnny Phillips. Phillips would go on to be Warren's right-hand man in the cocaine business, notoriously declaring a fatal war on the Ungi clan on the way. It was a turning point in Warren's criminal career. On the wings, he was exposed for the first time to members of the Liverpool Mafia, the white, middle-aged crime godfathers who controlled the big-time action in the city.

At that point in time, many of them were plotting the strategic switch from old-fashioned racketeering to drugs. It was a match made in heaven. Here was an extremely bright and hard 19-year-old black villain who was closer to the heart of the deep-rooted but essentially piece-meal drug trade in Toxteth than they were. It was a case of 'I've got the brains; you've got the cash. Let's make lots of money'. Numbers were exchanged and the seminal foundations of the future cartel laid down.

When he got out, Warren stepped up a gear, holding up a Securicor van with a pistol and a sawn-off shotgun. After smashing in the skull of a have-a-go hero, the gang fled with £8,000. Warren was caught and handed down five years. He continued his criminal education, consolidating his connections with the Liverpool Mafia and also networking with villains from Manchester and London.

On the outside the Liverpool gangs were making quantum leaps in their drug-trafficking enterprises. Heroin and cannabis abuse was spiralling out of control. In 1985 Tommy Comerford was convicted of a huge cannabis conspiracy and the Godfather of Toxteth, Michael Showers, was busy organising the heroin consignments for which he was later jailed.

On his release Warren was prevented from getting a piece of the action by a lack of funds. Instead he jumped on the scallywag bandwagon headed for Europe. For several years the city's top urchins had been plundering the sports shops of Switzerland and Germany, blazing a trail of havoc in the wake of their beloved football teams and shipping the exotically rare designer clobber 'zapped' from the shelves back to Liverpool. From mass sportswear theft, the phenomenon escalated to robbing jewellery shops and snatch raids. Some of the 'teams' had colourful names, such as the 'Cuckoo Clock' gang, distraction thieves from Croxteth's Smack City who specialised in stealing high-value jewellery from specialist cuckoo-clock shops in Switzerland.

Warren joined the *Trans Alpina* exodus, but in Christmas 1987 was caught stealing £1,250 from a super-sleek shoe shop in the chocolate box Swiss resort of Chur. Warren was jailed for 30 days after the judge heard how he violently attacked the female shop assistant before making off with the till.

Following his stint in jail, Warren returned to Liverpool and set up shop as a street dealer in Toxteth. His unique selling point that made him stand out from the army of grafters on Granby Street was that he served up heroin. Pre-Warren, a gang of vigilantes had kept Toxteth brown-free, using extreme violence and the catchphrase 'This is Toxteth not Croxteth. No smack'. Warren moved up the ranks quickly by warning off the vigilantes, exploiting the competitive advantage in heroin and opening the floodgates.

Over the next three years Warren moved up the Class A ladder from street dealer to wholesaler to importer. He befriended Liverpool Mafia boss Stan Carnall and flew to Amsterdam regularly. Carnall was typical of the older generation of white armed robbers who'd moved into big-time dealing. Paul Grimes knew of him and hated him. It was around this time that British Customs first became aware of Warren's smuggling activities. Intelligence reports and phone calls linked him to a one-off heroin run from the Dam to Liverpool.

As with the Toxteth riots and then his frontline heroin revolution, Warren was quick to take advantage of market changes to build his business. Modern commercial tools such as cheap international flights, computers, mobile phones, integration with Europe, deregulated banking and English as the international business language helped push his growth rates into mind-boggling figures. The free availability of firearms was also a factor, but the biggest drivers of all were as old as trade itself: supply and demand.

Two distribution networks set up by the £10 billion Medellin cartel to flood Britain with cocaine were simultaneously smashed in 1987, instantly cutting off bulk supplies. Meanwhile, demand was rocketing. Street seizures were at record levels and in June 1988 Britain's first crack manufacturer, Colin Borrows, Warren's business partner, was caught in Liverpool. From then on, crack would drive demand for cocaine, leading to a year-on-year exponential growth in usage. The Liverpool Mafia responded by setting up a home-grown network in alliance with south London gang boss Eddie Richardson in the hope of capitalising on the new trend. But the pioneering organisation, which had not yet got Warren fully onboard, was unfocused and flaky and unable to get off the ground.

In 1991 the police first became aware of Warren's independent smuggling operation after an informant in Operation Bruise, a Midlands-based task force targeting organised crime, named him as a maverick middle-ranking operator who specialised in 50-kilo-at-a-time shipments. It wouldn't be long before the Liverpool Mafia would realise Warren's full potential and headhunt him into an executive position and it wouldn't be long before his path would once again cross that of Paul Grimes. A collision course was in motion.

13

The First Consignment

In the winters of 1991 and 1992 Paul Grimes helped Customs and Excise sink the biggest ever cocaine smuggling operation in Britain's history up to that point. He led them to two consignments of cocaine smuggled directly from Colombia by the Liverpool Mafia. The first weighed 500 kilos. The second weighed 905 kilos.

Curtis Warren was later put on trial for the crime, but was dramatically cleared of all charges on a technicality. In the grand scheme of things, it didn't really matter. Grimes had led them to their man and from that point on they had their teeth into him and they weren't letting go. Sooner or later Warren would be taken out.

The story of how Paul Grimes infiltrated the UK's first drugs cartel begins in the late '80s in Amsterdam. Following the spectacular failure of the Medellin cartel to penetrate the British market, the rival Cali cartel decided to mount a rival bid. The Cali cartel, based in the Colombian city of the same name, had always played second fiddle to the wealthier Medellin mob who had grown powerful on their dominance of the US market, but with their crack-friendly cocaine and good European connections the Cali cartel planned to even out the market share.

The Cali's senior salesman in Europe was 22-year-old Mario Halley, a Colombian-born Dutch citizen whose job it was to drum up business. In the late '80s, he met a senior member of the Liverpool Mafia who was in Amsterdam trying to make connections to facilitate entry into the top end narco market. It was a match made in heaven.

Within months the Liverpool Mafia bosses introduced Halley to their rising star, Warren. In turn, Warren introduced Halley to a wealthy drug dealer from the North-east of England called Brian Charrington. Little did Warren know that Charrington was a police informant.

Charrington, a former second-hand car dealer who owned two aeroplanes, had grown rich on cannabis importation by sacrificing his partners-in-crime up to the police in order to protect his own operations. Even though Warren considered his own cell-structured network super-secure, unknown to him it had already been compromised.

In July 1990 detectives Ian Weedon and his boss Harry Knaggs of the North East Regional Crime Squad, based in Teesside, were green-lighted by top brass to handle Charrington as an informant codenamed Enigma One. The flow of intelligence would specifically concern up-and-coming drug deals.

They soon learned that Charrington was an expert at playing the double-agent game. At times, the information was long on generalisations and 'colour' but short on key details. Crucially, the crafty Charrington seemed to pick the timings at which to download his mental notepad to police when it suited him, not the operation. Some senior officers were frustrated that the drip feed meant they were missing the boat on important stages. These flaws would leave Charrington open to accusations that he was holding back in order to protect his own interests.

Meanwhile, on the other side of the world in the Venezuelan capital of Caracas the distribution arm of Halley's Cali cartel was putting the finishing touches to its plan to flood Britain with cocaine. A front company called the Conar Corporation, ostensibly an import–export firm, was set up by businessmen Marco Tulio Contreras and Jesus Camillo Ortiz Chacon to mask the South American end of the smuggling operation.

In March 1991 Curtis Warren and Mario Halley held a summit in Amsterdam. They were joined by Charrington, who later reported back to his police handlers that an imminent drugs deal was high up on the meeting's agenda.

Charrington claimed that a massive load of cocaine – a record 2,000 kilos – would be routed to Europe between July and November 1991 on a ship that had already been lined up for the run. Though Warren was later cleared of all charges, the intelligence was enough to spark a police operation that gathered momentum throughout the summer.

As autumn set in, the Liverpool team began to get their 'ducks in a row' in preparation for the deal. A long-standing friend of Billy Grimwood, who had secretly moved from warehouse robberies into drugs and become one of the richest criminals in Britain in the process, volunteered to underwrite the deal with his massive cash pile.

A second notorious Liverpool thief, Brian 'Snowy' Jennings, who was also a millionaire haulage contractor, was put in charge of organising the movement of the consignment after its arrival from the port of entry to a holding depot in Liverpool. A Manchester business acquaintance of Jennings called Joseph Kassar was drafted in to front the British end of the 'legitimate' import deal.

The plan was to conceal the cocaine hidden inside X-ray-proof lead ingots. During the subsequent court case, it was revealed that Kassar's responsibility was to arrange the paperwork to import 85 tonnes of lead ingots and 40 tonnes of aluminium and to make it look like a kosher scrap-metal deal. According to the prosecutors, Kassar then handed the deal over to his London-based cousin, Joey Nana-Asare. But he did not tell Asare the true nature of the transaction and pretended that it was a straightforward metal import with a 20 per cent forecast profit.

From then on there was a flurry of big-player movement on

both sides of the Atlantic. In September 1991, Curtis Warren and Brian Charrington flew to Caracas via France and Spain, disguising their trail as much as possible. Coincidentally, Mario Halley was also in Caracas at the time. Nine days later, while they were still there, the lead ingots left Venezuela, bound for Britain. During a pit stop in the Dominican Republic the load was transferred to an ocean-going freighter called the *Caraibe*. Warren and Charrington returned to the UK. The smugglers' plan was to drop the first 500-kilo load of cocaine in Britain and the remaining 500-kilo load in Europe. Based on Charrington's intelligence, it was assumed these loads were destined for the Italian Mafia and the Turkish *babas*.

Several weeks later, in late September/early October 1991, Charrington decided to tell his handlers of his trip for the first time. He reinforced his earlier intelligence that 2,000 kilos was winging its way to Britain, but astonishingly feigned ignorance on the subject of mode of transport and date of arrival.

A few days later on 8 October 1991 the North East RCS disclosed their information to the Customs and Excise for the first time. All hell broke loose, with Customs accusing the police of deliberately holding back on them until it was too late. To add insult to injury, Customs retorted by revealing that they had been independently looking into Charrington for months in Operation Python, as well as liaising with residual elements of the Midlands RCS's Operation Bruise. A wall of distrust went up between the two agencies. The upshot was that Customs began looking for their own way to get into the smuggling operation and crack it independently.

Almost immediately pieces of intelligence began to flow their way independently of Charrington and the Regional Crime Squad. The police in Caracas had got wind of the plot and in mid-October tipped off Customs in Britain that a heavy-duty load of coke was in transit. Crucially, they filled in the blanks left by Charrington and said it would come by sea and possibly be stashed in blocks of metal.

As Customs and Excise analysed the intelligence to find out if there were any matching metal cargoes due into British ports, Mario Halley had quietly slipped into Manchester airport to meet Warren. It was 16 October.

Two days later the *Caraibe* docked at Felixstowe. The court was later told that Kassar immediately ordered Asare to make ready the necessary arrangements to deliver the lead ingots to a storage depot called P&J Warehousing, owned by a Mr Singleton, near the Grand National racecourse in Aintree, Liverpool.

But first they had to endure a nail-biting wait for the ingots to clear Customs. Luckily, the recent intelligence from the Caracas police had been flagged up to the dock's search teams and as routine they began 'turning them over'. Unluckily, they did not possess a drill bit any longer than 25 cm and failed to find the secret steel-lined compartments within the lead that contained the coke. Later, it would be claimed that the Cali cartel knew in advance the exact length of Custom's longest drill bits and had buried the coke deep enough to beat them.

Over the next 12 days Customs took photographs of the load and explored further. But increasingly uncertain that this was the suspicious lead they were looking for, the officers were forced to let it go. On 30 October, 500 kilos of cocaine were waved out of the secure docks area into the possession of a firm of hauliers. Customs paid no further attention to the consignment. By rail and lorry it headed for Aintree.

The first week of November 1991 was a key stage in the saga for all parties. For the villains, the police and Customs and Excise it was a decisive, watershed period. Not least because it was the first point at which Paul Grimes got involved.

At the warehouse in Liverpool the cocaine was extracted from inside the lead ingots. Enter Paul Grimes' former partner-in-crime Snowball and his team of armed robbers. Crucially, they had been drafted in for the laborious task of drilling into each of the two-tonne ingots and removing the inner steel box, each containing an average of 16 kilos of white powder.

The tight-knit group of men were ideally suited for the task. As a front for their criminal activities they owned a demolition firm and were more than used to dangerous heavy-duty work. They were also equipped with the hydraulic plant needed to lift the ingots off the ground while they burrowed inside from underneath.

Their work was supervised by Conar Corporation executive Jesus Camillo Ortiz Chacon, who had flown in because he knew the exact position of the cocaine within each mass of lead. As Customs officers at Felixstowe had found out, without detailed knowledge the cocaine was near impossible to find.

Dripping with sweat, despite the cold November evenings, the extraction team worked through the night to crack open each one of the 32 ingots. On several occasions their hammer drills accidentally penetrated the cocaine parcels, showering the men underneath with white powder. The men grinned maniacally, not sure whether to put it down to their growing success-fuelled excitement or the side effects of the drug. As the air became thick with particles, an air-purifier was brought in. It was a good idea.

Then out of the blue the warehouse's insurers had decided to carry out a routine inspection of the building. Desperately, the owner tried to stall them until the job-in-hand was finished. By 5 November the extraction process was nearing completion and as Bonfire Night fireworks exploded in the distant sky, the irony of the celebrations under way was not lost on the gang.

At the same time, 350 miles away in London, Mario Halley had already begun spending his share of the profits. He was allegedly washing his loot by buying new BMW saloons to ship abroad for re-sale later.

The last phase of the operation involved destroying the trail of evidence. Events had moved fast, but it was still only the first week in November. Transport manager Brian 'Snowy' Jennings instructed his innocent brother-in-law, a skip-hire boss, to get rid of the lead ingots. The senior hierarchy of the operation had resolutely decided that they should be buried, preferably on a piece of secure land controlled by them, and left for good. Jennings' brother-in-law quickly found the ideal location – a demolition yard used by Snowball and his team on Liverpool's Dock Road. All parties were paid extra to bury the ingots and forget about them for a long time or until further orders.

By the end of the first week of November the main players were already moving large amounts of cash around their money-laundering networks. In Colombia, they had paid £7 million for 500 kilos at £14,000 apiece. In Britain, cut and 'bashed', the 500 kilos yielded an estimated bulk of 900 kilos, each worth £80,000 on the street. That equated to a cool £70 million profit.

To all intents and purposes the biggest cocaine smuggling operation in British history had just gone down without a single hitch. Even armed with pre-op intelligence the Customs and police had, somewhat surprisingly, not gotten a sniff. Now the main evidence was flooding out onto Britain's streets and rapidly disappearing up people's noses. Without a decisive break in the next few days the case would be lost forever.

14

The Key

Enter Paul Grimes – the key to unlocking the mystery. Within seven days of the consignment's arrival at Felixstowe, Paul had learned of it and gleaned enough hard, accurate intelligence to find out exactly where it was. He tipped off his handlers at the Customs and Excise and put them on the trail of the drug crime of the century.

If that wasn't enough there was a killer twist in the tale. Paul had stumbled across the deal purely by accident. As Paul Grimes revealed how he had infiltrated the gang, Customs officers could not believe their ears and their luck. The gang had made one mistake. They had gotten greedy. Not content with their share of the £70 million profit, Snowball and his gang decided to double-cross the cartel's bosses. Instead of leaving the lead ingots buried in the ground as ordered, they could not resist trying to fiddle a few shillings on the side.

Snowball and Jennings' brother-in-law dug them up and sold the 32 tonnes for scrap. And who did Snowball call to buy the lead? None other than his trusted old confidant and underworld scrap dealer, Paul Grimes. For the sake of a few hundred pounds they had sold out the biggest drugs cartel in British history.

As the wide-eyed customs officers listened, they had to bite their hands to stop themselves from laughing out loud. This was the breakthrough that Customs and Excise had been waiting for. It was, to say the least, explosive. Not only were they in possession of specific, checkable data, such as the location of the warehouse, the nature of the ingots and the identities of the criminals involved, they had a reliable mole now on the inside.

Smugly, the Customs and Excise officers debated the best way to break the news to their somewhat frantic police colleagues. An intense rivalry, compounded by mistrust, had now grown up between the two agencies. Customs officers were now openly questioning the value of the police's mole, Brian Charrington.

As if to emphasise the point, one week after Paul Grimes had begun feeding intelligence to Customs, Brian Charrington popped up once again. Whetting the appetite of Regional Crime Squad DS Weedon, he 'revealed' that a 500-kilo load had entered Britain. He boasted to the police officer that the operation 'had gone off perfectly right under the noses of Customs, who did not have a clue'.

Charrington was wrong. As he spoke, Paul Grimes was infiltrating the gang and hoovering up vital clues at a frenetic rate. Charrington was certainly talking a good game. Clearly bigging up his own value as informer, he showed his police handlers a bag containing £900,000 in cash. It was, he said, profits from the deal which the gang was 'washing' through a bureau de change in London.

But despite this show of histrionics, Charrington could not furnish them with any detailed information about the operation. Astonishingly, he claimed he had only learned the specifics after the load's arrival, pleading that he could not have warned the cops in advance. It meant that Paul was single-handedly left to shoulder the responsibility of bringing down the gang.

———

PAUL: It all started with a phone call from one of Snowball's team. It was the first week of November 1991. They asked me whether I wanted to buy 32 tonnes of lead. I don't know why I got onto the fact that there was something shady going on, but I did. Straight-a-fucking way by the way. Call it instinct. Say it takes one to know one and that. But I felt it in my bones that there was a big fuck-off caper going off and I wanted to get to the bottom of it.

Over the next few days I got into Snowball's head. I took him out on the town and got him pissed. After two pints, he was purely singing. Like a fucking canary and all. It's the egos with these pricks. They can't help themselves. They love telling you what great criminal masterminds they are.

Within minutes he's telling that the lead was used to smuggle a load of white into Liverpool. I'm like that, 'No!', and he's like that, 'I know yeah. Get paid or what?' He's getting real cosy now. With the ale and the glow of the optics at the bar on a winter's night and that. Next minute he's in bits telling me how he's cutting the yayo out of the lead and that, the bags are bursting open and they're getting covered in powder. He is laughing and clacking his fingers Granby-stylie.

'Showered with coke we was,' he said, like he's a fucking workie talking about a bag of plaster that fell on his head. But he's like that: 'We weren't arsed because there was piles and piles of it. Pure fucking Tony Montana, knowmean? Kis and kis [kilos] all over the show.'

'What?' I'm thinking, having to stop myself from falling over. Could already feel my good self getting half a glad on over this. Got to ring this one in, I'm thinking, no two ways. Snowball wasn't stupid enough to reveal who the Mr Bigs were at that stage, but I knew anyways that they'd have to be pure heavyweight to put up the money for this kind of carry-on. That went without saying. But the payoff was still to come.

I asked Snowball why he wanted me to get involved. He said that they wanted me to weigh the lead in, so that they could make a raise off've it. He laughed and told me that the Mr Bigs had told them to keep it buried and leave it well alone. But being pure scousers Snowball and his cheapskates wanted to diddle them and get the scrap money. Can you believe it? I could not understand how small-time these pricks were. It made me want to turn them over even more.

The next day I phoned my man at the Customs and Excise. Met him in a car on the Dock Road and filled him in. He gave me the go-ahead to infiltrate the gang posing as a scrap dealer. Then I phoned Snowball back with a best-price quote for the lead. I told them that I couldn't buy it personally because I couldn't give them the best price, so I'd phoned up a mate of mine, Mick Burns at M&A Metals in Ditton. He said he'd give them £10 or £12 per hundredweight. There was no ulterior motive by doing this; it's just the way I would have done it anyway.

The next day one of Snowball's team phoned back and told me that they were considering the offer. He even told me that they'd rung round several scrap dealers to get more than one quote to make sure they weren't getting ripped off. Could you believe these cheeky twats? Making millions off've the gack and that, and quibbling over a few quid on some jarg South American lead.

One week later, during week two of November, Snowball phoned me and said: 'We'll take the lead to your man.' Meaning we'll take it to Mick Burns.

The Customs told me that they wanted a sneaky picture of the ingots because they weren't sure what they looked like. So I took a camera. The next morning I arrived at their demolition yard at nine thirty. Snowball was on the Bri-Mac machine digging out the lead from the rubble. One of his crew tried to blag me off, saying that the lead had been ballast from a ship. They'd been buried ten feet down in the ground.

They filled a skip with about eight of these ingots, which in all fairness looked like massive buckets with eye hooks on either side. Then the skip was put on top of the wagon. The remaining ingots were loaded onto a 20-tonne tipper wagon and another lorry. A couple of them rolled onto their sides and I saw big holes in the bottom. I asked Snowball what the holes were for and he just laughed. One of Snowball's team had changed the number plates on all of the wagons just for the journey.

When we got to Mick Burns' yard they were unloaded and weighed and his secretary handed me an envelope containing the cash – the money for the scrap plus the VAT. I couldn't believe it. Snowball told me to take out the VAT, which was £700, and told me to tell the other lads that it was a cash deal and there was no VAT. He was not only ripping off the big bosses by selling the lead, now he was skanking his own team by diddling them out of the VAT.

He gave me £350. Could not believe him, la. Then he even tried to rip me off. He told me that my cut was £500, but I later found out that they'd agreed to give me a bag of sand (a grand) and he was going to shady half of it for his good self. Cannot trust anyone, can you? But the fucker was purely scuppered on this score because his boss went out of his way to give me the grand directly and it was wrapped in a cellophane bank wrap so no cunt could shave any off.

It had been too risky to take a photie for the Customs that day, but a few days later I took the Customs fellers to Mick Burns' yard where they were still stacked up so that they could eyeball them.

About a week after I'd delivered the ingots to Mick Burns' yard, Snowball's team were on the phone asking whether the ingots had been melted down yet. Obviously they were getting a bit jumpy because they had handed over a shit load of potential evidence against their bosses to a third party. If the bosses found out there'd be untold, to say the least. All's I said to them was that I didn't know if they'd been melted and it was nothing to do with me. 'One of them, isn't it?' I told them. Just fucked them off.

The third conversation was a bit hectic. The feller said that there were heavy people involved with guns. It was half a veiled threat. It was half to get across how important it was to find out they'd been melted.

A few nights after the ingots had been taken to Mick Burns' yard I took Snowball out on the piss again. What he told me was pure fucking explosive. The next day I met up with Customs. They were made up with what I'd given them so far and thought they had enough to bust the gang right then. They wanted to hit Snowball's yard there and then, but then I told them what Snowball had told me the night before. The gang were planning to bring in an even bigger load of cocaine at around Christmas time by the same fucking method. Loose lips sink ships or what?

The effect on the Customs was jaw dropping to say the least. Not only had I led them to the one just gone, but I was getting them into the next one. That would give them a good chance of copping for the gang red-handed. Get paid.

15

The Bust

Shortly after Christmas, on 12 January 1992, exactly as Paul Grimes had predicted, the second consignment of cocaine arrived in Britain. Bingo! The 32 cylindrical ingots contained a staggering 905 kilos of cocaine worth £150 million at street prices.

Acting on Paul Grimes' intelligence, Customs had been able to track the contraband continually throughout its journey through December from Venezuela to Felixstowe. The court was later told that Kassar arranged for the ingots to be stored in a holding depot in Derbyshire. The Customs' plan was to hold off from swooping on the gang until later, by which time it was hoped that as many of the suspects as possible would have been drawn into the net. Until then it would be a waiting game.

But suddenly the British authorities were rocked. On 18 January, police in Holland raided a warehouse and discovered 35 similar lead ingots containing 845 kilos of cocaine. Conar Corporation executive Jesus Camillo Ortiz Chacon, the technician who had bored out the cocaine from the Liverpool ingots two months earlier, was caught red-handed in the drilling position.

The Dutch bust caused the Cali and UK cartel to immediately

batten down the hatches. According to police, the Liverpool Mafia ordered Kassar to leave the ingots well alone, but he ignored the instruction and transported them to a second warehouse in Stoke-on-Trent. It gave Customs officers a chance to covertly examine the ingots.

Over the next few days a special search team worked secretly and silently to extract the cocaine from the ingots without Kassar realising. Each one yielded about 28 parcels of 90 per cent purity. The total, a whopping 905 kilos, was the largest amount ever recovered up to that point from a single shipment. Luckily, Kassar did not realise the coke had been removed and the court was later told that he continued to make plans for his own extraction process.

Over the next two months Kassar played cat and mouse with the Customs surveillance teams, moving the ingots erratically between warehouses around the North-west. At one stage the gang took away a single ingot on a flatbed truck for testing. To foil surveillance the ingot was shunted around for nearly a month before the villains felt comfortable enough to examine it. The gangsters quickly found out it was empty.

Knowing that the gang had realised they had been rumbled, D-day was quickly arranged by Customs. On 29 March, over a dozen men, including Curtis Warren and Joseph Kassar, were arrested and later charged with conspiring to import cocaine.

PAUL: It all went off. To keep me safe and to keep my role as an informant secret, the Customs hatched a cover story. Is right and that. The sketch was this. It would be arranged that I would be nicked along with the gang so it looked as though I was in the shit as well.

First they'd nick the Mr Bigs. Then they'd nick me. And then they'd nick Snowball and his firm of gobshites. To Snowball, the beaut, it would look like I was a pure stand-up guy, knowmean? Also, in the window of time between the Mr Bigs getting an early morning call and me getting collared I would be able to pump Snowball for more inside info. Devious, I know, but I was getting right into being a grass by then. Terrible, isn't it?

After the plan was sorted I was told by Customs to just go home and wait. Then one day I switched on the telly and lo and behold it was all over *Granada Reports*. A big drugs ring had been smashed. Pictures of the ingots came on. That Manc newsreader, Tony Wilson, was going on about it. It was clearly a big deal. He was getting a real hard-on over it, if the truth be told.

So was I. Was like that, 'Nice one. Pure jug for youse scoundrels now.' Rubbing my hands together with glee, I was. Just like Michael Owen does after scoring a goal. Obviously the news report was the signal that I would be nicked soon. After I'd seen it on the telly, I phoned Snowball up and met him the next day. He was keeping his head down working on a demolition job by Hill Road Hospital in Everton. I pretended to be half head done in about it all, a bit worried, if you will, and I asked him about the ingots I'd seen on the telly.

I said: 'What the fuck's going on? All this gear and all that.'

He's like that, going: 'Ssshhh. Calm down, will you. It's only telly talk.'

I'm secretly buzzing inside, but giving it loads on the panicky front for effect: 'What's all this fucking FBI and that? The Customs and Interpol involved in all this shit?'

Fairplay to the nugget, he just started laughing at me and said don't worry about it. 'I'll give you a ring later on,' he said, as cool as a fucking salad he was.

At that point, he thought none of it would go back to them. Of course, I knew it was coming right back to them, knowmean? It was going to be real horrorshow for them over the next few days, no two ways.

The next day the Customs raided their yard and ripped it to fucking pieces to find the gear, which hadn't been recovered from the first shipment. Of course, it was well gone by then. Then I phoned my Customs' hombre and had a meeting with him in a car on the Dock Road.

He said, 'We are now going to start nicking them all.'

I told him that I wanted to get nicked outside my sister's house in Huyton. It was just something that came to me. We fixed the exact date and time; a couple of days later. They wanted to do it early doors and all that.

'Forget about that,' I said. 'I want to have some brekky and go the gym and that first.'

So it was fixed for three or four o'clock in the afternoon. It was the 6 April 1992. When they came for me I was sitting in the Jag on my new phone. It was one of those big fuck-off, prehistoric NEC porties they had in old days. There was about three or four officers. I was just sat there on my cream doe-hide leather seats waiting for them. One of them drove my car down to the Customs' HQ on the Dock Road.

They arrested me. I was making all kind of phone calls to solicitors and all that carry-on to make it look like I was irate and that. I had to give a blag statement the next day to make it all look straight up. Of course, it didn't mention that I was the grass. It just covered my involvement with the ingots as an innocent and legit scrap dealer. End of.

To make it look legit to Snowball we also arranged that the only person I phoned in the family was me mam. Using my experience as a gangster I also designed a few nice details of my own into the cover story, to make it sing and that. Before I got nicked I had arranged to stash a load of bent booze in my sister's ken. It would appear to Snowball that I was still up to devilment, still one of the rooting-tooting lads and that. It was brandy and Scotch that had been robbed from a warehouse. In the phone call to me mam I told her to make sure they got rid of the whisky from my sister's before the rozzers got there. In code of course, 'bagack slabang' and that.

Sure enough, by the time the Customs turned my sister's over there was nothing there. In Snowball's eyes, it'd look like I was half a hero for thinking of the family first. I knew that was a nice detail which would impress him. The bottom line is this – when someone gets nicked on a big caper, the people involved are para to fuck. Constantly looking for signals, they are, that you're not talking and that. I had been a gangster all my pip. I knew exactly how they thought.

The Customs officers who were interviewing me knew that I was an informant so they were just going through the motions. They fixed bail so that I could go and get more info from Snowball. Snowball wanted to know why I hadn't used the solicitor the gang had sent down for me. He kicked off about it, but he was still none the wiser that I was turning him over. The prick. Then they all got nicked.

It was only at that point that I fully realised how big the big players really were. They were international super-heavyweights for sure. They had the money and the power to bribe busies and judges if need be. And if they found out I was the midnight mass, it was pure curtains for me – no two ways.

That's when I started carrying a shotgun round with me, just in case they fancied a pop. I even showed my shooter to the Customs fellers. They went mad, knowmean, but they understood that I was dead man walking. Even so, they said they couldn't sanction a shooter. But I kept it anyways.

I went down to Plymouth to get out of the way. My son Jason was still down there but he had deteriorated loads. He was using a lot of gear by that time. It broke my heart, in all honesty, but at the same time it hardened my resolve to give it to these bastards. While I was down there the police in Plymouth turned over the car and found the shotgun.

After doing a couple of weeks in Exeter jug I got out and told my Customs guys in Liverpool. They called me all the pricks in the world for getting caught, but they closed the court and told the judge that I was a top grass and what have you. They straightened it out for me and I got let off. I got 18 months' conditional discharge, which was a pure result, in all fairness.

In the run-up to the big drugs trial Snowball and the Mr Bigs tried to bribe me not to turn up in court. They used an intermediary called Paul. He was a painter and decorator for the council, but he was also a doorman, so he had all the usual underworld links – the perfect emissary to deliver such a message without being caught. He came to my flat in Hoylake and then we went for a walk along the prom. He offered me 25 grand not to appear in court and not to give evidence. I said: 'Yes, OK. I'll think about it.'

Then I got straight on the phone to the Customs. They said: 'Yes, we know all about it. We knew that they were going to give you 25 grand and we know that they are going to bump [refuse to pay] you as well. They are gonna get you out of the way and after the court case they are going to fuck you off and not give you the money.'

I said: 'Well that's not very good, is it?'

Later Paul showed me the 25 grand. I went to his house in Huyton and he showed me a shoebox with the notes all bundled up.

He said: 'If you get off to another country and not be around to give evidence, you can have this when the case finishes.'

I told him that I wasn't interested. After that, my wife started getting threats that the house was gonna get torched and that. I was getting told that I was a dead man. Was not arsed, by the way. I could well hangle these pricks. The funny thing was, though, that they didn't even know I was the informant. They were just pissed off 'cos I'd made a shitty statement saying that I'd got rid of the ingots. It went without saying that if they found out I was the rat they'd execute me within 24 hours. No back answers.

16

The Trial

On 1 July 1992, as Paul was preparing to take the stand against Warren in the narcotics trial of the century, his beloved son Jason died of a drugs overdose. It was a bitter irony. It was also Jason's 21st birthday.

Jason's frail, drug-ravaged corpse was found slumped in the street. When his father Paul identified the body two days later, he barely recognised the lifeless cadaver that lay on the mortuary slab before him. Jason's head looked unusually large and completely out of all proportion on top of his rake-thin, skeletal body. His face was taut, drawn and yellow. Paul broke down in tears. His son's body bore all the hallmarks of a smackhead. Where was the healthy, happy young naval recruit he had known and loved, he cried.

At the inquest it was revealed that Jason had overdosed on pills prescribed to help him cope with his addiction to Class A drugs. Paul Grimes' world came crashing down around him. He could not understand why it had to be his son. After all, hadn't he, Jason's father, crusaded all of his life against drugs? Had he not given up everything to fight that war? Risking his own life to destroy the peddlers he believed were responsible for the killer scourge.

For a brief moment Paul Grimes felt like exacting revenge with the barrel of a gun. Simply executing all of the peddlers of death he knew of there and then – those names on a secret hit-list he hoped to grass up in the future – would at least be some justice. But the Customs officers he knew talked him out of bloody revenge. They persuaded him to fight another way. The best thing for him to do would be to carry on informing and turn up in court to give evidence. Paul vowed to continue with his undercover crusade.

At Jason's funeral, Snowball, who had miraculously blagged himself out of prison on bail, turned up unexpectedly to pay his respects. Flush with drugs money, he offered to pay for a flashy coffin and big spread at the wake. Paul later revealed that he had to hold himself back from putting one in his head there and then.

In the run-up to the big trial Paul received several more death threats. Anticipating an attack, he got hold of two more guns: an .18mm sawn-off shotgun and a .38mm revolver. He carried them at all times and even took them to bed. He moved between different safe houses and during the day did business on the move. He even got a job as painter and decorator to cover his tracks and keep himself mobile.

At a pre-trial hearing in Manchester an escorting prison officer refused to be handcuffed to Paul or walk beside him, fearing an assassination attempt. In April 1993, the trial proper began at Newcastle Crown Court. Paul was secretly billeted at a local police training college and guarded by armed officers round the clock. He was driven to court in a bullet-proof limo and his arrival was covered by snipers on the roof of the court precincts. A tactical firearms unit brimming with Heckler and Koch automatics was on standby outside. No one was taking any chances.

PAUL: I got escorted everywhere I went. One time I got escorted from Exeter Jail to Manchester on a pre-trial hearing kind of thing. The two screws was all shitting themselves because we'd parked the car miles from the court and we had to walk through the streets the rest of the way.

One of the Customs officers said: 'This is fucking great, isn't it? We're sitting ducks.' He thought it was funny.

The other screw's arse went and he took the handcuffs off and I had to walk ten paces behind.

'If they shoot you that means they shoot me as well, so you can fuck off,' he said.

In the days that followed I had to start watching myself. I was worried about who was following me. I knew that I was a marked man. That's why I started carrying. I had a shotgun and a handgun. I got them off a mate of mine. He just gave them to me. It was a sawn-off, .18mm rounds. I stayed at different addresses and made sure that I was getting all over the place. If anyone would have come for me I would have used it. Oh ay. No back answers. The Customs knew I had them. I showed them to one officer. I showed them to him in the boot of the car. He just said: 'I've seen them.'

Then they took me to Newcastle. We went to some police-training place. It was like Frank Pentangeli in *The Godfather II*, the guy who goes over to the FBI. As soon as we got to court all the solicitors came to the back of the court to have a look at me. As though I was some kind of fucking freak or something. They wanted to see with their own eyes 'cos (one) they didn't think I was still alive and (two) they didn't think I'd be so crazed as to turn up. Was that ontop, in all fairness.

Going in the stand was a bit of an anti-climax. I wasn't arsed. Threw in a few funnies and all that, had the court laughing a bit. They brought up all the stuff from the past about being a gangster and that. I was like that, I'm a businessman. It was like that Italian Tony off've *The Simpsons*, knowmean? 'I'm not a mobster. It's a slur on my reputation and that. I'm just a legitimate businessman. Get off my case.'

Then they said I used to be a bouncer. I hate that word. I told them that a bouncer is what you buy from Mothercare for babies. The court was in bulk, to be fair. The jury was warming to me a bit. Then they started fishing, trying to get me to admit that I was an informant. Bad one, la, but I just blanked it and they couldn't say fuck all.

Then they made a big deal of me having a mobile phone. It was the dark ages in those days and lads like me with porties and that did look half shady, to be fair. It was all bollocks though, but I had to get them off've that subject in case they asked for the bills. That would have been catasrophic; it had the Customs and Excise numbers all over it. If they would have asked for records of my phone it would have shown me calling my handler. Bang ontop, knowmean? Game over. And then they also said that I was supplying all the boys with these phones as well. I didn't know nothing about it.

Curtis Warren was sitting in the dock with all the others: Snowball, Jimmy Mac, the other feller etc. All's I did was look at the jury so I didn't have to look at them. Bored of them I was. When I did look at them I smiled. I did what I had to do.

It was never revealed in court that Paul was the informant. The cover story that he was simply a scrap dealer who had agreed (innocently) to broker the sale of lead held tight, but other aspects of the prosecution's case rapidly fell apart. A row between Customs and Excise and the Regional Crime Squad over the best way to use Brian Charrington in the case blew up into a Government scandal.

At first Charrington was promised £100,000 in a secret deal by police as a reward for being an informant. Astonished Customs officers blocked the payment, pointing out that Paul Grimes had been a more valuable and honest source. Furious, Customs officers then charged Charrington with drugs offences relating to the first 500-kilo consignment, accusing him of double-crossing them and deliberately allowing the drugs to slip their net so he could make money from their sale. What happened next was unprecedented in British judicial history.

The police asked their local MP Tim Devlin, then parliamentary private secretary to the Attorney General, to lobby on behalf of Brian Charrington. It resulted in the Attorney General agreeing to act as a referee between the Customs and Charrington's lawyers in a secret meeting. One month later the charges were dropped.

A freelance reporter called John Merry got a whiff of the secret deal and started digging. Later, Devlin attempted to cover up the scandal, but the *News of the World* splashed the story over the front page. From then on it seemed the prosecution was fighting a losing battle. A string of other problems plagued the case. Halfway through the trial, before even a single defence witness had taken the stand, the judge dropped a bombshell. He let Warren walk.

Mr Justice May ruled there was insufficient evidence against him. All that anyone could prove was that he had made a number of journeys, met a number of people and made a number of phone calls. It was not enough. At the end of the day Warren had not come into contact with the cocaine.

As he left the courthouse, Warren turned to the Customs officers who had brought in the case and said: 'I'm off to spend my £87 million from the first shipment and you can't fucking touch me.'

All of the other defendants except Joseph Kassar walked – two at a later retrial. In his summing-up, the judge pointed out that there was no evidence that there was actually any cocaine in the first load of ingots. Paul bit his lip. If he could have given his evidence revealing his conversations with Snowball, and his admission to cutting the cocaine from the lead, the course of the trial may have been changed dramatically. But, ironically, that would have blown his cover. It was a catch 22.

PAUL: They all walked on a technicality. My first thought was, 'What the fuck's going on?' I was fucking furious. Oh ay I was.

I phoned my Customs feller up and said: 'What's happened? How did you fuck up?'

He was gobsmacked. He couldn't answer me. One thing I did know is that all of my enemies were now out on the street. Pure dead man walking wasn't in it.

17

The Intervening Years

On the face of it Paul's efforts to bring down the cartel had been a disaster. Warren and his main boys had walked and were back on the street. It seemed Paul had failed in his mission. But Paul was playing a long game. As a former racketeer he understood that, if anything, his intelligence had allowed the authorities to get a handle on Warren, get their teeth into him. He knew also that they would now not let go. Especially after their humiliating defeat in court. Warren was now the dead man walking.

In truth, the court case was the beginning of the end for Warren. Even as he staged an impromptu victory parade in Toxteth, regally lapping up the adulation from well-wishers from a convertible limo, the chain of events that would lead to his downfall was already in motion.

Almost immediately a specialist police surveillance unit was set up to track his movements. Then a joint Customs–Police operation was launched to specifically target Warren and his backer, The Banker. The collapsed court case had hardened their resolve and this time Operation Crayfish would not be plagued by the systemic in-house fighting which had weakened their last mission.

Unlike Grimes, Warren had failed to grasp the bigger picture. In a bid to sidestep the heat, he moved to Holland but carried on smuggling. The British police tipped off their Dutch counterparts and on 24 October 1996 Dutch SWAT teams raided six houses across the country affectionately known amongst the international drug dealing community as the 'Flat Place'. Coordinated raids in Britain at a further 20 addresses linked to Warren's cartel were hit at the same time. The pièce de résistance was a raid on a shipping container in Rotterdam. Inside they found a cargo of lead ingots, similar to those Paul Grimes had rumbled five years earlier, containing 400 kilos of super-grade cocaine.

A further 1,500 kilos of cannabis, 60 kilos of heroin, 50 kilos of Ecstasy and £370,000 in cash were recovered. A small armoury including 960 CS gas canisters, hand grenades, three guns and a cache of ammunition was also seized. Warren was later jailed for 12 years. He is currently serving his sentence in one of the toughest jails in Europe in Rotterdam, Holland.

Many of Warren's immediate associates were jailed for between three and ten years, but even more astonishing were the knock-on effects thereafter. Without the expert guidance of their leader, the Liverpool Mafia began to fall apart. Several key members were convicted of big-time drug and money-laundering offences simply because they messed up in Warren's absence. But the biggest prize of all was yet to come.

Warren's conviction directly led the Dutch team to one of the biggest drug dealers in the world. On 8 October 1998, Cali cartel godfather, Arnaldo Luis Quiceno Botero, the 'Mr Big' who had allegedly supplied Warren with cocaine, was jailed for six years.

An article in *The Observer* newspaper definitively explained the significance of Warren's capture and, by default, the key role played by Grimes in his downfall. Journalist David Rose wrote:

> The mythology of British villainy needs to be rewritten.
> Next to Warren the Krays were pathetic minnows. The
> Great Train Robbers and Brinks Mat robbers, who were

POWDER WARS

swaggering highwaymen from the pre-drugs era, were way down the division. The plain fact is Warren is the richest and most successful British criminal who has ever been caught.

Paul was buzzing.

PAUL: After the trial finished in April 1993 I just disappeared into obscurity. For the first time in my life I lived in the suburbs. On the Wirral, pure bank manager territory, knowmean? I was content to be just another Mr Average. I got up in the morning and went to work. I drove a Peugeot 205. Of a night I sat in and watched the telly. *Eastenders* and all that bollocks. Watching that shite was far more painful than all of the injuries I had sustained during a life full of violence. It was, believe you me.

Gone were the days of £1,000-a-night Chinese meals and champagne nights out with the lads. Gone were midnight raids. The lock-ups full of swag. The beatings. The dough on tap. Banging cocktail waitresses two at a time. The respect. The power.

Now I was ten-grand-a-year Joe Schmo. None of the neighbours knew who I was. I was just another loser, keeping his head down and trying to get through the day without any hassle. And do you know what? In a weird way, I enjoyed it. I felt free. For the first time in my life I wasn't a criminal. No one was after me. The moby wasn't going off 30 times an hour, at all hours, with villains on the phone saying this and that. Life was simple. There was a certain logic, in the world of the straight-goer, that was comforting, knowing that if you didn't go to work you didn't have enough 50 pences to put in the gas meter. Straightforward as that.

In normal life there was no *get paid*. Ever. That goes without saying. It was all simple textbook economics. No breaking the system. It was purely a case of do this, get that. End of. The system had been here for 2,000 years and there was no way of getting around it. And for the first time, at last, I'd found my place in it. I was conforming.

I got rid of all the businesses and got a job as a painter and decorator. Then as a security guard. It was a shit job, but I got a buzz out of it. I was guarding warehouses. Poacher turned gamekeeper, all that. I was good at it. A lot of people suspected me of having made a lot of goulash from my swashbuckling days and from the sale of the yards and that, but that was my business. I certainly didn't go shouting about it, knowmean, the taxman and that. At the end of the day money meant fuck all. I've always enjoyed living frugally and being super low-key. My new life as an arse-wipe security guard suited me down to the ground.

After the trial the Customs didn't offer me a witness-protection programme. To be honest, there was no need. My role as the grass never came out in court. Their cover story had held tight. Obviously, Warren and Snowball had their suspicions and that. And to boot, they were certainly pissed off that I'd given evidence as a legit scrap dealer. But in the furore of them walking, everyone seemed to forget about it. Of course I still carried a gun. That was my only vice. That was for my own self-protection.

Once when I was driving along in my little works van I suddenly saw Snowball out of the corner of my eye. He was driving a big wagon with ladders on. He reversed the lorry into me. Full on. Clearly trying to kill me, but I just got out and started laughing at him. In the past, I would have banged his head in the car door repeatedly and left him for dead, but I just walked across the road and called the busies. That was the new me.

A couple of months afterwards, one Sunday, I slipped back into Liverpool and went down to Heritage Market. I wanted to prove that I could go anywhere. Just to myself really, not to anyone else. I walked in and the first person I saw was one of Warren's men, the skip-firm owner who had sold me the lead. One of Snowball's team.

I just smiled at him. To me he was a piece of shit. He started giving it mouth. Language and that. He called me a grass and all that carry-on.

'Fuck off, you drug dealer,' I said to him.

With that, he walked away from me. Knowing full well that, even though I had turned over a new leaf, if he carried on his foolishness, he would suffer a thrashing – Sunday shoppers or no Sunday shoppers. I could have done him in there and then, but I really couldn't be arsed, to tell you the truth.

The girl who was serving me said: 'What was that all about?'

I raised my arm and pointed him out to the crowd: 'He is a drug dealer,' I said.

She said: 'I didn't know that. He comes in here all the time. I won't be serving him again.'

It was only a small thing but it was good. It gave me a bit of a boost, to tell you the truth. I had threats and all that. Even my brother Stephen was passing threats round. They were ashamed of me.

I started going into pubs and people would mark my card. A lot of people asked why I had given evidence, because no one knew that I was an informant. I just made out I was a businessman who had got mixed up in it all.

'Do you think I'm going to jail for those pieces of shit?'

That was my excuse and I just kept that going.

A few of the lads were on my side. There were still a lot of gangsters who were against drugs. They wouldn't dabble in that shit. They looked at it as that the people who did dabble in it were shit who killed people. One of them was an old mate called Little Mick. He'd made a lot of money selling bent ciggies and all that. In massive amounts. Huge lorry loads. He'd got into the building and was doing all right, but he was anti-drugs. He kept me supplied with guns.

There was lot of big names who were made up. They'd shake my hand and all that, but they never had the bottle to do what I did. They knew that I'd stopped a lot of gear coming into the country. They were amazed that I had the bottle to still walk around and all the carry-on.

One thing that didn't change was my hatred for the drug dealers. As a security guard in the shops I began noticing that most of the thieves I was catching were bag-heads. Stinking, alien-headed heroin addicts who stole batteries, razor blades and coffee to get through the day. They were pathetic, for sure, but I still felt sorry for them. In their dead, dark eyes I saw the ghost of my own son, Jason. I could see the estates and schools being swamped with Es, coke and brown. Cheap, strong drugs like there had never been before. The rave thing had opened up whole new markets and new outlets. Even door crews were well in on the act now.

I knew the teams that were bringing the drugs in and the crews who were knocking them out. I knew it was only a matter of time before our paths crossed.

18

Haase Backgrounder

In the years since they had drifted apart sometime in the 1980s, Paul Grimes was unaware that his old pal John Haase had become one of Britain's most feared gangsters.

Haase had made the transition from armed robber to international drug dealer at exactly the right time – and struck gold. In fact, senior-level villains in Liverpool now look back on the late '80s and early '90s with rose-tinted glasses, fondly remembering them as the glory years of drug dealing, in much the same way as Victorian mill owners must have looked back on the Industrial Revolution.

Haase was now a multi-millionaire heroin baron. At the same time as Paul Grimes was waging his one-man crusade against Warren in the early '90s, Haase was secretly expanding his empire. Haase had secretly pioneered the Turkish Connection to the UK; the trading route from the poppy fields of Afghanistan to the cafes of Stoke Newington, controlled by the fearless Turkish Mafia. Haase had grown so close to the Turk babas or godfathers, and his buying power was so huge, that he was granted direct access to the mujahideen warlords in Afghanistan. He often left his suburban home in Liverpool to fly to mountain redoubts in eastern Turkey in person to inspect the goods. He had come a long way since his days as a small-time crook.

Haase picked up his first conviction in December 1963 when he was given a conditional discharge for minor offences at Liverpool City Juvenile Court. One year later he was nicked for larceny and breaking into a shop, and in January 1964 he was sentenced to probation, again at Liverpool City Juvenile Court.

Like many a young Scouse rapscallion before him, he had invaded the relatively peaceful pastures of north Wales to pillage the rich pickings. In March 1964, he was given two years' probation at Llangollen Juvenile Court for unlawfully taking a mailbag. Two years later he was fined £5 at Liverpool Magistrates' Court for stealing a box of grapes. In April 1966, he was sentenced to six months in prison, suspended at Denbigh Quarter Session for larceny of lead.

In March 1969, he was sent to prison for the first time after he breached the conditions of his suspended sentence when he was caught taking a car without consent. A year later, in March 1970, Haase was jailed for 18 months at Liverpool Crown Court for burglary and theft. Then for a string of similar offences he was given two years' probation at Preston Crown Court in June 1972.

In March 1973, Haase got seven years for his part in five armed raids on post offices and betting shops and two attacks on police. Jailing him, Judge Rudolph Lyons said: 'The time has come for your reign of terror in Liverpool to come to an end. You are an evil, dangerous man.' A detective who worked on the case later told the *Daily Mirror* newspaper that a female employee who had stared down the barrel of Haase's trademark shotgun never recovered from the ordeal. The detective said: 'She was totally traumatised by what happened to her.'

By the late '70s John was the leader of a ruthless gang of armed robbers known as the Transit mob. Their trademark MO was to spring out of the back of a Ford Transit van, armed to the teeth, and pounce on their victims. But despite being super tight and supposedly impenetrable, they were caught and in July 1982 Haase got 14 years for armed robbery on two post office vans. Haase was then 34. Haase's co-conspirator, Danny Vaughan, was jailed for 13 years.

Haase always blamed a supergrass called Roy Grantham for informing on the Transit mob. Several years later Grantham allegedly committed suicide after mysteriously disappearing at sea on a boating trip. Underworld sources maintain he was killed in revenge for betraying the Transit mob.

The case was further complicated by evidence given at the trial by a second supergrass called Dennis Wilkinson. Wilkinson was a violent and sadistic veteran of the Scottish underworld. In the early '80s, he was arrested for attempted murder, indecent assault, extortion and robbery on a young man. On remand, he claimed that he had befriended John Haase and Danny Vaughan. Facing a possible 20-year sentence, Wilkinson swore under oath that Vaughan and Haase had confessed in the prison exercise yard to the Transit mob robberies. His evidence was crucial in convicting Haase and Vaughan.

Wilkinson later retracted his statement, claiming in a *Sunday People* story that he fitted up the pair on the instructions of a bent copper who had passed him Vaughan's confidential file and told him to memorise the evidence. Wilkinson claimed that he had perjured himself.

Seizing on an apparent miscarriage of justice, in 1984 friends and relatives of Haase and Vaughan climbed the 120-foot Wellington Monument in Liverpool to protest at their imprisonment. However, the protest, which later inspired the 'Free George Jackson' campaign in the soap opera *Brookside*, was in vain. It did not result in freedom.

Following his release in 1990, Haase realised that there was no future in armed robberies. He noticed that his contemporaries in the Liverpool Mafia were riding the crest of the drugs boom and he wanted a piece of it. What's more, Haase had the respect and the firepower to muscle in and that is exactly what he did.

Haase's point of entry into the drugs business owed itself to contacts he had made in jail and his nephew, Paul Bennett, a 30-something gangster who in the late '80s/early '90s was doing to heroin what Curtis Warren had done to cocaine. Bennett had excellent distribution networks in Britain. Whilst Haase had been in jail, he had cultivated a contact of one of Turkey's most powerful babas, known as the 'Vulcan'.

This mysterious crime boss controlled the wholesale poppy market in Afghanistan and the trafficking lines through Turkey, the Balkans and around the Caspian Sea known as the 'southern route'. His vast wealth ensured that every time the Vulcan had been sent to jail, he had managed to buy himself out. The police complained that his organisation was immune because he owned politicians, judges and senior law officials.

The Vulcan was impressed enough with Haase to put him in the safe hands of his own son-in-law, a heavyweight heroin baron called Yilmaz Kaya. Haase introduced Kaya to Bennett. Recognising that Haase had the muscle and the experience to run a large criminal enterprise the Turks were more than impressed. They began dealing directly with Haase. Business boomed.

Within a relatively short period, Haase had taken over a large slice of Liverpool's and thus Britain's heroin import. Between 1989 and 1993 his trafficking ring was the biggest in Britain. Unique amongst the Liverpool Mafia, he did business alone. He was not a team player, more of a maverick who was suspicious of their cliquiness, taking comfort in the anonymity of doing business with firms far afield.

Haase feared no one. To prove it, he even leant on the untouchable Curtis Warren. Haase had met Warren in 1990 and helped him sell a consignment of cocaine, but when a business deal with one of Warren's top bosses had gone badly wrong, Haase stepped in. As punishment Haase kidnapped the gangster involved and 'taxed' Warren's crew for £50,000. The victim protested, using the defence: 'You can't do this. I work for Curtis.' Haase replied: 'So fucking what? Get the money or you will be killed.' The ransom was paid.

At the height of Haase's success there occurred one of the most extraordinary events in British judicial history. It mirrored the strange and sinister legal workings that had loomed large in the Warren case and in another striking similarity with the case, Paul Grimes was to become a key figure.

In the summer of 1992 Customs and Excise officers put John Haase under surveillance. Rightly they believed him to be the British-end kingpin of a Turkish heroin smuggling ring. Unable to infiltrate the gang, Customs officers decided to 'follow the money' in the hope of unravelling their modus operandi. They watched as nearly £2 million was handed over to a North London Turkish outfit headed by 26-year-old godfather, Yilmaz Kaya. The cash was spirited back to Turkey via Heathrow airport.

However, the real money was being made in Liverpool. Two of the Turks were regularly followed on frequent visits to Liverpool where they met Haase, who by then had firmly installed his nephew, Paul Bennett, as his deputy, and a dealer called Edward Croker to oversee distribution on the street. Watching in secret, the Customs officers looked on in amazement as bundles of cash the size of house bricks were handed over in a heavy plastic bag at the Black Horse pub in Liverpool.

In July 1993 Customs moved in on the gang. A staggering 50 kilos of heroin with a street value of £18 million were discovered in the bedroom of a safe house in Evesham Road, Walton. Haase immediately suspected that Customs had been helped by a secret informant. He blamed a businessman called John Healey, who was indebted to Haase for over £1 million. Haase raged that Healey had ratted him out in order to avoid paying back the money and that it was a fit-up. His protestations fell on deaf ears.

Two years later, in August 1995, the eight men involved were jailed for a total of 110 years. Haase, then 46, was sentenced to an unprecedentedly severe 18 years, as was Paul Bennett, then 31. They had £840,000 in cash confiscated. Croker, then 31, was jailed for 14 years and had £110,000 confiscated. All three Liverpool gangsters had pleaded guilty to conspiracy to supply heroin. Judge David Lynch said: 'It is rare that the courts deal with people so high up the ladder. It must be marked by a heavy sentence.'

The five Turks involved – Suleyman Ergun, 26, Mehmet Ansen, 54, Yilmaz Kaya, 29, Bulent Onay, 39, and Manuk Ocecki, 37 – also received hefty sentences. It was a major coup for the Customs and Excise, who were still reeling from the fallout of the collapsed Warren case.

A senior Customs investigator who worked on the case said:

> We were delighted with the result. For us it was a turning point in the fight against the big players. We had managed to bring down a complicated international gang successfully. And we were confident we could do it again.
>
> The sentences were deservedly harsh. Without time off for good behaviour. And we were confident that Haase would get as little as possible off because he is notoriously uncooperative – he was expected to be released in 2013. We couldn't have wished for better. He was a dangerous man best kept off the streets.

19

Freed

Under the Criminal Justice Act 1991, the earliest Haase would be considered for parole was 2002. Failing this, he would normally have been released two-thirds of the way through his sentence in 2005. But 11 months after he was sentenced on 4 July 1996 a bombshell dropped – and seemed to explode with nuclear force. Haase and Bennett were mysteriously released from prison after striking a secret deal with the then Tory Home Secretary, Michael Howard.

The scandal sent shock waves around the nation. The *Sunday Mirror*, the newspaper that broke the story, splashed it across the front page under the headline: 'Two-Faced Howard – Heroin dealers jailed for 18 years . . . then HE frees them after 11 months in secret deal.'

The 'full shock story' on pages four and five revealed 'the scandalous secret the Home Secretary didn't want you to know'. The details of the deal were unfolded. It was revealed that Judge Lynch, who had jailed Haase and Bennett one year earlier, had been urged by Customs and Excise to write to Mr Howard recommending that their sentences be reduced. No one quite knew why at that stage, but it was hinted that the pair of hardened gangsters had turned informants.

Astutely, the paper pointed out that if that was the case then why were Haase and Bennett parading around Liverpool as cocky as ever without a care in the world following their sensationl release? Surely if they had grassed up top underworld figures they would be in hiding in fear for their lives?

The article appeared as follows:

Sunday Mirror 01/09/1996

REVEALED . . . THE SCANDALOUS SECRET THE HOME SECRETARY DIDN'T WANT YOU TO KNOW

It was, in the words police use among themselves, a result. The two ringleaders of a highly organised international gang who smuggled millions of pounds worth of heroin into Britain had each been jailed for 18 years. John Haase, 46, and Paul Bennett, 31, were sent down with the words of Judge David Lynch ringing in their ears. 'It is rare that courts deal with people so high up the ladder as you, and it must be marked by a heavy sentence.'

But just 11 months after their cell doors slammed shut behind them, the two crooks were swaggering down the streets of Liverpool – set free by Home Secretary Michael Howard, who received a letter from the judge after a plea from Customs officials.

Yes, the same Michael Howard who has demanded powers to increase criminals' sentences and promised the British public that a life sentence must mean a life sentence.

Yes, the same Michael Howard who went to court last week to halt early release of prisoners. Yes, the same Michael Howard who attacked drug dealers in the House of Commons, telling MPs: 'The Government is determined that those who persist in causing human misery and ruined lives should get the punishment they richly deserve.'

Last night the astonishing deal was greeted with disbelief by police, anti-drugs campaigners and parents who fear their children could be among the 1,000 people killed by heroin each year. 'I just can't believe these two are back out – we thought they were going to be off the scene for a long, long time,' one Liverpool detective told the *Sunday Mirror*.

A spokesman for the drugs charity Turning Point said: 'These two were major players in bringing the deadliest drugs into Britain. I am amazed that they are out on the streets so early.'

And Karen Griffiths, whose 18-year-old heroin addict son committed suicide after kicking the drug, said: 'This is outrageous. I can't see how these men can have got out after having served so little time. They are just going to do the same crimes over and over again.'

Haase and Bennett led a gang that specialised in the Turkish Connection, running heroin into Liverpool, which in the '80s was so awash with the drug it was known as Smack City.

Bundles of cash the size of house bricks were handed over in heavy plastic bags in the Liverpool pub the Black Horse and taken back to Turkey. Some of it was the gang's profits and the rest was reinvested to buy more drugs. When police and Customs swooped they seized a massive 190 lbs of heroin, one of the biggest hauls ever.

Haase and Bennett admitted conspiracy to supply heroin, and also had about £840,000 each confiscated. In total, the eight-man gang, including five Turks, were sentenced to 110 years inside.

At their trial in August last year, Judge Lynch told Haase and Bennett that the courts often dealt with the pitiful wretches who sell heroin on the streets to feed their own addiction, and rarely got an opportunity to punish the ringleaders. But following a request from

Customs officials, the judge wrote to Mr Howard with his recommendation that the sentences be reduced. The deal was done. Less than a year later, Haase and Bennett walked free, and it's hard to guess who is more amazed – the Liverpool police, or Liverpool's crooks.

One senior detective said: 'Locking up two major drug players was seen by many police officers as a great victory. Now they are out again and one can only assume they must have come to some arrangement with Her Majesty's Customs.'

One of the city's better-known crooks was equally stunned: 'The two of them were seen strolling down Dale Street together last week – the whole of Liverpool's underworld knows they are out. They even went to see one of the main guys who run the city's nightclub doormen. It's all very sinister – but they are simply brazening it out.'

Judge Lynch refused to comment about the case, but has told colleagues: 'I would like to discuss the details of this but there are certain restraints.'

When the Home Office discovered the *Sunday Mirror* was about to reveal details of the scandal, a senior aide to Mr Howard asked that the story should not be published. He denied that the request was being made to save Michael Howard's embarrassment and suggested we speak to a senior Customs investigator involved in the case. The Customs man said: 'If you want to quote me, people who help us get credit for it.' He admitted that Haase and Bennett were up to their necks in smuggling heroin, and that they turned informer only after they were arrested and remanded in custody – to save their own skins.

The Customs investigator said the two crooks could be in danger after informing on their former associates. But Haase and Bennett have made no attempt to hide or change their identities. Instead, their underworld reputations have been hugely boosted as men who can get out of an 18-year sentence.

And the decision to release them will cause further embarrassment to already under-fire Home Secretary Michael Howard. Five months ago he launched what he claimed was his toughest crackdown yet on Britain's criminals in a White Paper called 'Protecting The Public' – and he promised to target drug dealers. He told MPs in the Commons dealers were a 'scourge on society' and added: 'They prey on the young and innocent. They wreck people's lives.'

Mr Howard promised that his tougher sentencing policy would lead to a dramatic decrease in crime figures and clean up our towns and cities. He added: 'These proposals are tough and so they should be. They need to protect the public and build a safer Britain. Our duty and task is to protect people's freedom to walk safely on their streets and sleep safely in their homes. We have taken action to ensure that the balance in the criminal justice system favours the law-abiding public, not the criminal.'

Last night a Home Office spokesman said: 'We do not comment on individual cases in which the Royal Prerogative has been exercised.'

But there was growing outrage at the secret deal to free the two drug smugglers. Liberal Democrat MP Alex Carlile said: 'The Home Secretary must make a statement about this case.' Furious mother Karen Griffiths blames pushers who tempted her son into trying heroin for causing his death in 1995.

Yesterday Karen, 38, of Tonyrefail, South Wales, said: 'It was probably people like these two who gave my son heroin and caused his death. People have got to realise that our children are at risk from people like this. It's time someone took notice of what's happening on our streets. Byron was the apple of my eye. I really loved him more than anything but when he got into drugs there was just nothing I could do. I saw him change from an innocent teenager into someone I didn't even recognise as my own son.' Mother-of-two Karen has now set up a support group for other parents in South Wales whose children are addicted to drugs. She added: 'I wouldn't want any other mother to go through what I had to with Byron. People have got to act before it is too late. The problem is not going to go away.

'It's escalating, and the release of people like this after spending so short a time in jail is just adding to the problem.'

Drugs charity Turning Point was also shocked to learn of Haase and Bennett's early release from jail. Last night a spokesman said: 'Given the amount of heroin they were caught with, it does seem amazing that these two convicted drug dealers have been released early from an 18-year sentence.

'I can only assume that the information they provided to Customs and Excise was of invaluable assistance.

'But that will be of little comfort to the families and friends of the 1,000 people a year who die in this country from heroin addiction alone. And the others whose lives are scarred forever by becoming hooked on drugs.'

The main news story was followed by a strong comment piece on the leader page. It read:

THE VOICE OF THE SUNDAY MIRROR
Heroin kills at least 1,000 British youngsters every year. Countless more lives are destroyed by the billion-pound racket.

Michael Howard is a Home Secretary who revels in his tough-guy image. The hardliner cracking down on crooks and soft-sentencing judges alike. Evil Paul

Bennett and John Haase were major heroin barons jailed for EIGHTEEN years.

Judge David Lynch said the courts usually dealt with 'pitiful wretches' caught up in the heroin twilight zone. 'It is rare that courts deal with somebody so high up as you are and it must be marked by a heavy sentence.' Strong PUBLIC words. ELEVEN months later the pair were secretly freed in a strange deal involving the Home Secretary, the judge and HM Customs. An action that defied all the tough words.

When the *Sunday Mirror* discovered the truth, a senior Home Office official tried to persuade us NOT to publish. He suggested the freed drug tzars were giving 'sensitive' help to the authorities and might be at risk.

Or was it another case of trying to spare Howard's blushes and keep YOU, the public, in the dark?

What's the story, Home Secretary?

The exclusive was picked up by *The Observer* and the *Sunday Telegraph* and followed up the next day in *The Independent*. Tragically for the Home Secretary, the story also made the front page of the middle-England agenda-setting *Daily Mail*. The headline screamed: 'Howard in Drug Gang Deal Shock'. For Howard it was a total sickener.

Hysteria mounted again when it was revealed that Howard had recommended the Queen exercise the Royal Prerogative of Mercy. Merseyside Police and Members of Parliament vented their anger and surprise. One senior officer told the *Liverpool Echo*: 'I was absolutely flabbergasted when I heard they were out. Deals go on but this is an extreme case.'

Knowsley North MP George Howarth demanded assurances that the public were safe from the convicted drug barons. The Labour Home Affairs spokesman said: 'Given the recent history of armed violence on Merseyside, which is often associated with drug barons, I find this decision surprising to say the least. For that reason

I am writing to Michael Howard seeking an explanation.'

Michael Howard defended his decision, describing it as a 'wholly exceptional case', adding that it would have been 'inconceivable' to ignore the call of Judge David Lynch. In a confusing statement Howard went on:

> He said that were it not for the special circumstances of the case in terms of the lives of the men and safeguarding future operations he would have passed a sentence of five years instead of the eighteen years which he has passed. I think we have to look at this in the context of the real world. If I would have taken any other decision I would have been open to the most serious criticism.

When contacted by reporters Judge Lynch said, 'I cannot speak to you.'

Two days later on Wednesday, 11 September 1996, the Haase scandal was still going strong in the national newspapers. *Daily Mirror* reporters Frank Corless and Patrick Mulchrone were the first journalists to track down the recently freed prisoner to his Liverpool 'lair' and ask him for a comment. Haase responded with a threat: 'Get away. I'll hurt you,' followed by a string of four-letter abuse. He then landed a kick on terrified Corless as his grinning girlfriend, Debbie Dillon, looked on.

But the real story was yet to come out. Why had two of Britain's biggest and most violent drug dealers suddenly been released 11 months into an 18-year stretch? What had moved a right-wing, hang-'em-and-flog-'em Home Secretary to put his career on the line and plead for a Royal Pardon? Why was the deal shrouded in secrecy? Why had Howard tried to stop the story of their release from getting out?

Clues as to the answers to some of these questions lay in a series of shady events which occurred in Liverpool in 1994. Over a three-month period between February and May seven

POWDER WARS

huge arms caches were mysteriously discovered by police.

They included 150 weapons, such as Israeli-made Uzi sub-machine guns, AK-47 assault rifles and thousands of rounds of ammunition. One haul – the biggest ever on Merseyside – included 80 brand-new Italian Armi Technique 12-bore shotguns worth £30,000 still in their boxes. Another stash gave up ten sub-machine guns, five silencers, three magazines and 229 rounds of ammunition. The first find, in February, yielded 13 automatic weapons. On 31 March, buried wartime rifles were dug up in Formby. Four discoveries in April turned up pistols and a machine gun in Fazakerley, AK-47s in West Derby, a Czech pistol in Stanley Park and, among other weapons, an elephant gun in Ellesmere Port.

The circumstances surrounding each find were tantalisingly similar. Many of the caches were found in abandoned cars, which seemingly had been specifically bought for the purpose a few days before. Police were directed to the secret locations with remarkable accuracy. In all cases, although guns were recovered, no arrests were made.

Nonetheless, the finds were sold to the public as a major coup in the fight against organised crime. Confidently, investigating officers immediately ruled out a terrorist link and said the guns were definitely heading for the criminal underworld. It was just the success Merseyside Police had desperately been looking for. The city was reeling from a recent spate of gangland shootings. The success of Curtis Warren's drug operation was causing friction between those favoured distributors who were growing rich on his business and those gangsters who were being kept out of the loop. The rivalry would eventually lead to the shooting of David Ungi on 1 May 1995.

Big photo calls were staged by the police in which serious-looking officers posed with the staggering array of weapons they had taken off the streets. The press conferences were reminiscent of the RUC displaying captured IRA weapons in Northern Ireland. It was unprecedented on the mainland. Experts, like celebrity cop John Stalker, were wheeled in to ominously explain how Merseyside had become a 'staging post for gun-runners' but that the good news was that police were getting on top of it.

However, other experts, mainly underworld watchers, quietly noted that there was more than met the eye behind this little charade. Could it have anything to do with John Haase and Paul Bennett, they wondered, who at that time were awaiting trial on massive heroin charges? They could only speculate. Cryptically, Michael Howard had let it be known that information Haase and Bennett had provided 'proved to offer quite enormous and unique assistance to the law-enforcement agencies'.

Zoom forward to 1996 after Haase and Bennett were released from prison. Speculation that they had turned informant reached fever pitch. Wild conspiracy theories abounded about secret deals with MI5. It was a fact that the domestic spy service had been ordered by then PM John Major to wage war on the now out-of-control Liverpool Mafia. Had they recruited John Haase?

On 25 May 1997 the *Sunday Mirror* added fuel to the fire with another explosive story. The exclusive revealed how within days of his release Haase had twice made contact with a shady 34-year-old underworld fixer called Simon Bakerman. Mind-blowingly, Bakerman was Home Secretary Michael Howard's cousin. The paper hinted at awkward questions which could be posed in the light of this new information. Had Bakerman acted as a secret go-between in the shady deal? The article went as follows:

Sunday Mirror 25/05/1997

MICHAEL HOWARD, HIS CROOKED COUSIN
AND THE TWO DRUG BARONS HE SECRETLY
SET FREE?

However much Michael Howard might wish it, this is the case that simply refuses to go away.

Last summer, as Home Secretary, he authorised the release of two international drug dealers just 11 months into their 18-year prison sentences.

John Haase, 46, and Paul Bennett, 32, had admitted

masterminding a £15 million heroin-smuggling ring from Turkey to Liverpool.

If the decision had been taken by a civil libertarian minister keen on alternatives to the prison system, it would have raised eyebrows at the very least.

That these men were freed by the only Home Secretary in living memory tough enough to satisfy the hawks of the Tory Party conference provoked astonishment bordering on disbelief.

At the time, Mr Howard explained that the two drug dealers had provided vital information to Customs investigators, who in turn had recommended to the trial judge that their sentences be reduced, and he was merely doing what the judge asked.

This is pretty rich coming from a Home Secretary who established his formidable reputation – not to mention landing himself in courts from Strasbourg to the Strand – by NOT doing what judges asked.

But that is in the past. Today, the *Sunday Mirror* reveals that within days of his release, John Haase had twice made contact with a small-time crook called Simon Bakerman. Bakerman, 34, is known to associate with some of Liverpool's most notorious criminals.

He is also Michael Howard's cousin.

He carries a photograph of the former Home Secretary in his wallet and often boasts of his family links to Mr Howard.

He told the *Sunday Mirror*: 'I see Michael's mother all the time. I last saw Michael when he came to my mum and dad's house for tea after Chelsea played at Liverpool last season.'

His mother Freda Bakerman told us: 'I am related to Michael through my father. I do keep in touch. We're a very close family. I speak to my aunt, Michael's mother, three or four times a week.'

In 1985 Bakerman was given a six-month suspended prison sentence at Liverpool Crown Court for attempting to obtain money by deception.

He inflicted injuries on himself to convince his parents he had been beaten up over a £2,700 debt, then phoned his mother and pretended to be held hostage in a warehouse – all in a desperate attempt to con money out of them.

It is not, of course, Mr Howard's fault that family duty requires him to take afternoon tea with a convicted criminal.

After all, we can choose our friends, but we cannot choose our relatives.

But there is more. The *Sunday Mirror* has discovered that the decision to release the two drug dealers was taken by Michael Howard alone, without reference to his Prisons Minister, Ann Widdecombe.

She might have expected to be consulted, but the files marked Top Secret landed only on his desk.

The unanswered questions surrounding this case continue to mount. The drug dealers' release was first uncovered by a crime reporter on the *Liverpool Echo* newspaper.

Before he could write it, he suddenly quit his job and now lives in another part of the country under a different name following a visit from Haase and Bennett.

Before the *Sunday Mirror* broke the story last September, we were placed under enormous pressure by the Home Office not to publish it.

When Sky News ran an item on the case, they were called by the Home Office and asked to pull it.

And just hours after we spoke to Simon Bakerman, we received a threatening telephone call from a prominent Liverpool underworld family warning us not to publish anything about his criminal past.

Mr Howard says Haase and Bennett were released because they provided vital information about other criminals.

Underworld figures in Liverpool say this is laughable, and they have a point.

Two supergrasses who have committed the ultimate sin of informing on their criminal colleagues would be in hiding, in disguise, in fear for their lives – not, like Haase and Bennett, strolling the streets of Liverpool without a care in the world.

As a credible contender for the leadership of the Conservative Party, Mr Howard cannot afford to have the smallest question mark hanging over his judgement.

If the decision to release these two men was justified, it should be easy for Mr Howard to prove.

Let him now announce the name of a single criminal who has been arrested, charged, prosecuted, convicted or jailed as a result of information provided by Haase and Bennett.

Until he does, the *Sunday Mirror* will continue to ask the awkward questions that Michael Howard seems unable to answer.

More awkward questions were raised when it was revealed that Bakerman's father Warner had serious charges in connection with cannabis smuggling against him dropped. Another embarrassing article appeared in the *Sunday Mirror*. The story went:

Sunday Mirror 08/06/1997
RELATIVE OF EX-MINISTER HOWARD GETS OFF DRUG RAP
Former Home Secretary Michael Howard's role in authorising the early release of two convicted drug dealers has taken a new twist.

Mr Howard sparked outrage last year after rubber-stamping the release of heroin barons John Haase and Paul Bennett 11 months after they got 18-year jail sentences in 1995. He said they gave vital information to Customs in Liverpool where they had run an international smuggling ring.

Last month we revealed how a cousin of Mr Howard, Simon Bakerman, was in contact with Haase days after his release. Today, we can reveal that Bakerman's father Warner was arrested in a drugs bust in Liverpool but charges were dropped.

Accountant Warner, 62, was held after the discovery of a consignment of cannabis in a lorry-load of oranges. A local underworld figure said: 'He had heart problems and the next thing was let go – but he soon seemed fine.'

A Customs spokesman confirmed: 'The charges were dropped before it reached the committal stage.'

We asked Mr Howard how many arrests there had been based on Haase and Bennett's information. We also asked why Ann Widdecombe, then Prisons Minister, was not consulted over their release and if he was aware that Simon was associated with Haase and Bennett. A spokesman said: 'Miss Widdecombe was not consulted because her duties did not involve sentencing of prisoners, and Mr Howard was not aware Simon Bakerman was connected to Haase and Bennett.

'You could not expect him to tell you of arrests resulting from Haase and Bennett's information.'

The speculation mounted. Questions were tabled in the House of Commons. Fleet Street reporters were dispatched to Liverpool to get the facts. But the astonishing truth of how Haase sprung himself from prison would evade them all.

20

The Great Escape

The truth is that it was a very clever con. John Haase paid members of his gang and underworld associates to plant the guns and a quantity of drugs so that he could tell the authorities where they were and claim the glory – and a sizeable chunk of time off his sentence for cooperating with the law.

Normally, informants would tell the police or Customs about real crimes that are being or about to be committed. In Haase's case he carefully choreographed the planting of evidence so that it appeared that crimes were in progress. But in reality they were stunts. Phoney set-ups, make-believe incidents carefully staged to convince the police that they were stopping the bad guys. But no one was ever caught.

Despite 19 'raids' in which more than 150 weapons were 'seized' there was not one single conviction. Police invariably arrived at the location of a tip-off to find a deserted 'safe house' or an abandoned car with a holdall full of guns in the boot. All fingerprints had of course been wiped clean. All of the vehicles had mysteriously been purchased for cash a few days earlier by untraceable men who, despite numerous appeals in the press, never came forward.

And that's just the way John Haase planned it. Because no one had been dobbed in he could retain his street credibility. He would be able to convince other members of the Liverpool Mafia that technically he was not a grass. He was still a stand-up guy who could be trusted. Not only that, Haase knew he would be revered as the gangster who had conned the Government into releasing him.

This explained why Haase had been able to walk back onto the streets of Liverpool within days of his release without a care in world. Instead of being shot, Haase was congratulated by members of the Liverpool Mafia who lined up to meet him at a series of rug-joint parties.

In fact the only people Haase 'grassed up' in his numerous put-up jobs were corrupt law officials – a crooked prison officer, a corrupt CPS manager, a rogue solicitor and a bent copper. This super-selective targeting of 'enemy' fall-guys clocked up extra brownie points on the street. The villains were happy that Haase hadn't actually grassed any villains up. The break-out was a triple-whammy success. The most audacious escape plan since Steve McQueen went over the wall on a stolen German army motorbike. Haase became an instant underworld legend.

One of the gangsters who supplied weapons to Haase for his scheme was the notorious Glasgow godfather Paul Ferris. In his book, *The Ferris Conspiracy*, he explained how his gang sold £20,000 worth of firearms to an envoy sent by Haase specifically for use as plants.

PAUL FERRIS: A guy from Liverpool visted Rab on behalf of John Haase. Haase was on remand accused of dealing in a large quantity of heroin and set to go down for a very long time if found guilty. His friend reckoned he could have his sentence reduced in return for a consignment of illegal weapons.

Rab and I debated the implications. I pointed out to him that McGraw had been running this trade for years. The people selling the guns would get paid top dollar, the police could kid the public they were getting guns off the street, no one was arrested or jailed and Haase would get better treatment. It didn't resolve all the dilemmas but on balance it was reckoned to be within the code.

Haase's friends bought £20,000 worth of weapons, including 50-calibre tripod-mounted machine guns, machine pistols, handguns, a rocket launcher and some plastic explosives. The bundle was handed into police. Haase was originally jailed for 18 years – not a great result. After 18 months, Michael Howard, the Home Secretary, announced that Haase was to be released immediately for helping Customs and Excise smash a Turkish drugs ring. Haase claimed that the early release was for the weapons, the Turkish story being the official cover-up.

Haase's devious operation nearly came to light after a close brush with the law. Some of the guns were transported from a location outside Manchester to Liverpool by two stunning-looking women who were close to Haase. The idea was that a couple of dolly-birds, who looked like they had been on a shopping trip to Manchester, were unlikely to get a pull off the police. But the ladies' sports car was stopped almost immediately for speeding on the East Lancs road. The boot was crammed full of assault rifles and hand-grenades. The scantily clad girls did their best to distract the traffic cop away from the boot, flashing their legs and cleavage. It worked. He let them go with a ticking off without searching the car.

In another extraordinary incident, the operation nearly came crashing down amid fears for public safety. Haase's men planted a cache of explosives and several small arms in a car near a pub called Black George's on Park Road in Liverpool 8. The pub was run by the Ungi family and Haase hoped the find would implicate them, and at least mean they were in for a bit of harassment.

But the plan backfired when the car was stolen by joyriders before the police could seize it. A massive operation was mounted to find the car and eventually it was spotted by a patrol car being driven at high speeds by a teenager and his pals through the streets of Walton.

The joyriders were awestruck when they were suddenly roadblocked by nearly 20 police, an armed response unit and a bomb disposal unit. The explosives were found in the boot untouched. The kids hadn't even noticed it and were never told. There was a collective sigh of relief.

Other clues were missed. Haase insisted that he conducted all the negotiations with his Customs handlers in person. The deal was brokered at a series of secret meetings and phone calls at the prison where Haase and Bennett were on remand. Also present were Haase's solicitor, Tony Nelson, and a Customs officer called Paul Cook. During one of the meetings Cook outlined the number of years Haase could expect off his sentence in return for quantities of weapons seized.

Little did he know that Haase was taping the meetings using a mini-digital recorder strapped to his leg. It was an insurance policy in case the authorities reneged on the deal. Later officers discovered the illegal device and confiscated it. But Customs men went ballistic, fearing that potentially compromising conversations had been recorded. They threatened to call off the deal. Haase insisted that there were no other copies in existence other than the electronic files on the tape that had been seized. He was lying. Copies had already been smuggled out of the prison and buried. Not realising they had been duped, the officers resumed talks.

Haase continued to feed the authorities the locations of the phoney arms caches. But the Customs and Excise and police remained blissfully unaware that the weapons and drugs stashes they were finding had been planted especially. In a top-secret report, Customs and Excise innocently documented each find and praised Haase for his cooperation.

The report was penned by Haase's Customs handler, who cultivated him while they were on remand for the 55 kilos of Turkish Connection heroin from 1993 to 1995. The report submitted by a Customs officer to the trial judge revealed how Haase approached Customs shortly after their arrest in September 1993, indicating that they wished to be considered as informants.

The Customs document, signed on 9 August 1995, states that both Haase and Bennett 'indicated through their solicitor that they wished to cooperate with the prosecution'.

The Customs officer added:

> As from October 1993, the defendants commenced the flow of information to the prosecution. The information given in my opinion falls into several categories.
>
> Information which produced an instant positive result and led to the authorities making an arrest, recovering stolen property, seizing drugs or firearms and ammunition.
>
> From their information over 150 illegal firearms were recovered, including Kalashnikov assault weapons, Armalite rifles, Thompson machine guns, Bren guns, Uzi sub-machine guns and over 1,500 rounds of ammunition.
>
> Other significant results were the seizure of 7,534 Ecstasy tablets, five kilos of amphetamine, 58 litres of methadone, the recovery of 100 LSD tablets, the locating of a skunk (cannabis) factory, 200 cannabis plants and a machine gun.

In conclusion, he stated:

> The number of arrests made do not do justice to the quality of information given by these defendants.
>
> It is a rare occurrence when the authorities have such a rich vein of information on quality criminals, more so when that information can, by other means, be shown to be genuine and 100 per cent accurate as in this case.

> I consider that their continuing value to the police with regard to the recent use in firearms has a great deal to offer as does the intelligence they can impart relating to serious drug importations.

The report played down the low number of arrests – two related to growing cannabis and another in connection with three illegal firearms. The report stated:

> The number of arrests made do not do justice to the quality of information. Over a period of 20 months they (Haase and Bennett) have continued to supply information relating to serious offences concerning firearms and drugs.
>
> Around 150 weapons were seized.
>
> A plethora of intelligence has been gained and introduced into the authorities' system, the value of which should not be under-estimated.

But, despite the arms finds, criticism of the releases followed, particularly as there were never any arrests of note made by the authorities. This, according to the document's author, was because: '. . . the need to take the weapons off the streets was seen as the main priority. Situations did not arise where extensive observations could be undertaken.'

But the Liverpool underworld knew the truth. One gangster told the *Liverpool Echo*:

> John got people to hide the guns here, there and everywhere in Liverpool while he was behind bars awaiting trial. Police and Customs spent two years doing cartwheels round the city finding them. He's no supergrass – the number of arrests proves that. He tricked the system into letting him off a lengthy stretch in jail. Police and Customs were happy because they got

a load of guns to boost their figures. No one ever
stopped to think and ask why?

The Customs report confirms that three arrests were made,
supposedly from his tip-offs – two related to growing cannabis
plants and another to do with the seizure of three guns.
However, no convictions are mentioned in the report.

Another claim was that:

> the defendants, at great personal risk, supplied
> information that there was a loaded firearm concealed
> within Strangeways Prison for the use of a fellow
> prisoner standing trial for a double murder. They
> explained how a prison officer had brought the weapon
> into the prison and gave details of his outside contact
> and a mobile telephone number. The loaded gun was
> found and the prison officer identified. They identified
> [name removed], a solicitor who is criminally linked to
> numerous drug dealers. They identified a serving police
> officer who was assisting the criminal fraternity.

The report stated:

> Haase and Bennett, again at great personal risk, supplied
> information that there was a loaded firearm concealed
> within Strangeways [prison] for the use of a fellow
> prisoner standing trial for double murder. They
> explained how a prison officer had brought the weapon
> into the prison. The loaded gun was found and the
> prison officer was identified. The case was widely
> reported to the press. Suspicion fell on the defendants
> [Haase and Bennett] who, notwithstanding, completed a
> questionnaire relating to the events for the Greater
> Manchester Police.

The double murder suspect, who was convicted days later, said he was fitted up by Haase. The report stated that Haase and Bennett helped smash a banknote forgery in southern England and exposed a corrupt CPS official.

The report continued:

> They supplied information relating to a major drugs target having contact within the CPS in Liverpool. They identified a solicitor who is criminally linked to numerous drug dealers. They identified a serving police officer who was assisting the criminal fraternity.

Liverpool MP Peter Kilfoyle revealed how he had been gagged from talking about Haase by Michael Howard. He told the Commons he was about to do a television interview about the release of the two, when he was called by Mr Howard who asked him not to comment as it would put their lives at risk.

Kilfoyle said:

> These two villains were on the streets, bold as brass, up to their old tricks but I deferred to the Home Secretary's privileged information and did not go out and get involved in publicising what was happening. We had a situation where a self-styled tough home secretary extraordinarily pardoned these truly vicious, serious criminals.

Kilfoyle said a senior source within Merseyside Police confirmed that the police now believed Haase had planted the guns. Mr Kilfoyle said it has been further alleged that all the weapons were bought for £82,000 from decommissioned stock held in a Midlands Police depository and a North Wales store. The Liverpool Walton MP added, 'I am very careful with these allegations because so many have been made. But only something that requires further investigation is being raised in the course of this debate.' Mr Kilfoyle also said there was a very strong case that Haase and Bennett were behind the Strangeways incident to win favour with the authorities.

'There are grave concerns that Customs and Excise have been misled by two practised liars in Haase and Bennett who manipulated their handlers.'

Customs minister Dawn Primarolo said Customs officers behaved appropriately throughout.

For all the hullabaloo, for all of the outrage, for all of the political posturing – at the end of the day none of it really mattered. The deed had been done. The bottom line was that John Haase was now firmly back on the street. Free to renew his war on society. Free to rebuild his criminal empire. If he so chose.

This time, though, it would be different. Many people now perceived him to be 'untouchable'. A gangster who had been 'made', green-lighted, granted a get-out-of-jail-free pass by none other than the Home Secretary himself. It was a passport to the super-league. Senior customs officers and policemen were in despair. If John Haase turned to organised crime again, how could they bring a man like that down?

21

Big Brother Security

Not surprisingly, within weeks of his release from prison in 1996 John Haase was back in business as a Liverpool Mafia godfather. Bigger, badder and better than ever before. Brimming with confidence and driven by a hunger for money and power that was as frightening as it was unfathomable, Haase's nihilistic emptiness was painful to be around. Friends shied away from looking into his thousand-yard-stare eyes, cowering like weak dogs from his visceral, brutish outbursts.

Haase was a real-life Scarface, fired up by the same cut-throat ambitions that had driven film director Martin Scorcese's refugee drug dealer from Cuba to make it big, whatever the cost, in Miami. The world is yours, Haase convinced himself. The ink on the Queen's Pardon was barely dry when Haase set to work rekindling his heroin and cocaine contacts. The Turkish Connection was re-established with a vengeance and heavyweight shipments of brown and white began to flood in.

Then Haase began to diversify his criminal empire at break-neck speed; wholesale gun-running, money laundering, extortion, kidnapping, cigarette smuggling, armed robbery, organised hijacking, contract violence, protection rackets, debt collecting. The crime spree was breathtaking in its velocity, range and depth and there was nothing that anyone could do about it. The authorities and the rest of the underworld had to stand back, backs against the wall, as the unstoppable tornado swept through town destroying everything in its path.

Haase's return to crime made a laughing stock of the Home Secretary and the Customs officers who had lobbied for his release. In the controversial secret report that had been submitted to the trial judge and then sent to Michael Howard, Haase's handler, Customs officer Paul Cook, had concluded: 'It is my considered opinion that such is the impact of this case on the defendants that, for differing reasons, it is highly unlikely that they would revert to a life of crime upon their ultimate release.'

Those words would come back to haunt the authorities.

For the Customs and Excise, Haase was too politically charged a target to take on. He was a walking media time bomb. His every move seemed to make headlines and heap embarrassment on the Government. The situation was further complicated by the fact that Haase was technically still a registered informant. Since January 1994, shortly after he had first turned informant on remand and begun feeding Customs information on the whereabouts of guns and drugs, Haase was registered as a fully fledged, signed-up, official grass.

That meant that he could use the fact that he was still 'on the books' as a defence at any time to explain away his criminal activity. It wouldn't be the first time a supergrass had turned around and said: 'I was only committing crimes so that I could gather intelligence and turn it over to the authorities.'

The tricky relationship between Haase and Customs and Excise was exacerbated further because officers continued to meet Haase following his release. This was not to warn Haase to desist from gangsterism or to probe him for criminal intelligence as would be expected of an informant. Customs officers met Haase in order to discuss how they could limit the damage being done to the Government by his case in the press, to keep him away from reporters and to return property.

These meetings were detailed in a witness statement later given by Haase's handler, Paul Cook. Cook revealed:

> My dealings with John Haase and Paul Bennett since that time (of their release) are as follows:
>
> 1. In 1996 I attended the release of Paul Bennett with Mr (Tony) Nelson, his solicitor, and then returned to my office.
>
> 2. In late 1996, as part of my duty of care after media articles appeared in various newspapers, I attended Manchester airport where I met Paul Bennett and his family arriving back into the UK from a family holiday in Mexico. I arranged an overt search of their baggage by uniformed Customs officers after which I took Paul Bennett to a hotel near the airport to meet Mr Nelson and John Haase. The reason for my actions was to allow their legal representatives to discuss matters with them in advance of the press.
>
> 3. I subsequently attended the office of Mr Nelson. I believe this was around December 1997, when Mr Nelson, John Haase and Paul Bennett were present. The reason for this was to return property. A general discussion took place regarding how they were contending with any difficulties. At that time general information relating to other individuals was volunteered by Paul Bennett.
>
> 4. I have since received a number of calls, that have diminished in time, from Mr Nelson during which he gave general details of individuals who were concerned in drugs. I have no record of the dates of these calls.
>
> 5. At some time in 1998 I received a call from Mr Nelson and then John Haase concerning a threat against an individual. I passed these details to a member of Merseyside Force Intelligence Bureau.
>
> 6. On 3 August 1998, I received a letter from my Assistant Chief Investigations Officer.

7. On 11 June 1999, I telephoned Mr Nelson to inform him that Paul Bennett was wanted in connection with a cannabis importation. I asked Mr Nelson that, if possible, he contact Paul Bennett and arrange for him to surrender for interview. I received no news after this request.

In 1998, just at the time when the authorities should have been trying to get closer to Haase in an effort to monitor and curtail his resurgent racketeering, they cut off all links. A bombshell memo from Customs boss Steve Rowton to Haase's handler, Paul Cook, dated 3 August 1998, and referred to in Point 6 in the above statement, read:

Restricted – Management
John Haase and Paul Bennett
We spoke. As you know there is sustained political interest in the activities of Haase and Bennett. In order to safeguard our position we must maintain our distance. You are therefore directed to have no further dealings with Haase, Bennett or their representatives. If they should contact you, for whatever reason, you must report the matter immediately to either me or HODO.

Steve Rowton

The memo seemed to sum up the helplessness of the situation. Customs and Excise had their hands tied as Haase ran amok. It seemed as though Haase had them exactly where he wanted them – dancing to his tune. As Haase stepped up his drug dealing and gun-running, he set up a legitimate front business, a 'security' company called Big Brother, to cover his tracks.

In the old days gangsters bought nightclubs or went into the olive oil business to front their rackets. But this was '90s Britain and door teams were now the building blocks of organised crime. 'Security consultancy' was the perfect business to mask a multitude of sins.

Haase realised this and set up Big Brother with a two-pronged business plan in mind. One side of the operation was to 'take over' the doors (provide bouncers) for as many of the nightclubs and pubs in Liverpool as possible. The other side was to provide security guards for commercial premises such as building sites and shops. This would not only generate revenue, but also provide a pool of hard men to use as footsoldiers in his crime war on society.

Last but not least, the business would provide excellent cover for organised crime.

In the classic mobster tradition, like Al Capone, Haase maintained to his public that he was a 'legitimate businessman' plagued by insinuations that he was a racketeer because of his shady past. 'It is a slur on my reputation,' he would say.

The parody bordered on the comical. In an interview with the *Liverpool Echo* Haase managed to keep a straight face as he lied:

> I am going straight, running an efficient business and doing it well. I am a poacher turned gamekeeper. Half my life has been spent locked away behind bars. I feel as though I have wasted so many years.

Haase gushed that finding a woman had softened him up:

> I met Debbie in a pub in the city and it was love at first sight. Suddenly I had a girlfriend who I wanted to be with more than anything in the world. It was a big big gamble for Debbie deciding whether to stay with me. We spoke and she discussed things with her parents. I promised her that I would go straight and that things had changed. And her parents' view was that if she loved me she should give it a go. Thank God. I am happier

than I have ever been in my life. I get on great with my in-laws and have reconciled with my mam and dad.

Haase played the old community benefactor card as he went in for the PR (over)kill:

I sponsor a Sunday football team, Pineapple FC in Dingle, and I enjoy watching them. I keep fit and enjoy skiing. When I got out I was discussing what to do with my mate John Melvin. We thought about renovating houses. But John suggested that I should go into the security business. After all, I know a lot about security having been a criminal for so long.

Menacingly Haase added: 'I am endeavouring to provide an expert service to my clients and have not received any complaint from either a client or a member of the public.' Knowing full well that anyone who complained would be hit so hard and fast they would never dare to speak out again. The complaints department at Big Brother was not known for its customer relations. Disgruntled clients were often hospitalised and their houses blown up.

The payoff from Haase's extraordinary PR puff was an Orwellian masterpiece, so diametrically opposite to the truth as to be absurd: 'Life is so different for me now and I just hope that the public will give me the chance to show that I have changed.'

Behind the scenes Haase continued to rob the public blind and lure their children into a twilight world of drug abuse en masse. His reign was an orgy of non-stop crime. His team of rapid-fire, round-the-clock racketeers, addicted to cocaine and explosive violence, got up in the morning and literally drug dealt, extorted and armed robbed their way through the day.

In the morning they would take delivery of six kilos of heroin, in the afternoon they would send a cache of guns to Scotland and in the evening they would petrol bomb a nightclub. And then they would go to work, as doormen on Liverpool's buzzing but brutal nightclub scene. There they would fight gun-slinging turf wars with rival door teams, kidnap drug dealers and broker the sale of swag – lorry loads of stolen whisky and designer sportswear worth hundreds of thousands of pounds.

Haase's PR smokescreen seemed to work. Big Brother security won a string of lucrative legit contracts. Astonishingly, Haase's company took over the security at a parish church, a story so preposterously absurd it made national newspaper headlines. An anonymous member of St Mary's Walton-on-the-Hill church in Walton, Liverpool, who was too scared to be named, told the *Sunday Mirror*: 'It's crazy! How can you have a man like this looking after a church? It's like having the Devil to stand at the gates of St Peter.'

The impropriety of a convicted drug dealer running a high-profile security firm, which guarded the public at prestigious venues such as McDonald's at Liverpool FC's Anfield Stadium, sparked further controversy in the press. In the *Sunday Telegraph*, industry bosses called for Haase to be closed down and for urgent regulation to prevent him from starting up again.

This was all very worrying for the police and Customs and Excise. How could they take on Haase? How could they get close to him? How could they gather the evidence to put him away again? Putting Haase's 'political protection' aside, there were very definite technical and logistical problems associated with mounting an operation against him.

Haase's organisation was virtually impenetrable to outsiders. His inner circle were all old hands, hardened criminals whom he trusted as much as he could trust anyone. Having been through the supergrass system, Haase knew the threat posed by informants and was too cute to be caught out by the standard techniques.

Worryingly, like many modern criminals schooled in the cloak-and-dagger world of drug trafficking, Haase was an expert in counter-surveillance. He had access to state-of-the-art anti-bugging devices and secret video cameras. A cell of expert trackers able to watch and follow law enforcement officers who were watching them was on stand-by round the clock. They had blacked-out surveillance vans, long-lens cameras and scrambled walkie-talkies. The shadowy team could be deployed to set up a kidnap or secure an environment at short notice on Haase's orders.

Highly paid private detectives able to pull phone bills, medical records and bank details were on the payroll. Ex-directory phone numbers and addresses of rival criminals and police officers were just a phone call away. Haase also had corrupt policemen, lawyers and prison officers in his pocket. All in all, it was a nightmare scenario for police and Customs officers wishing to mount an operation against him.

Haase's inaccessibility was further assured by the constant presence of bodyguards. Even his wedding looked like a scene from *The Godfather*, Scouse-style. Haase's busty bride, Debbie, arrived at Brougham Terrace Registry Office in Liverpool in a cream Rolls-Royce wearing a white dress. One onlooker said: 'There seemed to be a lot of bouncers on the door, checking everyone who went into the wedding. Security seemed very strict.'

In short, the conclusion was bleak; it seemed as though Haase was victorious and there was nothing or no one who could stop him.

22

The In

Reload, Paul Grimes. In 1997, Paul came out of supergrass retirement to take on Britain's Public Enemy Number One face to face.

The match had an air of the comic book fight about it. Grimes, like an ageing superhero, pitched against his old friend turned archrival and evil super villain, in a battle between good and evil. But that is where the fantasy ended. The bitter, cold reality was that Grimes would have to risk his life every day in one of the longest-running, most dangerous and technically sophisticated undercover operations in the history of British law enforcement.

If Haase even suspected that Grimes was a plant, Customs officers were sure that he would 'disappear' instantly, never to be seen again. His assassins would come with smiling faces, as his friends, probably Haase himself, and Paul would have no idea of the fate that awaited him except that it most certainly would involve torture and end with death. Everyone on the team, including Paul, recalled the tragic fate of supergrass Roy Grantham, who had previously crossed Haase. Grantham allegedly committed suicide in very mysterious circumstances. No one doubted Grimes was taking a terrifying risk.

The operation to bring down Haase was technically a joint probe between Customs and Merseyside Police. Paul's direct handlers remained Customs officers, to whom Paul fed his intelligence. Much of this information was passed to Merseyside Police, who did much of the operational and surveillance work, putting it to good use. Paul often couldn't tell the difference between them, so, out of habit, he referred to them all as Customs.

The first difficult task was to get Paul 'in' to Haase. The infiltration would be risky. Paul had had zero contact with Haase for over ten years, since well before the Warren trial. Would Haase have heard the rumours that Paul had been the informant who led to Warren's downfall? Would he have got specific intelligence about Paul's role as a supergrass from the corrupt officials he had on the payroll? Would he have Paul checked out? Would he bring Paul into his inner circle or keep him at arm's length?

The success of the operation would depend on Paul's skill as an undercover investigator and on his ability to deceive Haase and win his trust. They also needed a lot of luck. Which luckily they got. The start of the operation was blessed by a fortuitous twist of fate.

———————————

PAUL: It was pure luck that got us into John Haase. It just started out with a chance meeting and I took it from there. Million-to-one, it was.

In 1997 I was working as a security guard for a firm called Sovereign. They were a good firm run by an ex-army feller. I'd been working for them for about four or five years after the Warren trial. I wore a pair of black nylon kecks, a bit shiny from over-washing, and a pair of Dr. Martens that had seen better days. I looked like a grim version of a busie.

It was as though my former life as a gangster had been brainwashed from me completely. I was now a totally reformed and reprogrammed member of society. I was Alex from *Clockwork Orange* after going through Ludoviko treatment. If a scallywag in a Ford Probe (baseball cap skewed insolently to one side) gave me road rage, I'd smile nervously and turn the other cheek.

To all intents and purposes I was now a fully fledged member of working-class society. I knew my place. Pure sheep, knowmean? Getting ragged by my boss, the taxman and any other cunt that wanted to have a go. I winced away from violence and crime and wanted for nothing more than a Sky subscription and a Ford Sierra. Of a Saturday Night I watched *Casualty* and of a Sunday I went to B&Q. If I was lucky I'd cop for a Big Mac Value Meal on the way home. I was Tony Blair's Sierra Man. No fucking back answers.

I'd given up the life of devilment completely. A lot of it was because I'd got involved with a girl from Hoylake. She didn't like gangsters at all. So I sat on the nest with her waiting for something to happen. That was until Haase came along again. I wanted this cunt badly. This one was purely personal. Haase had been a friend to me. He was one of my own. Old school, he was. Staunch as they come . . . or so I fucking thought.

Unknown to me he'd got into the gear, the brown, la. It was like finding out that your da had been fiddling with the kiddies and that. It was that bad. I'd first found out that John was mixed up with the brown when he got nicked in '93 or '94 with the 80-odd kis. I had to read the *Echo* twice. John Haase? Scag? No way, la. But it was bang on. For me that was the final nail in the coffin for the villains in Liverpool.

I had heard bits about what had gone on afterwards, with Michael Howard and all that caper, but I had blanked myself off from it all. I'd heard that he'd turned the Government over to get out of jail. But I'd also been told that Customs were still interested in him.

At the time I was guarding shops, stopping smackheads robbing razors and that. I moved all around for security reasons but sometimes I had to go to Liverpool. I didn't like working in Liverpool for obvious reasons, but there was no way I was going to allow them cunts, Warren and co., to dictate my life. I was in constant fear of being popped. But I'd made a decision and I had to live with it.

One day I was doing a Sunday stint in Netto in a place called Garston in Liverpool. Vera Aldridge comes into Netto. Vera was John Haase's ex-wife. Even though John had got a new bird, Debbie, Vera was still very close to him. She was very loyal to him. If you said a bad word about him she'd knock you out. She was a tough girl. They'd only split up because Haase had spent so much time in jail and Vera had hit the bottle out of loneliness. She was in Netto buying some cider. I didn't recognise her at first. But she come over and said: 'Paul.'

There was a bit of small talk and that. 'How's the job?' and all that carry-on then. I got talking to her.

'How's John?' I asked.

'Yeah. He's sound.' Blah, blah, blah. As she was getting off I said: 'Tell him I was asking about him.'

In all honesty, I knew he'd go for that. Curiosity killed John, knowmean? Always had, kidder. Lo and behold, the following Sunday he turns up in Netto. Is right and that Grimesy lad. Myself had not lost the magic touch.

I got talking to him and all that. He said sorry about your lad and that carry-on, referring to our Jason. Fucking cheek of him. Here's fucking Britain's biggest brown merchant flooding the fucking nation with tackle and he's saying sorry for killing my son. Mad, these drug dealers, aren't they? But I said fuck all. Did not mention about him in prison and then getting out or nothing like that.

At the end of the day I was still Haase's mate in a weird way. I was actually half-glad to see him. Old mates and all that. But it came down to drugs again. I knew he had been down for drugs and that disgusted me. He'd stepped over the line and got into something he'd never dealt with. When I went to work for him it was even worse. He used to brag about it and all that carry-on.

I could see he thought I was on my arse working in Netto like a prick and I knew he'd play the big gangster card, James Cagney and all that 'I can take you away from all this'. He couldn't resist it. I could read him like a book.

Next minute it's: 'If you need a job give us a ring.'

Gives me his phone number as though he's handing me a passport back into the big time and gets off. Get paid. Haase told me that he had set up Big Brother security. But he said he'd only managed to get a couple of contracts, nothing major. No doubt because he was too busy running amok. He needed someone who knew the business, someone he could trust.

The next day I phoned my handler at Customs. Was half-buzzing, in all fairness.

'He's offered me a job. What do you reckon?' I said.

He said: 'It's up to you but I'll think about it. If you find anything out. Definitely.'

I knew they were umming and arrhing. They were worried. The offer had caught us on the hop. Out of the blue. They were worried about my safety and the political fall-out if it came ontop. What I basically said then was that if I go and work for him, and find out anything that's not kosher, are you interested? And he said yes, but he put a rider on it.

He said: 'It's up to you what you do, Paul. But we'll take it on board and we'll monitor what you find out.'

That was their way of covering their arses. Pure Hutton-speak, knowmean? So a couple of weeks later I phoned Haase up and he offered me bits of work, working on sites, doing security. Cash in hand and all that. I ran a couple of sites. It was tedious work. Just sitting around in shitty cabins with only a kettle for company. John was nowhere to be seen. He was back at the office, running his rackets over the phone or out doing people in.

The first office was in Crosby, then after a few months he moved it to an old mortuary next to the docks. It was a fitting place. Haase was so paranoid that he had CCTV cameras put everywhere; in his own office, on the stairs leading to the door, to watch comings and goings, and on the car park. He was like Tony Montana in *Scarface*.

That's where I needed to be – at the Dock right next to him. But it was early days. There was no way he was going to let me close to the action straight away. He'd let me stew first on the sites for a bit until he trusted me to bring me in. If I hinted that I wanted to be more involved, he would have suspected. It was going to be a case of slowly, slowly, catchy monkey on this one. I'd have to worm my way in. I was constantly on the scan for ways of rising up the ladder, 'cos that meant getting closer to John.

For instance, there was a supervisor there, but he wasn't doing his job properly. I wangled it so that John gave me his job. Snidey, I know, but all in the name of truth and justice! Then I started to bring in bigger and better contracts, persuade the clients to take more men, things like that. At first Big Brother only had three contracts; a DIY store, a flat conversion and the Stanley Dock Market. But soon it was 20, including good payers like McDonald's. We had the contract for the Heritage Market – the biggest indoor market in Europe. That was 367 man-hours a week, 22 guards on Sunday, worth £10,000-a-month. The thing is, the more work I got him, the more money he made, the more he started trusting me, telling me things about the criminal side of the operation.

At first he just mentioned he was doing ciggies, smuggling them from abroad, but even though they were £1 million-plus deals and he was making as much from them as the drugs, I wasn't arsed with all that. Personality-wise, he'd turned into a tyrant. He'd done so much time, he'd gone crazy. Did not give a shit about authority or anyone. He'd hit the self-destruct button.

It took me about six months before he invited me to get involved with the real villainy. And, la, was I surprised?

23

Round-the-Clock Rackets

Paul was shocked at the sheer intensity of Haase's criminal force. Having been a gang boss himself, Paul was no stranger to how an organised crime unit worked. To keep the kiddies fed, there had to be a production-line mentality. But this was in a different league altogether. This was the General Motors of gangsterism. It defied belief.

PAUL: The first time I come across Haase up to no good was just on the off chance – it was a minor thing.

One day I walked in the office about half-eight in the morning. Haase was sitting at his desk cleaning guns. I just looked at him and he started laughing. I went to the offices a few more times and took a note of the crew Haase had got around him. There was a few old faces – for instance Haase's nephew, Paul Bennett, the drug dealer who had got out of prison with him in '96.

Bennett had a sidekick called Baz who was a bagman. He specialised in running drugs and guns. There was also an ex-boxer called Chris No-Neck, who was expert at testing consignments of drugs for purity and so on. He was also a heavy who Haase used to twat people. There was Kenny Doorteam, who ran Haase's door operation, taking care of security on nightclubs, pubs and hotels. (It was a big earner.) Thomo was a student at the university doing a degree in sociology or psychology, something like that. He was also one of Haase's heavies.

Paul was a half-caste lad who was Haase's main drug courier. He went all over the country picking up tackle for Haase and bringing it back to the office for testing and distribution. Paul was Haase's main man for drugs, but he looked like a student. All of Haase's drug people were like that. They dressed like beauts. They looked like harmless students with scarves and woolly hats and suede jackets and that. The police wouldn't look twice at them. They should have – on a good run they'd be carrying up to six kilos of brown each.

A lot of big villains were coming and going from the office, buying and selling tackle and that. All the time, there was new motors with new faces pulling up in the car park. Was a big operation. I started passing that on to the Customs.

Haase did a lot of debt collecting, mainly for other villains, on deals that had gone wrong. There was a hard core of boys whose job was to fill people in, kidnap them, tie-ups, whatever. Griff was one of them. He was a karate expert. His job was to simply knock fuck out of people. He made plenty of money out of it. To me he was an ordinary feller, he was an auld feller, but because of the kung fu and karate, he had a good dig on him.

At first this was the only type of stuff John allowed me to see – the knocking fuck out of folk, the low-level stuff. One day we went to this feller's house, I think he owed Haase money. Griff broke his jaw straight-off, no back answers, with one dig. Haase's methods were often too crude for some clients. A demolition man called Joe then came to see Haase wanting a so-called debt recovered. Joe said a solicitor from Crosby had had him over for all kinds of money. Joe just asked Haase to go up there and have a quiet talk with him, get it all sorted on the QT. Gentleman's agreement and that. Not Haase. He steamed straight up there, into the solicitor's office and smashed fuck out of it. Could not believe it, la. This solicitor was well connected to the busies and the judges. He wasn't a fucking gangster, he was a civilian and a fucking brief to boot. But John didn't care. These were the new rules. 'I'm John Haase – I'm invincible' was his attitude.

There was no money in the solicitor's office. So Haase found out where the solicitor lived and sent someone down to smash his windows in and blow his car up and all that carry-on. The solicitor got on his toes in fear for his life. In the end, Haase put so much pressure on the solicitor that he called in the busies. Joe the demolition man got pulled in for it. But Haase couldn't give a fuck. His attitude was 'If the busies interfere in my business they'll get the same treatment.'

I started to pass things like that on to Customs. One morning Haase said we were going to Blackpool. Is right, I thought. Works day out, see the illuminations and that. There was me, Kenny Doorteam and another heavy who was also a drug dealer who drove a four-by-four. We travelled up with Haase.

We were going to lean on this businessman who had let Haase down on a big ciggie deal. Basically this businessman, who was just a normal feller in his late 30s, had promised to invest £50,000 into a deal to buy £150,000 worth of bent ciggies abroad. This wasn't a particularly brutal escapade compared to Haase generally, but it's a terrifying example of how ordinary people can have their lives ruined if they try to make a quick buck.

John set the ciggie deal up with his foreign investors, and if it went well, they expected to make £1 million in profit. The thing is, is that the Blackpool man backed out at the last minute. He'd probably realised he was out of his depth. Fair enough, he's got the right to do that. Not with Haase, he hasn't.

Haase blamed him for fucking up the deal. He said that the ciggies couldn't come to Britain without his financial input and the deal couldn't go through. Haase said he was having problems with these people from abroad, who were in on the deal, and they couldn't bring in the two wagonloads of ciggies. So we went to Blackpool, picked this feller up and kidnapped him. They battered him and all that. They took him down into the basement of the Dock, an underground warehouse, where no one could hear his screams. Put handcuffs on him and tortured the poor cunt. Fucking bats and knives and everything. Put him in bulk and dumped him.

Before they threw the Blackpool feller out, Haase told him that he had to come up with £5,000 a month, every month, until the £50,000 was paid off. (Even though there were no cigarettes.) And then, because he had fucked up the deal, he'd have to come up with the (forecasted) profits that they'd lost out on. The opportunity cost, if you will. That could be up to £1 million. Bad one for him, la. Haase basically was going to tax this poor cunt for the rest of his life. I'm afraid that's what happens when you get mixed up in the rackets. Them's the rules. So this feller had to bring down £5,000 from Blackpool every month.

Haase kept everything running smoothly because he was punctual and systematic. On the Blackpool payday every month he would phone me up and tell me to be at the Dock at eight or nine o'clock to meet the Blackpool feller, take the parcel and put it in the company safe. The next morning he would sit there counting the money.

A couple of times the Blackpool lad missed payments. On the dot, Haase sent a crew member up to Blackpool, instantly, to throw bricks through his windows and set his car on fire and all that. That was a bit of gentle remittance advice in Haase's opinion. Within hours he would get paid. The payments were crippling this feller and he was having to borrow off his friends and family to keep them up. Haase didn't give a fuck.

One night the Blackpool feller turned up for his monthly drop-off. He was dressed like a normal feller with a pair of trackies on and a top. I felt sorry for him. He probably owned a porn shop on the sea front and thought he was a bit of a wideboy, but now he had met some real gangsters and it had come badly ontop for him.

I suspected immediately that he didn't have the dough. He hadn't parked his car in the Dock, the usual place. He'd left it in a backstreet where we couldn't see it, obviously so Haase couldn't confiscate it off've him when he gave him the bad news. That's how I knew he didn't have the money.

I opened the door to him and he said 'All right' and I knew his arse had completely gone. He was terrified. I could see it in his face. I took him upstairs to see Haase. He was in the front office and I went in my back office. I switched on the CCTV monitor, which gave me a picture of what was going on in Haase's office. Haase didn't know I could get access and I'd also put some tape over the red dot on the camera in his office so he never knew it was on.

I could see the Blackpool feller telling Haase he had nothing with him and he'd just come down to tell him he couldn't get the £5,000, blah, blah, blah. It was the pitiful body language of a man under extreme pressure. Kenny Doorteam just fucking chinned him and cut all his eye open. The next thing is Haase was shouting for me to come in to his office to clean him up. He just pointed at the crying Blackpool feller as though he was a piece of shit and said: 'Sort that out.'

They didn't feel sorry for him. Haase simply didn't want evidence in the form of blood going everywhere. I got the first-aid box and put butterfly stitches on his eye to stop it bleeding. We had a good first-aid box in the office at all times for obvious reasons. The blood was going all over the show so I had to put gloves on 'cos of the fucking Aids thing and all that. Haase was pissed off 'cos the longer it took to put the gloves on, more blood was shooting out. But it was lucky for the Blackpool feller. While I was there fixing his eye, I knew they wouldn't whack him and I knew from experience as a villain that it was one of those situations that could have ended up in someone getting killed.

I made a big deal of the wound, making out it was worse than it was, just so Haase wouldn't set the goons on him further. Also I knew if I played for time, the more blood would spill out and the more evidence there'll be to clean up in the event of something going badly wrong. No one wants a body and a scene all bladdered with blood. They didn't like that. That night the lad didn't know how close he'd come to getting popped.

By the time I'd finished, Haase was more worried about the blood up the walls and all over his office. A few minutes later he was shouting to me to let the Blackpool lad out of the building. I breathed a sigh of relief. By then Haase and the crew were all laughing about it. Haase was saying: 'He didn't half give him a dig, didn't he?'

He was really thick like that, he thrived off it. He had a look in his eye, like bloodlust. I think he'd have come his fucking load in his pants on it. He loved the power of being able to order his heavies to knock fuck out of people – while he just stood there like the commandant. I thought he was an owt nowt fucking prat for that side of him, to tell you the truth.

There was half a happy ending though. A few days after his dig, the Blackpool feller phoned up the office to thank us. The lads were like that: 'Why the fuck are you thanking us. We broke your jaw the other night.'

The Blackpool feller said that he'd gone to hospital to get it sorted and as the doctors were examining it they had found a cancer growth in his cheek. So the Blackpool feller was like that: 'Nice one. If you hadn't had twatted me I'd have probably died and what have you. Every cloud had a silver lining and that.'

Even if you were close to Haase, if it came down to money, it was just business. Even for his partner. Paul Bennett owed Haase some money, but when he couldn't pay it back, Haase seized a mobile home from outside Bennett's kennel. It was a Dodge and the registration was JFK. He started to rent it out to clients as a temporary security HQ on building sites until it made back the dough Bennett owed him and then he sold it in the Loot for £3,500.

But Bennett didn't moan about it because he knew that he owed his whole existence to Haase. The only reason he could operate was because Haase was there to make sure no one fucked with him. For instance, Bennett was doing drug deals on the side, and on one, he fucked up. He ended up owing a lot of money – £1 million no less – to two black lads who were making a name for themselves in the city. Today they are very hard hitters in fact, tie-up merchants and that, who have moved out of the ghetto and now own a security company on the Wirral.

One of these teamsters came down to the Dock in a T-reg Porsche. John had to do a deal with him. They came out of respect. He said to John that if it would have been anyone else Ben would have been done in. But because he was Haase's nephew they'd given him a walkover for the time being and were coming to John to respectfully get it sorted.

Haase was like that: 'Ben's been out of order. I'll get it sorted.' But if John hadn't stuck up for him, Bennett would have been in deep shit. I think he resented Haase for having that hold over him.

One strange thing that did happen though was that my middle son, Heath, started to work for Haase. Ever since Jason had died Heath had gone off've the rails. He had never been the same since he had been forced to ID his older brother, who he adored, on the mortuary slab in Plymouth.

It started off innocently enough when Heath used to come and visit me of a night while I was guarding the sites. Then behind my back Thomo offered him a job as a security guard. I was fucking furious when I found out and told Heath to get out, to get as far away from Haase as poss, but he wouldn't listen. Then John started to suck him into the rackets, like the fucking Fagin wretch he was, knowmean? I took Heath aside and warned him to stay well clear of Haase, but he just smiled. It was as though he revelled in rebelling against me. Haase was paying him top dough to buy his loyalty.

I couldn't tell him direct that Haase was doomed. I toyed with the fact of telling him that I was working for Customs. But there is no way Customs would have gone for that – it would have compromised everything. Son or no son, he was just a young lad.

24

Protection and Extortion

After a typical day of violence, Haase would shift his attention to the protection-racket side of his business. Under cover of darkness his specialised extortion team would petrol-bomb nightclubs, pubs and hotels whose owners had refused to allow Haase to 'take over the door' – i.e. provide bouncers.

PAUL: It was just villainy all the fucking time. Kenny Doorteam ran the door side of the operation. He was a hard hitter himself but he needed Haase as backing so he could muscle in on the doors all over town.

If Kenny couldn't get a door he used to cause trouble for the people who owned the door until he got it. Haase didn't let up until he got it. Every month Kenny had to make sure that the door side of things put a good few grand in Haase's backbin. So the pressure was on him to 'grow' the business. That meant stabbings, shootings and firebombs.

One day Chris No-Neck came into the office and said he was having problems with a door. It was just like a business meeting. A course of action was decided on immediately. Haase, No-Neck and Kenny went to see the feller to try to persuade him to come on board for the big win. No-Neck smashed both his hands in, Kenny done his jaw in and Haase cut him up with a knife. Sliced his throat. No-Neck punched him that many times his hands swelled up just like two balloons. Put the poor cunt in pure bulk. Straight to hospital.

Every day there was pure devilment like that. If clients weren't persuaded by a tolchocking [beating], then their businesses simply went up in flames. End of story. Heath was the top arsonist who did it; he became a specialist at it. There was a club in Bootle which wouldn't pay up after repeated demands; they refused to give Kenny the door, so Haase dispatched our Heath down there to blow it up with a petrol bomb. End of. Get paid.

Heath was getting in too deep. Had a word with him: 'It's fuckin' serious, this fire palaver. Someone will get killed.'

But he was too big for his boots now. Fucked me off he did. In the end, I thought, 'Right, you little cunt. If you've got more loyalty to Haase than to me then I can't protect you. I'm going to have to turn my back on you.'

It was a gut-wrenching dilemma for me. What the fuck do I do? Stand back and let my son turn himself over or let the cunt carry on and teach him a lesson? On the first two arson jobs I actually went with Heath. I drove him to the fucking buildings with the fucking petrol. Other dads drive their lads to the match and that. I was taking mine to carry out his work. I was just trying to keep a look out for him.

Haase paid Heath £2,000 to do it. I thought Heath was ripping him off by charging him that much, in all fairness. Everyone knew the going rate for a firebomb was no more than five tonne. But that's how much Haase regarded Heath's professionalism. Haase always took care of his crew.

Then there was the Sporting Club. The feller who owned it owed Bennett money. Bennett come to see Haase about it at the office. A decision was rubber-stamped. Heath was awarded the contract. Two weeks later Heath went to work. Again, I drove him there. His *modus operandi* was always the same. He pinched a ladder and run up onto the roof. He took away some of the slates off the roof to make a hole, poured in the petrol and set it on fire. End of story.

Haase phoned me up to ask if it was burning. Haase didn't know I was with Heath doing it so I had to pretend to drive all the way over from the Wirral to check. He was into that – quality control and that. Job done. All in a night's work. Onto the next one. That's what Haase did with every building he couldn't have – he burned it down. Heath set another club in town on fire and smashed up another – to force the owners to hand over the door. They did.

Then Kenny wanted to go after the big hotels and clubs. There was this one called the Devonshire Hotel. A lot of businessmen stayed there and it had a big nightclub attached to it called Reds. Pure goldmine, it was. Kenny came down to the office and they had a meeting about the best way to go about it. Haase planned the takeover like a military operation. First they went after the club Reds. There was only one slight problem. The door was run by an old pal of Haase's called John Lally. Lally was old school. He was hard. But Haase didn't give a fuck about any friendships. He sanctioned Kenny to take it anyway.

First the club got smashed up and then Haase sent Heath down to petrol bomb it of a night. He didn't manage to fire it, but Heath carried on doing the damage with sledgehammers and bricks. Then Kenny approached the management and said he could stop it, so Lally got fucked off. We got the door. Get paid. Haase was ruthless. But he was always careful to make sure he was never around when the damage was being done. The dirty was always done by someone else.

Then Haase and Kenny turned their eye on the hotel and car park. Heath smashed up the hotel. Then he done all the cars in so that we ended up with the screw on the car park. Every single car in the car park – about 50 including rows of BMs, Mercs, everything – owned by the guests who were staying at the hotel were smashed up. Sledgehammers, baseball bats, the works. The next morning it looked like a riot scene. Eventually, after a campaign of hassle, we got the full contract for the Devonshire.

After that, Heath had to carry on doing little bits of damage to the hotel and cars so that it didn't look too suss. So that it looked as though we had nothing to do with it in the first place and that we were gradually reducing the damage now. It was textbook protection racketeering and it worked like a dream. The money rolled in, but Haase wanted more. He was a 24-hour-a-day gangster. He couldn't sleep. He used to phone me up at three and four o'clock in the morning to ask me about jobs.

Then Kenny wanted another club. The Buzz club where all the footy players and the Spice Boys used to go and that. So Heath did the business there. Then Kenny started going after the big clubs in town. Haase ordered a drive-by shooting at one of the superclubs in town. A security guard got shot in the hand. Kenny got Chris No-Neck to do that. He jumped out of the car all ballied up, ran up and just shot them point blank. All the taxi drivers chased him up the hill. But he made it to the getaway car. Heath supplied the car for him. I don't know whether Heath was driving, but No-Neck did the shooting. [Chris No-Neck later denied pulling the trigger. He blamed it on a hitwoman called the Horsebox. No-Neck said, 'They had me down for this shooting but it wasn't me. It was actually a bird who shot him. Fucking right. They call her the Horsebox. I think because she's dead goofy. She was the one who shot that bouncer in town.']

In the end Haase didn't get the door, but the doorman who got shot in the hand ended up working for Kenny anyway. He never knew that Kenny had been involved. Kenny made a lot of money for Haase. He was getting a nice bunce out of it as well. Kenny only paid his men £50 a night and he taxed them £5. Kenny used to pay Haase a nice few grand every month on the dot. If he didn't pay he would've been stoved as well.

But Haase wasn't satisfied. He couldn't bear the fact that once the clubs shut and his doormen went home he wasn't making money. He wanted money coming in round the clock. So he hit on the idea of actually robbing the pubs and clubs he was meant to be protecting. Who would ever suspect the team who run the door of an armed robbery of the takings?

He actually done the heists himself with a shooter and a balaclava. I couldn't believe it. One of the country's top villains, worth millions, doing blags, but he got a buzz out of it. I think it took him back to his youth, like a proper villain again instead of some fucking drug-dealing fucking organised crime king sat behind a desk.

One night when I was off I got a call from the police saying that one of the clubs we had the door on had been robbed and my doormen had been held up. I shot down there in the car. When I got there the police were jumpy. As I got out of my car the armed-response busies pounced on me, pointing their Hecklers in my grid. 'Woh!' I said. 'I'm the security manager. Back off.'

One of the doormen had been twatted in the head bad style. He was badly injured; two weeks off've work and all that. This was an act of war. Whoever was responsible for this outrage was going to pay. No one fucks with my men. The next day I went into the office. I was fuming.

Haase simply smiled and said: 'Who the fuck do you think did it, you stupid bastard. It was me you tit.' Couldn't believe, la, that he'd do such a thing, that it was him who had done the robbery. He had held up his own men and battered them. Couldn't believe he'd treat his own men like that.

On another occasion he robbed a club owned by a feller who was well connected to the Bhoys – the IRA. But Haase didn't give a fuck. Big Brother had been asked to give an estimate to install video cameras in it. CCTV was a very successful side of the business. During his guided tour of the premises the manager shows the Big Brother technician called Mark the safe, stuffed full of goulash after the Bank Holiday, and the other security bits and bobs. He even gives him the fucking four-digit alarm code.

'Got to ring that one in to Haase,' thinks Mark. Just got to, haven't you?' he says.

Haase told the video man to give him the layout, paid him off, and then he burst in there in the middle of the day, ballied-up with bats and that. The next day Haase handed me a bag and asked me to get rid of it. Then he counted out the money on his desk. There was tens of thousands and thousands. Haase gave me drink out of it – a couple of hundred quid. He fucking loved that balaclava. I think that was the only thing he thought was real crime.

People were always getting leant on all over the place. It didn't matter who they were. Even normal businessmen who had contracted us to do security. Or even people who had asked for a quote and then decided to go with someone else. Oh no you don't! After a beating they came round to Haase's way of thinking. Then if they tried to press charges they were beaten some more.

That's what happened to a nightclub owner called Roy Carson. After Haase knocked him round, he filed charges. But he soon withdrew them. It was same with everyone who brought charges. The statement issued by the CPS always ended with the same line: 'I can confirm the case has been discontinued after the complainant withdrew his evidence.' Too right he fucking did.

Haase was treating Liverpool like his own fucking fiefdom, knowmean? He had his little spies all over the show, ringing it in when someone badmouthed him. Hitler youth or what, la? One time someone spotted a bit of graffiti on the back of a toilet door in a pub off Park Road, near Admiral Street. It said that some gobshite robber had shagged his own daughter. Haase hated kids but he would do anything for his daughter. This graffiti really sent him wild. Two carloads of fellers were ordered down there that moment to do this one feller in. The robber who did the graffiti done one, got on his toes.

If you crossed Haase you got hit hard. Revenge was how everybody stayed in line. Haase bragged about a feller who'd let him down over the 18-stretch for the heroin. The feller had betrayed him in some way. When he got out Haase cut him up to fucking bits. If he held a grudge, he never forgot. Telling you, la. Would literally take it to the grave.

There was another feller called Flannagan – a tax man, an extortionist who had tried to steal money from Chris No-Neck while Haase had been in jail. Haase went down to see him. By this time the Customs and the busies were following him 24 hours a day with secret video cameras. Haase just walks up to Flannagan and cut his throat in the middle of the fucking street.

The busies who are watching him nearly fucking choke. This was on video. Panic breaks out.

'What the fuck do we do?' they are shouting down the radios.

But the control room is saying: 'Leave off. Get out of there. We can't nick the cunt.'

They couldn't nick him 'cos that would have brought the whole operation ontop, there and then. No back answers. They just have to carry on filming it.

Flannagan falls to the floor, blood gushing from his neck. Haase leaves the poor cunt where he found him. Left for dead.

Next minute Haase finds out that Flannagan is alive, on a fucking life-support machine, in the ozzie.

'What? Cannot believe this,' he says, in genuine total fucking disbelief. 'Is this fucking Flannagan taking the piss or what?'

Next, he jumps in his fucking Beamster and is heading up to the ozzie to switch off the life-support machine. Bombing round the corridors looking for him, he was. Mad, isn't it? Luckily, he didn't find him. That's what happened if you didn't pay.

Another time Haase told me to go out and buy some acid. Gallons of it. 'I want the strongest acid there is,' he said, with a weird look on his grid.

He knew that I could get hold of hydrofluoric acid 'cos I had been in the stone-cleaning business. It's the strongest acid known to the human body. Just eats you it does. You need goggles and big rubber gloves on to just open the top. The antidote is fucking torture. The most painful injection ever – a big spiked ball on the end of a hypodermic needle full of alkaline.

Next he moves in an auld bath and puts it in the basement where we had a massive cannabis factory on the go. He tried to blag me off that the acid bath was in case the busies raided the premises. He said he would just throw the bags of heroin and cocaine he had in the bath so the evidence would dissolve.

But later I found out that it was for an acid bath to dissolve someone alive. Haase wanted it to torture someone. Don't know who it was for, but the acid bath was prepared for this feller, whoever he was, at the Dock. It was powerful enough to liquidise a body in an instant.

Haase had never forgiven the Ungi crew for insulting his bird all those years ago. When David Ungi, the one who got shot, was getting buried, Haase planned to throw a hand grenade at the funeral. Haase didn't like him at all. He vowed that this feud would go on and on whether he was dead or not. I think Haase may have been inside at the time, on remand for the scag, but he got his team to get the grenades together nonetheless.

But none of his boys would do it. Not because they were scared, but because they thought attacking a fucking funeral was out of order. How much of a sick bastard is he to think that? A funeral is a funeral, no matter what. You don't do things like that. His boys talked him out of it. They told him that if he launched a grenade attack it would fuck his chances of doing the deal with Michael Howard.

Haase loved footy. He played five-a-side and he even sponsored his own Sunday league team out of a pub called the Pineapple on Park Road. They had Big Brother on the front of their shirts and Haase even paid to have an all-weather pitch done up for them. He was always down there giving the groundsmen loads of abuse, that is, for not making the pitch better. Then he got into doing security for the big Premier League (or whatever it was then) footy clubs in the North-west and North-east. He had stewards on the team coaches and round the grounds.

Haase was one of those villains who would be torturing someone one minute and then helping old ladies across the road the next. He hated it when kids were being disrespectful to the old folks. One day a gang of teenage scallies were harassing an old biddy who lived in the same block as him. He'd told them to fuck off, but you know what kids are like these days. Hard-faced schoolie birds chewy-swinging and giving it loads and that back.

One night they were sat off in a bus shelter causing the old folks grief, terrorising the bingoites hobbling back from the Mecca and that. Haase witnesses this and is pure disgusted, stops in his Beamer across the road and phones one of the lads on his portie. The next minute two cars full of lads pull up with cans of yellow paint. They throw it all over the hooligans, just fucking head to toe drenching the little cunts in yellow paint. Never came back, la. Never seen them again. It was same yellow paint that Heath used to use to damage people's cars and that. Used to buy it bulk. It was a tool of the trade – the gangster trade.

25

Drugs

Of all his criminal activities, Haase kept the drugs side of his business closest to his chest. It was the riskiest. It was the crime the authorities were determined to nail him on. Haase put measures in place to decrease the risks. A loose cell structure meant that certain crew members didn't know what the others were up to – even if they were closely involved with the same drug deals. No one knew the bigger picture except Haase.

Drugs also brought with them the added risk of 'have offs' and 'tie-ups' – being robbed by other gangs. Liverpool's second generation of drug dealers had spawned a ruthless new phenomenon – specialist gangs of kidnappers and torturers who preyed on drug dealers, 'taxing' them of their super profits. They often burst into rooms where deals were going down, masked and armed with assault rifles, to relieve dealers of their 'tackle' and tens of thousands of pounds in cash.

Though Haase was still feared and revered himself, reputation was not necessarily a defence against attacks from the new breed of irreverent young bucks. Therefore Haase was forced to boost his security during 'drop offs' with old hands like Paul Grimes as well as banks of CCTV cameras Haase used to monitor entrances, exits and stairwells.

In this role Paul Grimes was able to get snapshots of information about Haase's drugs network. He was able to pass on this piecemeal picture to his Customs handlers. For example, Paul manoeuvred himself into a position whereby he was able to be present when up to six kilos of heroin were delivered into the office at fortnightly intervals. Paul was convinced that there were many other deliveries but Haase only allowed him to see this specific arm of the operation. At times Paul believed that these single-figure consignments were the vanguard of much bigger loads – mere test samples to be distributed amongst the many gangs who bought from Haase. But he could never get total proof.

Paul was also able to penetrate Haase's Scottish connection – the large-scale trafficking of cocaine to gangs north of the border.

PAUL: I first realised there was drugs involved when I became Haase's right-hand man and I was in and out of the office.

One day I was guarding a site at Dunningsbridge when he called me and said: 'I want you back at the Dock now.' When I got back there, it was about four o'clock in the afternoon. Haase said: 'A black feller will arrive soon. He'll be in a cab. Let him in. If anyone tries to come in behind him do them in.'

Sure enough, a scruffy black lad turned up. He had a leather coat on with fur inside, a woolly hat and he had a student's bag on his shoulder. I showed him up to Haase's office, then I kept watch on the front door through the CCTV monitor.

At that stage I didn't know what was going on. I'd been working for Haase for about nine months. I knew about all the guns and the firebombings and what have you. But then Haase called me in and said: 'Call him a cab,' pointing at the student.

There was just them two sat there at opposite sides of the desk. On the table was four bag-of-sugar-sized parcels of beigish, off-white powder: heroin. I was fucking gobsmacked to be honest. I never knew he'd got back into the brown. I thought he'd learned his lesson after being jugged for the 55 kilos, but it was there, as clear as powder. One of the bags had a split in it, obviously where Haase had tested some. Them two were just sitting there talking about football or whatever.

That was worst thing – Haase thought that having a load of tackle on your desk in the middle of the afternoon was the most natural thing in the world. It made me sick. To me it was just like having a load of anthrax or fucking Semtex in your lap. It just spelled death.

After the black lad, Paul, had gone, Chris No-Neck arrived. That was for the official testing. Once they'd got the percentage purity, it went into sales and distribution immediately. This was a sigma six organisation. Richard Branson had fuck all on it. Haase would be on the moby shouting all kind of orders to Bennett. Then he'd get off into the night, leaving No-Neck to deal with all the gangsters who started arriving from all corners of the city, to take samples away.

That was the drill every two to three weeks. That evening, shortly after No-Neck had arrived, I said to Haase: 'You don't need me any more tonight, do you?' and I got off. As soon as I got outside I phoned my Customs handler and told him exactly what I had seen.

Haase would send Paul all over the country collecting and delivering kis of drugs. I always knew that Paul was out of town on a drugs run 'cos Haase would leave the Dock and go to a phone box on the Dock Road to call him. He would never ever make or take drugs-related calls from the office.

Haase must have trusted Paul to courier his tackle. Then I found out why. Paul had once got nicked in Africa or somewhere with a load of gear. Haase had paid a lot of dough to get him free. When he got out he looked like he'd been in a concentration camp. He owed Haase big time and I think he was working off the debt moving tackle around for his saviour.

One of the Turks Haase used to deal with kept phoning the office. His name was Kaya. I couldn't even pronounce his other name. He was the boss of the Turkish Connection who had supplied Haase with the 55 kilos he got nicked with in '93. Kaya used to phone him from the jail, but he wouldn't take the call. Then his sister kept phoning up. Haase just blanked it. Haase said that he owed their family money and that's why he was fucking them off.

But I got the impression that there was more to it. He wasn't letting me in to that side of his business. That's what he did. He kept the big things secret. Haase wasn't taking their calls 'cos he knew that the phones from the prison were monitored. He didn't want them to make a connection with Kaya and him with all the shit that was going on. He knew that after he conned the Government they'd be on red alert to catch him with that crowd again. I think he'd call them back later from a phone box when I wasn't there.

The Customs wanted to bug the offices, both at the Dock and at the old funeral parlour. At first they wanted to put an audio bug in his phone-fax machine at the Dock, but they couldn't get into the building. Haase told me that he had chosen the Dock specifically so that no one could get into it. I think he had Customs and police in mind especially. Haase had deliberately designed a full range of counter-surveillance measures into his HQ.

First off, the Dock was a keep within a castle. The walls were ten feet high and two feet thick. Haase had 24-hour guards on the door and on the gate into the car park. Sometimes there was a man inside. There were scouts and spotters, anyone from taxi drivers to deliverymen on the payroll, who kept the premises constantly under surveillance from moving, unmarked, unconnected positions and patrols, looking for warning signs. A moody van, a passer-by, it was likely that any surveillance unit watching Haase would be being watched themselves.

The Dock had a state-of-the-art bell on it. It was cameraed-up to death. Sometimes Haase would come back to the office at four in the morning and spend hours looking at the CCTV monitors to make sure no one was trying to get in. Then when he'd finished with the live pictures he used to go over that day's tapes to clock who'd come and gone. Scouring the screen for anything suspicious.

I couldn't believe anyone would take care of the details like that, but he was clever enough to realise that only he alone could truly look after his security. Other people got lazy. So even with their best penetration teams, Customs could get nowhere near the Dock. Then my handler asked me whether I could remove the fax machine for a few hours so that they could install the bug. I agreed. But then they got cold feet and told me they were going to find another way.

Then they decided to have a go at the old mortuary office. They were desperate. We both knew that was the only way to get proper evidence. I met my handler and gave him the alarm number. Drew a map of the office and pointed out Haase's desk. They gave me 250 quid as expenses.

I waited for them to break in and place it. It was a tense time, totally ontop to be truthful. One wrong move and it would have blown the whole operation. Haase would have shut down dealing and I would have probably been exposed.

On the night the Customs had gone in, I got a call at three in the morning. It was a Customs feller. They had managed to break in and put the bug in, but they couldn't reset the alarm on the way out. Total downer. That would give the whole game away, brought it ontop straight away. Whoever arrived first in the morning to open up, they'd notice it.

I jumped out of bed and shot over in the car. I checked all the system, but I couldn't find the fault. Each minute we were in there, there was more chance of being tippled. The electrics must have been fucked up by the Customs team. I told them that we'd just have to take a chance on it and leave it be.

I got in early the next day to check the lay of the land. By a million-to-one chance there was a load of workies outside, digging up the road and fixing the drains. There was a fucking power cut. They'd cut the wires. That got us off the hook big time. There was a big stewards' inquiry as to why the alarm wasn't on and not working. So I just blamed it on the workies and no one said fuck all.

POWDER WARS

26

Gun Deal

The bug in Haase's office began to pay dividends. The benefits were twofold. Firstly, with each whirr of the tape Customs caught more damning evidence against Haase himself from his own mouth. Secondly, police were able to make discreet use of the first-hand intelligence they were picking up and act on it immediately to stop crimes and make arrests in the short term.

This was a delicate and high-risk operation. Obviously, the police had to be very careful to make sure that the arrests were not being linked to Haase's premises – otherwise the underworld would have quickly realised there was a bug plus an informant in there. But despite this, many arrests were made.

A car got stopped in the Mersey Tunnel with a bootful of guns. A Mr Big gun dealer on the Wirral was raided and found with incriminating evidence all over his house. There were many more. It was only a matter of time before Customs and police went in for the kill and took out Haase himself.

PAUL: The crew were making a lot of dough – millions. There was always money.

No-Neck says he wants to get married in Mexico, sombreros

and all that. Haase says: 'Sound. No problem. Here's £10,000.'

'John, I need a new car.'

Haase says: 'Yes, you do. Here's a Peugeot 406.'

'John, I'm going on holiday.'

Haase is like: 'Have a nice time. Here's your spends.'

The lads constantly had their hand out – and like a feudal fucking Lancelot riding amongst his teamsters, Haase boxed them off for anything they wanted. There was so much money. In the end, No-Neck had two weddings – one in fucking Meckico and one in Liverpool. Knowmean, how fucking *Hello* is that? But it didn't matter. Running out of dough?

'Sound, lad, just fucking rob some more. Low on tank there, kidder? Is right. Here's five kilos of beak. See you later.'

In between knocking out the tackle, there was plenty of time for general crime. There was the Asian feller, who was a big duty-free ciggie broker. He worked for a firm but Haase had him boxed off. So that when there was big artics coming in from France with loads of ciggies, the Asian feller would give Haase the nod on it. The consignments would be had off, no back answers. The Asian feller would then pretend to his other bosses that he had been legitimately robbed so that he wouldn't have to pay the real owners and Haase would cop for the lot. All's I had to do was open the gate when the load arrived. Haase gave me £2,000. He'd give Heath £4,000 for getting rid of the van or the truck. Laughing, Heath was.

Haase was making millions off've the ciggies. Literally fucking millions. That's what the Customs could never work out. Was making fucking 20 times more off've the ciggies than heroin and cocaine. No cargo was less than 50 grand's worth. The profit was one thousand per cent, week in, week out. Buy them on the continent for £3 for a 200-bifter carton. And sell them for £30 in England. With no jail or nothing if you get caught. Get paid or what?

One night I gets a call: 'I'm having trouble with coloureds.'

What he meant was that a team of heavy hitters from Toccy

had declared war on his door team. Kenny had taken over the door on a famous bar called Kirklands where the footie players used to go and that. Kenny had smashed the windows, gibbed the black door team and now they'd turned up mob handed outside. Oh dear! These were well-known bad lads, but Haase didn't give a fuck.

'Go down there and tell Kenny to give them a kicking. I want to see their blood running down Hardman Street.'

I took my telescopic flip stick and told Kenny to stop talking and do them in, but he just kept on negotiating in the bar. There was a call-out and Haase sent a vanload of 15 doormen down as back-up, but Kenny was trying to avoid a war. Haase was fucking furious.

Haase was like that: 'I couldn't give a fuck about all that doorman stuff, standing there saying, "I'm on the weights," and all that, just fucking waste them.'

That night he had the six Toxteth gang bosses' cars firebombed outside their L8 pads. Whoosh! End of story. End of problem. It was an audacious warning to them, which surprisingly they heeded.

That was Haase's favourite trick. You'd be sitting there on the couch watching *Coronation Street*. Next minute you'd look out the window and your car would be on fire. Two other door firms weren't handing over their door quick enough on another club. Whoosh! One of their cars goes up. Then the doorman is twatted. The second one is the same. Whoosh! Beatings. Get door. Get paid. It was always the same system.

Heath was doing it all. In the end, he got sick of it. He was sent to Scotland to pick up £22,000 in cash for a ki of brown and some other bits and bobs. He phones me up. 'Half tempted to do one with dough,' he says.

I was like that: 'Go 'ead, lad. Just fuck off with his dough.' But when it came down to it, Heath didn't have the bottle to fuck Haase.

Haase was buying a lot of swag off a feller called Mick the

Pallet who owned a pallet yard down the road. He was a old-style hijacker, pure wagon haver-offer, but he only went for high-value loads. The wagon drivers were involved. They were always paid off to look the other way when their lorries were stolen. Mick could never work out why he kept getting turned over by the busies. It was because the Customs were watching him drive his had-off lorries into Haase's yard and that's how they were finding out about what he was robbing.

One time he had off £500,000 worth of designer clobber which was in a lorry going to Wade Smiths. Wadies is a kind of department store for scallies with all the latest labels in and that. The footie players and the drug dealers go there for clobber. Posh and Becks and all that carry-on. Haase bought £150,000 worth of Versace suits for £10,000. I had to move them into the back office.

Haase was like that to everyone: 'Just pick what you want.'

All the lads were walking round in it, little skinny suits on and that. Shiny shirts with big fucking Chinese dragons on. Looked a bit mad to me, but it was a good seller. It was getting moved all round the city by a fence in his private hire cab. Anyone who came to the office left looking like Steve McManaman on a night out, knowmean?

One of my jobs was to go to Haase's flat regularly where he gave me ten or so mobile phones to get rid of. He constantly changed them. Then I'd go to a mobile phone shop on Edge Lane and buy a dozen more pay-as-you-goes. I went there that often that the shop assistants called me the man with no name 'cos no names were ever given. Every time he and the team changed their phones I had to give the numbers to Customs.

I seen him cleaning guns another two times. Then one day he bought a .38mm handgun off've one of the doormen along with 100 rounds of ammo. Was purely meticulous in his armament deals, he was. Sat there and counted out every fucking bullet on his desk, until he was convinced that he hadn't been ripped off. Then he went downstairs in the cellar of the Dock and pinged off a few rounds.

I was feeding the Customs that much fucking stuff they would have needed a small army just to keep on top of it all, know where I'm going? Didn't know the exact cases the Customs and the busies were going to pin on him, but I just kept the info flowing anyway.

John was doing a lot of gun-running to a firm in Scotland, but because of all the fucking chaos I could never get a hangle on it. But Heath kept telling me how it worked – 'cos he was right in the thick of it. Was simple. Every time the Jocks wanted shooters they sent a bagman down to Liverpool. Heath got the gear off've Haase and he drove out to meet the crazy Jocks on his motorbike.

Then in August '99 Heath told me that the next shipment was on the cards. This was the first time he'd told me about a delivery before it went off. Get paid. I gee'd the Customs up good style and told them to be ready. Then Heath went away on holiday. He must have thought it would go off when he got back, but suddenly the Jocks wanted their firearms. They must have had a blag planned or whatever.

It could've easily have been done without Heath, but by this time Haase thought so much of him that he put it off until he got back. Could not understand it, la. Only needed someone on a bike. But Haase was insistent – want Heath, la. No back answers.

When Heath got back, John was made up. Then on 7 September Haase called me and said: 'Get down the Dock for 12.'

When I got there he just told me to stay on the gate. Another one of the lads, called Baz, was guarding the door. Heath arrived on his bike. He told me he was doing a gun drop to the Jocks. He went in Haase's office and when they both come out Haase put a small bag on top of the bike's petrol tank. That was it. Heath got off.

Baz threw his mobile phone on the floor and stamped on it. I said, 'What the fuck are you doing that for, you silly cunt? All's you have to do is change the SIM card, not smash the fucking handset.'

But he just laughed. Fifteen minutes later Heath comes back after delivering the guns to the Scottish courier. I says to John immediately that I'm getting off, jumps in the van and fucks off. Outside the Dock I phoned Customs and give them the gen.

Paul did not know it, but at about the same time as he was on the phone to his handler, the police swooped on the car driven by the Scottish courier. In the front passenger footwell was a sports bag containing an Uzi sub-machine gun and a Smith and Wesson Magnum revolver – the most powerful handgun in the world, made famous in the *Dirty Harry* movies. The ammunition included 49 rounds of .38mm and 170 of .9mm, including 70 hollow-point bullets, which like dum dums, are designed to expand on impact and destroy internal organs.

Following Paul's warning several weeks before, the police had been on alert to catch the gun dealers red handed. Listening extra carefully to the conversations picked up by the bug in Haase's office police were able to mount a sting operation. For many months now, a Customs surveillance team had video cameras trained on the main entrance to the office to watch the comings and goings.

Haase had been observed in contact with Heath seconds before he had left the Dock offices on his motorbike. A police surveillance team had tracked Heath's motorbike to the Atlantic Cafe in Walter Street, north Liverpool, where he drew up next to a gold Renault Laguna. A few words were exchanged.

The hired car had been driven down from Scotland by 46-year-old Walter Kirkwood, from Dumbarton, under orders from one of Scotland's leading underworld figures. Both engines were still running when the driver's electric window had buzzed down and Heath heaved the black Head sports bag from his shoulder and into the car. Nothing was said during the actual handover. Police watched as Kirkwood checked the contents before tossing the bag into the foot-well and driving off.

Both vehicles headed off in separate directions: Heath's 750cc FZK Yamaha back towards the Dock and the Laguna towards the M6 motorway. As Kirkwood stopped at traffic lights near the Bell Tower Hotel, Kirkby, armed police surrounded the car. As evidence against Haase, it was solid gold – he was in the frame in person, the crime was contemporaneous and the continuity of evidence had been preserved throughout. The police knew that they could arrest Haase immediately and there would be enough to stick him away for a long time. But they didn't.

During the sting, police had been very careful and discreet in order to prevent Haase finding out that the mission had been compromised immediately. In fact, Haase did not know that Kirkwood had been arrested. Luckily, when Kirkwood did not return to Scotland his bosses battened down the hatches, maintained radio silence and did not inform Haase, presumably in case the message was intercepted and was used as further evidence to link the two gangs. It was good organised crime practice, but it also meant that Haase carried on committing crimes unaware that the 'busies were onto him'.

PAUL: Even I didn't know that Kirkwood had been nicked. So it was business as usual. About two weeks later I had a big argument with Haase. It was over a ridiculous thing. Basically, there was a feller who was robbing the old paving stones from the Dock next door. These flags were worth a fortune and every day he did it he gave me £1,000 for not grassing him up to the owners. I gave five tonne to Haase. But the greedy twat wanted more.

Could you believe it? The fucking tank he was on with his heroin and Uzi fucking machine guns. But that's what these fellers are like. They want a piece of even the most trivial of crimes. He told me to stop the men from having them off and I told him to do it himself. He exploded and I told him to stick his job up his arse.

By then it didn't matter to Customs too much that I had quit. The surveillance was picking up everything and I had a feeling it was all coming to an end anyway.

He wasn't wrong. One month later, on 25 October, Haase was arrested at Liverpool Lime Street train station after returning from a trip to London. In a huge and detailed Customs and police undercover surveillance operation, officers had followed Haase and a drugs mule called Kenneth Darcy as they left Liverpool from Lime Street station earlier that day. Even the men sitting in the Railtrack ticket booth who sold Haase his train ticket were undercover officers. So were the cleaners who mopped the forecourt and the guards on the train.

Haase and Darcy travelled in the first-class carriage. Under Haase's instructions, their journey was being monitored by No-Neck, whose job it was to see if Haase was being followed. After arriving in Euston, Haase made a call from a telephone kiosk to a mobile phone before both he and Darcy caught a black cab to a Turkish restaurant in Stoke Newington, north London. It was clear that Haase's Turkish Connection was still going strong.

Upon arrest Haase had more than £3,000 in cash, mostly made up of Scottish notes, while in the lining of Darcy's coat a plastic BHS bag was recovered containing a kilo of heroin – 984 grams to be precise. It was the end of Haase.

27

The Case

On 26 October 1999 more arrests were made during a police raid at Haase's Dock office at the Stanley Heritage Market. The following day he was charged with conspiring to supply heroin in relation to the kilo police had tracked from London.

A separate firearms offence stated that 'on 7 September this year in Liverpool, he conspired with other persons to possess or sell prohibited weapons, prohibited ammunition and Section One ammunition, contrary to the Weapons Law Act 1977'.

Ken Darcy, the drugs mule Haase had travelled to London with, was charged with drugs offences. Paul's son and Haase's main lieutenant, Heath Grimes, was also charged with firearms offences, as was Barry Oliver, who had allegedly been in the Dock on the day of the gun transaction. Oliver was in a bad situation. At the time of the offences he was out of prison on Home Office licence after being convicted of manslaughter. He had set a man on fire. If found guilty, Oliver would automatically be sentenced to life.

The situation was further complicated because Haase's right-hand man Paul Bennett was wanted in connection with a £1 million cannabis importation. Over the next few months the case became a stock exchange of plea bargains and deals, as some of the parties, awed by the level of secret intelligence against them, desperately battled to get the shortest sentences possible. But Haase and Heath were in for a bigger shock. When it dawned on them that Paul Grimes was the secret informant, the grass, they could not believe it. A lifelong friend to one and father to the other.

Haase first realised that Paul had betrayed him when police unearthed a secret cache of guns hidden underneath a floorboard in an old warehouse next to his office. The warehouse was so vast that Haase was convinced that only a tip-off could have led police to the specific hiding place. The only other person who knew the secret location was Paul Grimes. He had been there when Haase had buried them. Paul had kept look-out and blocked the doorway into the huge room as Haase had pulled up a floorboard and stashed the weapons in the cavity underneath.

As the interviewing police officers asked Haase whether the guns were his, his heart sank. 'How the fuck did they find them,' he asked himself. There was only one explanation. He'd been turned over. In a weak and unconvincing rebuttal, Haase limply tried to say that the guns were not his but actually owned by Paul Grimes. Deep down though he knew he was in deep trouble.

On the drugs-related charge Haase felt more confident. The great irony of the bust was that the kilo of heroin found on drugs mule Kenneth Darcy was not technically Haase's. Chris No-Neck had set up the deal. No-Neck had been badgering Haase to get him a kilo of brown in the run-up to the trip. Haase had first visited the Turks in London on Saturday 23 October, two days before he was busted, to talk business and pick up one kilo. But he agreed to get a second kilo of heroin for No-Neck as a favour on the following Monday. The Turks had been informed that on the Monday a courier would arrive at their cafe to pick up the parcel.

The following day, Sunday, Haase had told No-Neck that the heroin would be ready for him. Haase explained that although he would be travelling to London again on the train on Monday, he wanted Darcy to go by coach so that there was no connection between them. However, on the Monday Darcy missed the National Express coach after No-Neck gave him the wrong times.

Haase was observed bollocking No-Neck from the end of his mobile phone as he stood on the concourse of Lime Street station.

'Chris, you piece of shit. You have fucked these very simple arrangements up.'

In the end Haase agreed to allow Darcy to travel on the train with him and even paid for his first-class ticket. It was the worst decision of his life. On the return journey later that day, they were both arrested, Darcy with the gear on him.

Haase never contemplated grassing up No-Neck, but he decided early on that his case strategy would be never to plead guilty to possessing the heroin. After all, the drugs were not found on him. He would try to cut a deal on a lesser charge.

As a bad postscript to the already ruinous situation Haase found himself in, the Turkish cafe that had supplied the heroin was raided one year later. Some of the Turks secretly blamed Haase for leading the police to them.

Meanwhile, Heath was facing the first big rap of his life. For a while, Paul kept visiting him in prison and pumping him for information. Heath had not yet tumbled that Paul was the grass. It was a ruthless ploy, especially towards his own son, but Paul was so determined that drug-dealing Haase would be destroyed he no longer cared whether Heath went down with him or not.

Paul rationalised it in his head; even though it was his own son he had still chosen to get mixed up with Haase and drug-dealing. In his book, that was unforgivable and he deserved to be taught a lesson. It was tough love. Paul agonised over his treatment of Heath. It felt like he had already lost one son but was about to lose another – by his own making. By his own double-dealing hand.

Matters were made worse when Christine, Paul's ex-wife and

Heath's mother, accused Paul of the basest and most unnatural treachery. 'How can you send your own son to prison,' she wailed. 'You fucking bastard cunt. God will never forgive you for this.'

Paul felt like he was living in a Shakespeare play. He wrestled with both his conscience and his paternal instinct. He remembered how he had held Heath in his arms as a baby. How he had bathed him, changed his nappies and shushed him to sleep. How he had provided for and protected the helpless, crying child until he was old enough to stand on his own two feet. Now he was going to unravel that beautiful, life-giving process and destroy his creation like an abortion. Could he do it? Could he stick the knife in and turn it? Could he look Heath in the eyes as coldly as he had looked into Haase's and betray him?

Paul then made a last desperate bid to save his son. He would throw Heath a lifeline. If Heath took it, it would be his decision. Paul approached his Customs handlers and asked if they would show leniency to Heath if he turned Queen's Evidence. After much toing and froing, they came back and said that they might be interested in doing a deal, but that they also felt it wasn't worth talking about – in their eyes Heath was staunch. He would never turn grass. He looked up to Haase too much. He saw Haase as a father figure. He would never do it. Paul was pained by the father analogy, but he persuaded Customs to let him have a go.

———————

PAUL: Everyone started getting nicked. Haase, Heath, the lot. The busies even turned my flat over to make it look as though I was a legit suspect. For a short while no one knew I was the grass.

When it come down to it I couldn't throw Heath to the lions just like that. But if I wanted to give him a second chance I had to move fast. I wanted Heath to get bail so I could have a talk to him, but the busies were like that: 'Are you fucking joking?'

Then I said to them: 'Look, I can tell you where there are more guns hidden.'

They were non-committal but I went for it anyway. I knew that they were ripping the Dock apart, but there was no chance they'd ever find anything. Special fucking SWAT teams or not. It was the largest building of its type in Europe. They'd been at it nearly eight days and found fuck all.

So I took the police to the spot. They found the gear. There was a Colt handgun and a magazine, a Brevett pistol with a mag, a sawn-off Parker-Hale 12-bore shotgun, 200 rounds of ammo and 25 shotgun cartridges. There weren't as many shooters as I'd seen him put in there. Was like a fucking IRA cache at one stage, but he must have been selling bits over the months, getting rid and that.

The busies were made up, but they still kept Heath in the nick. I was going back and forth seeing Heath, pleading with him to save himself by fucking Haase. I give him the phone number of this busie to ring if he decided to change his mind. But I could tell he was a bit ashamed of me, his auld feller being a midnight mass and all. He kept going on about his security.

'Dad, I've got to think about me bird and me house and that. If I talk, they are gone. Blown up. You know that.' Heath was terrified of Haase.

I said: 'Look, the busies will put you on a programme, take you to fucking Australia or somewhere with a new fucking identity. They'll take your bird. Fuck Haase. He won't be able to find you.'

After that he phoned the special busie who hangles witness protection people. They took Heath out of the nick and drove him to a secret meeting at a hotel in Chester. The busies offered him the deal, but when it came down to signing the form his bottle went. He looked at the busie. 'I can't do it . . . comebacks,' he whispered.

Afterwards the busies were on the phone: 'What the fuck is going on, Paul? I thought he was up for it.'

After that there was nothing I could do. I had to start making statements and telling tales. It was a whirlwind of magistrates' appearances, where I had to stand up and say what I was going to say in front of their briefs. I was escorted back and forth by armed police. I was the prize, no doubt about it. No cunt was taking any chances on me. Everyone knew that Haase wouldn't think twice about killing me. Especially after he definitely found out I was a grass.

They found out for sure only after I'd tried to persuade Heath to turn. Heath must have told Haase and his worst fears were confirmed. It was after one of the committals. They brought Haase into court. He was giving it moody stares. I wasn't arsed. I just kept wondering why his hair had gone so grey so quickly. It was jet black two weeks ago and now it was like a fucking silver fox, knowmean? Transfixed by it I was. Can't be down to worry. This cunt could do 20 years in jail and not give a fuck.

Then I burst out laughing. The vain bastard must have been dyeing it all along and now he's in the jug he mustn't be able to get hold of the old Grecian 2000. Haase was always meticulous about his hygiene. Always washing his fucking hands, in bleach and everything. Hygiene was unbelievable. Howard Hughes, la, he was.

The busies moved me to a new house. A team of lads went into my pad, boxed everything up and moved me out. They told me to find somewhere I wanted in any area. I chose somewhere in Wallasey. Next thing I get a phone call telling me to go up to the council. They had a place for me. Then they got me a job working for a security firm in Manchester to keep me on the move.

Was a tense time to be honest. There was a lot of stress. I started rowing with the bird I was knocking about with and we split up. My head was wrecked with it all, in all fairness. The only thing that kept me going was the gym. That and chilling out with a joint afterwards. *Pumping Iron* and all that.

One time I went round to see her, there was the usual

slanging match and she called the busies. They searched me and found a little bit of weed. Could you believe it? The irony of it. Me at the centre of this massive case and being nicked for possession. I got fined £45 at the mags. Did not even try and call it in to the other lot to see if they could get me off. After all, fair's fair, isn't it?

Next thing I have to give evidence against Heath. Then his mam was on the phone saying I gave Heath up, blah blah, blah. That I'd go to hell and that. But what could I do? The busies offered me the full witness-protection programme. It even come up in court. Anywhere in the world. New ID, new house, new job, new fucking life.

But as far as I was concerned that was handing victory to Haase. That was like running away from him and everything I'd ever fucking known. I told the busies to fuck off. I told them that Paul Grimes was the name I was born with and that was the name I'd be dying with whether it was at the hands of John fucking Haase or not. I said I'm staying where I am, here in Liverpool, and facing up to these cunts. As far as I'm concerned I'm not changing my fucking life for them.

It was a lonely life. I spent a lot of time waiting inside special rooms in courts, with bored fucking busies with Hecklers next to me, reading old copies of the *Radio Times*. I'd have to wait all fucking day so that the prosecution could ask me two fucking questions. Then I'd have to go back again to answer one other fucking question . . . sitting there all day. A farce it was. Just walked in, gave me evidence and walked out. Sometimes Haase was there. They'd stare at me as I walked out. The system was fucking ridiculous.

The police were right, though they didn't know it yet. From his prison cell, Haase was already plotting to kill Grimes. Not out of revenge, but to stop him appearing in court and giving evidence. The plan was more complicated than a straightforward assassination. Haase was desperate to find out exactly how much Grimes had told his Customs handlers. At that stage Haase did not know about the bugging and the masses of intelligence the Customs had on him. What he did know was that if there was such data in existence much of it would be inadmissible against him, especially without Grimes standing up in court to back it up.

Haase's grand plan was to try and negotiate a deal with the courts. He was a past master at plea bargaining. Had he not pulled off the greatest sentencing deal of the century? Haase was totally confident he could do it again. But first he needed to find out exactly how much Grimes had given his masters.

Haase instructed one of his specialist surveillance teams to track down Grimes to his new safe house and observe his every movement. Within days his men had found it. The next step was to log his routine in a bid to determine the best time to snatch him. The plan was to bundle him into a van, kidnap him, torture him to find out what he had told them, kill him and dump him.

Paul's safe house was an anonymous flat in a council tower block in Thornridge, Morton, one of three high-rises close to the entrance of the Wallasey Tunnel. Haase's surveillance team discovered that they could see into Grimes' flat from an observation point on top of an adjacent tower block.

A former member of Haase's gang, who has been interviewed by the author, revealed how one attempted snatch raid was called off at the last minute.

One night as the team were scaling a fixed wall ladder, which gave access to the roof, they heard noises. When they reached the top and peeked over the edge of the roof wall, to their horror they found a specialist police surveillance unit already in position in the exact place they had been in just hours before.

Luckily for Haase's team, the officers were consumed by peering through their binoculars, checking on Paul Grimes sitting in his flat and scanning the estate for suspicious movements. The officers had not seen or heard Haase's men even though they were yards away. Haase's team quickly and silently climbed down the ladder from where they had come and escaped from the estate unchallenged. They later found out that although Grimes had bravely refused the offer of close protection, the Chief Constable had ordered his officers to secretly protect their star witness without him knowing. That was the purpose of the surveillance team.

Haase realised he would have little chance of snatching Grimes. Time was running out. If he was going to do a deal with the prosecution, he would have to make soundings before the trial started. In a last-ditch attempt to find out who knew what, he turned his attention to the Customs officers who had helped gather the evidence against him.

Haase instructed his team to find out the identity of Paul's main handler. Shockingly, within days they were able to find out the name of the Customs investigator that Paul had liaised with since the days of the Warren trial, Dominic Smith. Although this officer had handled Grimes at the outset of the Haase investigation, he had moved on and was now only one of a number of officers who Paul had passed information to. Nevertheless, this officer was the main port of call for Paul and his most trusted confidant. Haase gave the order for his men to track the Customs officer's every move.

Unknown to Dominic Smith, he was photographed at his home and outside his office at the Customs HQ in Manchester's Salford Quays. Using long-lens stills cameras and video equipment the team recorded him at secret meetings with Paul Grimes and at liaisons with other informants on unrelated cases. From these encounters the team learned the identity of several underworld figures who were feeding information back to Customs and Excise.

Once Haase's reconnaissance had been completed he gave the order to kidnap the Customs officer. It was unprecedented. To kidnap a serving law enforcement officer was unheard of. It was an unspeakable crime, well outside the unwritten underworld code of conduct, but Haase did not give a fuck. He was a desperate man, determined to do what it took to get off. Haase instructed his men to snatch Dominic Smith and torture him to find out what he knew but to avoid killing him. Some of Haase's men were uneasy but they understood to refuse would mean certain death. The operation got under way, but from the outset there were problems.

Owing to the Customs rules of officers working in pairs, the investigator was never alone. His home was protected by a sophisticated alarm and he drove everywhere, competently and at high speeds, making him difficult to ambush. Several times the trap was set – but never sprung for one hitch after another. Eventually Haase had to drop the plan. Time was running out fast. He would be forced to try and negotiate a deal with the prosecution without any aces up his sleeve. He would be playing blind.

28

The Deal

Haase instructed his solicitor, Tony Nelson, the lawyer who had brokered the deal that freed him from the first 18-year sentence, to instruct his barrister, the eminent Lord Carlile of Berriew, to start talking to the prosecution.

Seemingly, a compromise was reached without delay. The essence of the deal hinged on Haase pleading guilty to lesser charges. In return for the much desired, cost-saving guilty plea, the prosecution would bless a deal to give Haase a short sentence. The jail term would be slashed because of mitigating circumstances. In short, Nelson believed that if everybody played the game Haase might 'cop' for no more than six years. Not exactly a walkover, but the best of a very bad situation. Haase was still convinced that if he had killed Grimes and 'gotten to' the Customs investigator he would have been looking at instant freedom.

Nelson pushed Haase to take the deal. In a letter to Lord Carlile, dated 5 December 2000, Nelson states:

> I have told our client [Haase] that you have very successfully persuaded the prosecution to agree to one substantive charge of selling firearms in relation to Indictment 1 on the following basis:

a) That there was no harm to the public.

b) That there was no terrorist link.

c) That this was an isolated and 'one off' event.

The letter goes on to reveal that 'if one takes into account all the mitigating features that you have agreed with the prosecution towards damage limitation', then Haase would expect a sentence of between six and seven years. Furthermore, Nelson stated that this could be reduced to between four and five years if Haase pleaded guilty to the charge, saving the state the cost of a lengthy trial.

Nelson continued:

> I heartily agree with you and did say, if you recall, spontaneously on the telephone that you could not have negotiated a more handsome basis of plea on behalf of your client, short of the prosecution withdrawing from the action.

The second charge relating to the heroin deal was also the subject of intense plea bargaining. Seemingly, Lord Carlile was successful in having the indictment reduced to a money-laundering charge, reasoning that Haase would admit to putting up the money to purchase the heroin but not conspiring to actually deal in the drugs. Furthermore, the amount of money said to be laundered was reduced from £10,000 to £3,500.

In the same letter Nelson stated to Carlile:

> With regard to the second indictment, again I feel that Leading Counsel [Lord Carlile] once more has excelled in that the laundering is limited to £3,500 and again the case law would show sentence of between eighteen months and three years for that level of laundering and again credit will be given and a one third reduction after a plea.

In short Haase was being offered four to five years for the guns and approximately 18 months for the money laundering; a total of about six years. John reasoned that with time off for good behaviour that meant four years, and taking into account the time spent on remand, he'd be out in 2003.

'Is right,' he thought. He was 51 years old at the time. It meant he would be out by the time he was 55 – just in time to start preparing for his retirement. Haase agreed to the deal and pleaded guilty before the trial kicked off. Haase was particularly satisfied with himself. He had pulled off another extraordinary legal coup.

There was one other small matter. Haase claims that a secret clause was inserted into the bargain late on in the negotiations. It stated that he would never be allowed to talk publicly about this deal or the deal he had done over the previous 18-year sentence.

From the bargain, Haase had got what he wanted. But it had not all been plain sailing. At a critical point in the negotiations Lord Carlile suddenly resigned, seemingly fed up with Haase's unrelenting and often contemptuous hard-line approach to the legal system. Haase claimed that they fell out after he instructed Carlile to summon the former Home Secretary Michael Howard as a witness. Haase claimed Carlile was horrified at the prospect and immediately resigned. But after a brief hiatus the problem was smoothed over and Lord Carlile came back on board.

With the six-year deal apparently set in stone, Haase had to sit back and await sentencing while his co-defendants were tried.

First up in January 2001 was Barry Oliver, the security guard who had allegedly been at the Dock offices on the day the guns were handed over. His co-defendants, Heath Grimes and Walter Kirkwood, like John Haase, had entered guilty pleas. The court heard how Customs monitored the deal using electronic surveillance. David Steer, QC, prosecuting, said:

The officers obtained authorisation to insert a secret audio transmitter inside the office. They also started to monitor recordings made by a video camera that was trained on the front door of the offices to record all comings and goings. The observations led to Kirkwood being tracked by armed police officers as he drove his gold Laguna along the East Lancashire Road on 7 September 1999. When it stopped at traffic lights at the junction of Moorgate Road, Kirkby, the police swooped and Kirkwood was arrested.

Mr Steer said that Haase, Oliver and Grimes were not arrested at that time and observations continued until 25 October 1999, when Haase was arrested at Lime Street station after stepping off a train from London. Two days later police searched the market office building at Stanley Dock belonging to Big Brother security. The search of Haase's office and the surrounding warehouse space lasted eight days.

At another hearing Liverpool Crown Court heard how Customs officers had placed Haase high on their list of targets soon after his surprise release from jail in 1996. Senior Customs officer Steve Rowton revealed how his unit had acquired an informant within Haase's organisation from early on. The statement clearly referred to Paul Grimes but did not name him for security reasons.

Rowton, who was a drugs and crime coordinator for the British Government based in Washington DC, had also worked on the Warren case. He told the court:

> Between June 1997 and June 2000 I was assistant chief investigator for the National Investigations Service of HM Customs and Excise in the North-west. I was told we had someone very close to Haase. He gave us access to Haase's office premises so that we could carry out the technical work that needed to be done.

On 21 February 2001 John Haase was sentenced. In court, he looked relaxed. He had an air of confidence about him, born from the certainty that the case was a done deal. He was getting a six. No back answers. He stood up to receive the sentence, eyeing Judge Holloway and his barrister Lord Carlile mischievously. After all, was not this the same Lord Carlile who had agreed to the reduced sentence with his solicitor Tony Nelson in a quiet out-of-court settlement? Not only had the deal been signed, sealed and delivered, but Haase had seen it in black and white.

As the judge went through the formalities, Haase smugly concluded that it was all a game and that he, the one and only John Haase, was a major fucking player. He had bought his seat at the table through hard graft and was now able to look the likes of Lord Carlile in the eye and deal with them on an equal footing. He had arrived. John Haase was up there with the lords, the MPs, the ministers, the Michael Howards of this world and he was in a position to tell them what to do.

Then the sentence was read out. John Haase was jailed for 13 years. For Haase it was total devastation. He was dumbstruck. He felt he had been well and truly turned over. When he recovered his composure, angry, Haase shouted from the dock: 'I didn't plead guilty for this.' But he was quickly sent down and taken to the cells below the court under escort. The sentence consisted of seven years for selling the guns and six years for money-laundering.

In sentencing him the judge made reference to the infamous decision which saw Haase freed 11 months into an 18-year sentence.

Judge Holloway said: 'Mr (Michael) Howard is not given to bouts of light-headedness or light-handedness. One is entitled to assume that the Home Office investigated the details before agreeing to accept the Royal Pardon.'

Superintendent Dave Smith of Merseyside Police commented: 'We realised Haase was starting up his operations and was beginning to be a threat to society again.'

Mixed fortunes awaited Haase's co-defendants. Heath Grimes, then 26, received four years and Walter Kirkwood, then 46, received three years. Barry Oliver snatched the only result – he walked after the jury returned a not guilty. Haase immediately vowed to appeal. His PR campaign kicked in at once. In a letter to the *Echo* from Strangeways Prison in Manchester, Haase cried: 'I am devastated. I feel like my life is over.' But the stunt backfired when the headline 'Whinger' was splashed across first editions. After pressure from Haase's camp, the critical tone of the piece was softened for later editions.

From his cell Haase protested to anyone who would listen that he had been stitched up. He argued that the deal he had agreed to, the six-year sentence, had been a false offering all along. He said that it had deliberately been made to coax him into entering an early guilty plea and stop him from going to trial. Haase said that the conspiracy had been hatched after he threatened to blow the lid on the secrets behind the deal which had freed him from prison in 1996. After he threatened to call former Tory Home Secretary Michael Howard as a witness, Haase claimed the deal mysteriously was put on the table. Haase believed the authorities would have been seriously embarrassed by a trial.

To back up his conspiracy theory Haase revealed the timetable of events in the run up to the deal, recorded in the diary of an associate.

Monday, 4 December 2000
Offered deal of 10 to 12 years. Refused.
Tuesday, 5 December 2000
Haase tells his counsel Lord Carlile that he intends to call Michael Howard as a witness.
Wednesday, 6 December 2000
Crisis meeting arranged between Haase and Nelson and Ackerley (Junior counsel) in Strangeways Prison.
Nelson sends letter to Carlile about six-year deal.
Lord Carlile resigns.

> *Thursday, 7 December 2000*
> Haase in pre-trial hearing.
> *Friday, 8 December 2000*
> Haase offered new six-year deal. Accepts. Carlile takes
> up case again.

Haase also faced stiff political opposition. In the Commons, Liverpool Walton MP Peter Kilfoyle called for an immediate inquiry into how Haase was released from the 18-year sentence in the first place, and accused the Home Office of naivety in their assessments of Haase.

Kilfoyle said: 'I just ask you to consider whether more damage was done by allowing Haase and Bennett back out onto the streets, or what could be usefully achieved by pretending that you could handle people like these.'

Two months later, on 17 April, the trial of Kenneth Darcy, the drugs mule who had been caught with one kilo of heroin at the same time Haase was arrested, was free to get under way. Darcy, then 42, was sentenced to six years in jail after pleading guilty to possession with intent to supply. David Hislop, defending, claimed Darcy believed he was simply there to watch Haase as he knew the man 'had enemies'.

29

The End

Mission accomplished. John Haase was behind bars and his crime empire in ruins. A top-level drug- and gun-running racket had been smashed beyond repair forever.

Today Haase is a high-risk Category A inmate who frequently spends time in solitary confinement. In early 2004 he was moved from HMP Full Sutton in Yorkshire to HMP Whitemoor in Cambridgeshire, on a disciplinary charge for being found in possession of a mobile phone. He refuses to work and is due for release in 2009. But aside from incarcerating target one, what else had been achieved by Paul Grimes' mission?

A hard core of dangerous criminals had been taken off the streets including Walter Kirkwood, Ken Darcy and Heath Grimes. Dozens of other dangerous criminals from all over Britain had also been caught and convicted using intelligence supplied or originated by Paul Grimes during his period inside Haase's organisation.

Merseyside Police were singled out for praise, their bravery and surveillance skills attracting particular commendation. Many of the suspects were monitored whilst doing business with Haase and his associates, unaware that they were being observed. Weeks, sometimes months, later police swooped upon the targets. Many never linked their misfortune to Haase. The total number of convictions which resulted from the operation is still a secret, known only to the senior Customs and police officers involved in the case.

What price had Paul Grimes paid? Today he is a penniless divorcee living in a shabby council house in a tenement block usually reserved for old-age pensioners. The flat was provided by the police as part of the witness–protection programme Paul is subscribed to. The logic is that old people's residences make good safe houses because security is often better than usual and OAPs are more vigilant. Last year it saved his life. An elderly neighbour raised the alarm after three masked men clad in dark clothes were spotted hiding in a shadowy stairwell underneath the entrance to Paul's flat. The men were lying in wait for Paul to return from work; they were assassins engaged to eliminate him. On another occasion, there was a failed attempt to burn him alive when his house was firebombed. On two occasions his attackers hid in big communal rubbish bins ready to ambush him. They were unsuccessful.

For security reasons Paul spends four nights a week sleeping at the homes of a select band of trusted friends. The life of a witness in hiding is often lonely and grim. The hundreds of thousands of pounds Paul had made from crime in his early days has long gone. Paul has never asked for nor received any financial rewards for his undercover work. His lifestyle is frugal and basic and Paul often struggles to make ends meet. His small, dingy living-room is decorated with pictures of Red Indians, his only interest now, and the floor is littered with pirated DVDs of the latest blockbuster movies. Pride of place on the mantelpiece above the fireplace is a Royal Navy passing-out photograph of his late son, Jason Grimes.

For security reasons, Paul's life is regimented by routine. Every day he is obliged to ring in to his local police station to confirm that he is still alive and to report suspicious activity. Although, these days, he admits the system has lapsed.

THE END

Paul lives in constant fear of his life. With the help of his police protectors a job was deliberately chosen for him that keeps him on the move over a wide geographical area. Paul works as a mobile security guard and is often sent to different locations in the Northwest, Yorkshire and the Midlands. He frequently covers more than 1,500 miles in a single week. None of his work colleagues know his true identity.

Personally, life as an undercover informant has cost Paul his marriage and a string of relationships. He has been disowned by his brother, Stephen Grimes, and most members of his family. Most painful of all, Paul believes that his son, Heath, who he sent to prison, will never forgive nor talk to him again.

Was it worth it?

PAUL: The truth is I have lost everything. There is no doubt about that. And still I may yet lose my life. I am a real-life dead man walking, no two ways. Every car that pulls up, every knock on the door, creates a ball of stress in my shoulders. Every day I wait for the gunmen to come.

Worse than that is the loss that I have suffered personally. My wife, my family and my son, Heath. Only God will be able to explain to me why the fight which I started to protect my sons from drugs has ended up costing me another son, Heath. That's fucked up. It's something I'll never be able to get my head round. But if you asked me to do it all again, would I? Too fucking right I would. Someone has got to stand up to these cunts.

End of story.

Epilogue: Life in Hiding

As it transpired, the publication of the first edition of *Powder Wars* by Mainstream in spring 2004 was far from being the end of the story. The book sent shockwaves through the legal system, with questions being raised in the Houses of Parliament, the Metropolitan Police launching a high-level investigation into John Haase's phoney gun plants and a wrongly convicted man getting released from prison on appeal after serving 11 years of a 24-year sentence. A second prisoner has also launched an appeal, spurred on by new evidence first aired on these pages. The book was also behind one of the first requests for secret files held by the government under the new Freedom of Information Act. In an unrelated but equally surprising move, Curtis Warren, the drug baron grassed up by Paul Grimes, finally admitted that he was behind the 1991 lead-ingot cocaine-smuggling operation, despite the fact he was cleared at the original Newcastle trial. The confession was a victory for Paul Grimes, who always knew he had got the right man. It validated his brave actions and the account given in this book, and alleviated the disappointment he felt after the trial collapsed.

In short, the courageous decision by Paul Grimes to go public in *Powder Wars* has been a success. Over the years, alarm bells had alerted many journalists and politicians to a raft of miscarriages of justice in connection with the cases that Grimes had worked on – particularly John Haase's pardon. But their probes had fizzled out, their questions had floundered for lack of corroboration, and the guilty men went on unchallenged. *Powder Wars* changed all that. Suddenly, eight years after the events uncovered in these pages and as a direct result of this book, there was a massive flurry of activity.

Powder Wars sparked massive coverage in the newspapers and on TV and radio. Paul Grimes may have become an unlikely celebrity but there was also a serious underlying issue. The main line taken by much of the media was simple: Paul Grimes did a great job in putting John Haase away for 13 years in 2001. But, at the end of the day, he shouldn't have had to. If Haase hadn't been released from prison by Royal Pardon in the first place, Customs and Excise would never have had to turn to their number one supergrass to help put him behind bars again. In effect, the newspapers and magazines were pointing out that Paul Grimes had put his life on the line to right a wrong that was down in the end to former Home Secretary Michael Howard. The big question then was: why had Howard released Haase in the first place?

As a direct result of material first revealed in this book, the *Sunday Mirror* launched a long-running investigation into the scandal of John Haase's 1996 Royal Pardon, headed by myself. In a major exclusive, the paper quickly unearthed explosive new evidence of a £3.5-million corruption scandal. Though there was no evidence that the then Tory leader knew of any of the bribes or that he was guilty of any wrongdoing himself, new names came to light of gangsters who had helped hand over large sums of money to mysterious individuals and plant guns in fabricated caches in a massive plot to win Haase's freedom.

The fresh leads were nothing short of dynamite. A huge conspiracy to pervert the course of justice had been exposed – with witnesses to back it up. None of it would have surfaced without the groundbreaking revelations in *Powder Wars*. Witnesses who had read the story had at last felt compelled to come forward.

The Observer newspaper followed the *Sunday Mirror* with more revelations about Michael Howard's involvement, including a full-page comment piece by columnist Nick Cohen based on *Powder Wars*, in tandem with an article in the political magazine *New Statesman*. The heat was being turned up. The story was rapidly becoming a political issue – and one that continued to dog Michael Howard throughout the May 2005 election campaign. The allegations refused to go away, raising serious questions about Michael Howard's judgement in the run-up to polling day and casting doubt in some voters' minds on his suitability to be Prime Minister. The scandal may have been a small contributory factor in his crushing electoral defeat and subsequent decision to stand down as Tory leader.

Media interest soared. BBC Radio 4 used Paul Grimes' case to expose the shortcomings of the witness-protection programme and Five's Donal MacIntyre made a top-rating one-hour TV documentary called *Supergrass* about Paul Grimes' day-to-day life.

On a positive note for Grimes, his enemies continue to suffer, affording him a modicum of justice. John Haase is still in jail, furious that Grimes' insider story is continuing to hinder his chances of appeal and early release. Tony Murray, the gangster who was shot by Haase's accomplice while Grimes stood guard, has been jailed once more for drug-trafficking. For as long as they remain behind bars, the risk of revenge is greatly reduced.

Curtis Warren, the drug baron whose downfall was instigated by Paul Grimes, has had extra years added to his jail sentence in Holland for killing a fellow prisoner. Four years were added after he was convicted of the manslaughter of a fellow inmate, whom he kicked to death. Warren is also facing more time if convicted of a fresh set of charges. He has been accused of hatching a plot behind bars to smuggle 500 kilos of cannabis to the UK. Things went from bad to worse when £3.5-million drug profits related to him were confiscated recently by a High Court judge, who granted an order for the cash to go to the new Assets Recovery Agency (ARA). Mr Justice Collins said Warren had now claimed to have masterminded the 1991 operation – though he was acquitted at a trial in England – and that the money was therefore his. The judge said Warren wanted to offer the money to the Dutch authorities as part of a lump sum from his assets to avoid a longer term in jail following his drugs conviction in Holland. Grimes was delighted to read that, without the payment, Warren will face even more years in jail.

But the book's most important legacy to date has been in keeping with its main aim – its contribution to the search for truth and justice in the murky world surrounding John Haase and his dealings with police and Customs and Excise that led to his largely unexplained Royal Pardon in 1996. What follows is an overview of the events in parliament triggered by *Powder Wars*.

Shortly before the book hit the shops, and armed with handful of new leads and fresh evidence, I went to visit Peter Kilfoyle MP at the Houses of Parliament. Kilfoyle, a tireless campaigner for justice respected on both sides of the house, had been investigating the validity of Haase's Royal Pardon for eight years. His motive was simple: for years, Haase had terrorised his Walton constituency in Liverpool. Haase was, in fact, one of his constituents; he had lived in the Clubmoor district in a house at 1a Maiden Vale at the height of his criminal career. He had flooded the area with heroin, spreading death and misery on the district's run-down estates and fuelling a massive increase in crime. More specifically, the 50 kilos of heroin that Haase had been caught with in 1993, resulting in the 18-year sentence, had been discovered in the heart of Kilfoyle's ward, at a terraced house on Dane Street in the shadow of Everton FC's Goodison Park stadium. Kilfoyle was also chairman of a local anti-drugs group set up by mothers from the area. In short, Kilfoyle wanted answers. How could he explain to these mothers that the man responsible for getting their sons and daughters addicted to heroin had been pardoned? And even worse: how could he explain that the pardon was based on fabricated evidence? Kilfoyle had always suspected wrongdoing after Howard had effectively gagged him from going on TV to condemn the pardon shortly after Haase's release in 1996. Over a cup of tea in the Commons canteen, Kilfoyle and I agreed to pool our evidence in a bid to reinvigorate the quest for justice and to expose the truth for all.

The intrigue began shortly before *Powder Wars* hit the bookstands. Haase had been informed by a member of his gang of the book's impending release. I had offered Haase a right to reply to the allegations that were being made. In a shock move, Haase then invited me and Kilfoyle to visit him in prison, at HMP Full Sutton near York, to discuss the story. A spokesman for Haase had told us that his boss was maybe willing to spill the beans on the whole sordid affair in exchange for freedom – from his current 13-year jail sentence and from any prosecutions that may result in the future from admitting to crimes underlying his Royal Pardon. In essence, the cheeky Scouser was trying to cut a deal similar to the one that was under investigation – the bargain he had struck with Customs and the Home Office in 1996. Of course, Kilfoyle could not give any guarantees – he had neither the authority nor the inclination to do so – but he agreed at first instance to listen to what Haase had to say.

Key to the proceedings was Kilfoyle's power as a politician. I had already tried to get a visiting order from the Home Office in order to gain entry to see Haase, but, as he was a high-risk Category A prisoner, it was very difficult. Despite having Haase's permission, my formal application to the Home Office involved a police interview at my home to establish my identity and motive, as well as undergoing a strict vetting procedure. The outcome was that I was refused entry because I was a journalist – but as an MP it was no problem for Kilfoyle to get the passes to visit one of his constituents.

At Full Sutton, the crucial meeting nearly collapsed after Haase refused to talk in a private room set aside for legal briefings – he feared bugging. He abused prison officers and returned to his cell in an angry state of mind. Both Kilfoyle and I were disappointed. We had travelled a long way with high hopes of solving a mystery once and for all. After 30 minutes of coaxing and some helpful intervention from a member of staff, Haase agreed to meet us at a public table in the corner of the visiting room.

Haase was not the coarse, violent thug that Kilfoyle and I had expected. He was softly spoken, polite and businesslike. His hair was greying and he was dressed in a prison-issue denim-blue shirt and tracksuit bottoms. Haase started off by speaking about mundane details. But suddenly, when he thought that no one was watching, he whispered and signalled with his hands that he had important evidence about his Royal Pardon that he claimed amounted to corruption. It was a bizarre method of relaying such information, but he got his point across. The allegation was nothing short of mind-blowing – yet horrifyingly sinister.

In February 2004, we went to visit Haase at Whitemoor Prison in a place called March, near Cambridge, along with a lawyer, Mathew Thomas, and a legal secretary, Kim Stimpson. Haase's temporary transfer to Whitemoor from Full Sutton prison would soon become permanent. The legal team was on board to take down Haase's confession in line with the law with a view to preparing a sworn affidavit. The astonishing statement was taken down over two tape-recorded sessions in the course of a day. It backed up many of the revelations in *Powder Wars*. Haase confirmed that he had planted guns in phoney caches in order to pervert the course of justice and win a Royal Pardon based on fabricated evidence. He also claimed that money had changed hands to secure his freedom. Cash for pardons – what a story! Unfortunately, neither Kilfoyle nor I could make it public because we were bound by confidentiality to Haase to keep the scandal a secret – one of the conditions of the meeting.

Armed with Haase's startling new allegations, Kilfoyle lobbied then Home Secretary David Blunkett to launch an official investigation. He met with Blunkett in person and spoke to him at his constituency home in Sheffield on a weekend. Kilfoyle was keen to speak to Blunkett direct, for reasons of confidentiality and so that the process could be speeded up

Just one month after *Powder Wars* was published, on 21 May 2004, Kilfoyle made the campaign for an official inquiry into the Royal Pardon public by calling for an adjournment debate in the Houses of Parliament (by which an MP can bring up a matter of his or her choosing before the appropriate government minister). Drawing on revelations from this book, he made a sensational speech highlighting the scandal of the phoney gun plants and putting the allegations of cash bribery and corruption on the record for the first time. Frustratingly, he did not use Haase's statement as a source – his hands were tied by confidentiality – but he was able to refer to other allegations made by third parties. For the first time in the house, Kilfoyle named Michael Howard's drug-dealing cousin Simon Bakerman in connection with the Royal Pardon, allegedly linking him to 'large sums of money' changing hands. Another MP stood up and described the circumstances surrounding the pardon as 'scandalous'. Kilfoyle claimed in parliament that not only were the arms dumps bogus, but he had heard rumours that large amounts of money exchanged hands before Haase and Bennett were released, and that Mr Howard's cousin has been repeatedly mentioned in connection with the men and the money. Kilfoyle described the drug-dealers' release as 'strange' and a 'sordid saga' and demanded a ministerial inquiry. He asked, 'What made their case so special as to merit release? The repeated allegation . . . is that in some way, large sums of money were involved arranging these things.'

The MP stated that the money for the alleged bribes and gun plants came from a war chest funded by the sale of heroin. Kilfoyle claimed that up to 50 kilos of heroin with a street value of £18 million had slipped through the Customs net at the time of Haase's and Bennett's arrests. He said the heroin was later sold by gangsters in Haase's gang, who had not been arrested and were living freely in Liverpool, to raise money to fund their release. Kilfoyle added, 'They had a lot of money at their disposal, if that was the case, to . . . buy influence.' He went on: 'One name that is always mentioned in this context is Simon Bakerman.' Kilfoyle said that some official should have smelt a rat and prevented the 'travesty of justice': 'There can only be two conclusions. The first is that Customs and Excise, the Prison Service, police and judiciary and Home Office were all duped by Haase and Bennett.

'The alternative is that there was, at some stage, truth in the allegations that bribery played its part in securing the realease of Haase and Bennett. I do not want to believe it.

'Yet I also find it difficult to believe that no one within the system smelt a rat.'

He stressed that he had no evidence himself of bribery, but urged Home Office minister Paul Groggins to investigate the case. That day, Bakerman, 41, whose mother, Freda, is Howard's mother's cousin, denied that he was involved in the release of the prisoners. But the former millionaire financier said that he had gone to the police that week fearing for his life. Bakerman said, 'If someone tries to take me out, then it is so that I can't open my mouth to give the truth.'

The *Sunday Mirror* was the only national newspaper to pick up on the debate but in an article two days later on the following Sunday they were able to get the ball rolling in the media. Paul Goggins MP, parliamentary undersecretary of state at the Home Office, immediately responded to Kilfoyle's adjournment debate by saying that if there was enough new evidence, he would consider opening a new inquiry of some sort. It was a small step in the right direction – unprecedented in this case.

A few days later, on 28 May 2004, Kilfoyle wrote to Home Secretary Blunkett again to ask for immunity from prosecution for witnesses that may be prepared to come forward to give evidence about bribery and corruption. Events began to move at breakneck speed. Less than a month later, on 20 June, The Observer's tough columnist Nick Cohen piled on the pressure in a devastating comment piece. He revealed that Howard's press spokesman had tried to bury the story.

The article began:

> A few weeks ago, Michael Howard held a press conference as he toured the north-west. His spokesman told the journalists that the leader of the opposition would be happy to answer questions on all subjects except one, an adjournment debate in the House of Commons instigated by Peter Kilfoyle, the Labour MP for Liverpool Walton, on Friday, 21 May.
>
> It seemed an eccentric prohibition. The media are barely interested in parliament. It's a minor miracle if they cover Prime Minister's Questions, let alone a debate on a Friday afternoon, when most MPs have gone back to their constituencies. As it was, there was no need for Howard's spin-doctors to fret. With the exception of the *Sunday Mirror*, no one mentioned the debate, which was a pity because Kilfoyle was tackling one of the great, unexplained crime scandals of the 1990s.

Cohen criticised his fellow journalists for ignoring the story for so long:

> The reasons for their boredom are beyond me. The established facts about what happened in Liverpool are shocking enough. When it dealt with Haase, the satirically named criminal justice system slipped from its usual state of crisis into chaos. First, the Customs officers investigating his crimes, then the trial judge

and then the Home Secretary were conned by a master criminal. In a populist age, that can be enough to destroy a politician.

In the 1988 US presidential election, George Bush Senior devastated the campaign of Michael Dukakis, the Democratic candidate, by accusing him of allowing a murderer named Willie Horton to leave prison and carry out a brutal rape while he was governor of Massachusetts. Like Howard, the luckless Dukakis was following the advice of officials. It didn't do him any good because a politician who seeks the highest office in the land is meant to have the wit to exercise his or her own intelligence by asking pertinent questions.

Neither Howard nor anyone else responsible for dealing with Haase showed the smallest sign of possessing an enquiring mind.

Cohen argued that Haase should never have been released because he was too dangerous. In making his case, he drew on *Powder Wars*:

> Haase was an exceptionally dangerous criminal. He was jailed in the 1970s for his part in violent armed robberies and decided on release that there were better business opportunities in the heroin market. As the investigative journalist Graham Johnson describes it in his new book *Powder Wars*, Haase rose to become Britain's biggest heroin importer. He controlled the distribution at the end of what is known as the 'southern route', which runs from Afghanistan to Britain via Turkey and the Balkans. According to Johnson, Customs officers put Haase's gang under surveillance and 'looked on in amazement as bundles of cash the size of bricks were handed over' in a Liverpool pub.

Ominously, he ended with the prediction: 'The story may go away, but don't be surprised if you hear more about it in the run-up to the election.'

Cohen was right. About one month later, on 27 June, the *Sunday Mirror* unearthed three new witnesses based on evidence from *Powder Wars*. Three. Three gangsters told how they helped Haase walk free from jail by planting guns and Semtex in fake caches. They revealed how, on Haase's instructions from behind bars, they planted huge caches of guns and explosives in houses and cars across Merseyside.

Convicted heroin dealer Ken Darcy said, 'I got paid five grand for just two kilos of Semtex. It was planted in a flat in Liverpool and later found by Customs or police.' On another occasion, Haase's gang diluted three kilos of heroin to make six so that it would make a better find for police and Customs. Darcy added, 'When the police found it, along with loads of E tablets, plus loads of guns, it gave them better credit.' But the scheme nearly went awry after another cache was accidentally discovered by police before Haase could inform them. Darcy said, 'Fifty thousand pounds' worth of guns were put in a safe house in South Liverpool. But the alarm went off on the house and the police were called. The lads got away but the police found the guns before Haase could tell them where they were and get the credit for it.' Darcy claimed that Customs officers were meanwhile becoming increasingly suspicious that no one was ever arrested in connection with Haase's tip-offs, so Haase paid one of Darcy's associates £5,000 to get caught in possession of a gun. But the man was eventually freed on a technicality.

Another gangster, Paul Ferris, also admitted helping to supply £50,000 worth of weapons to Haase. He said, 'They were planted in a car in Holyhead ferry terminal in North Wales and a lock-up in Liverpool, and Haase said they were IRA. Customs never found out the truth.'

Suleyman Ergun, 36, was a member of the gang who supplied Haase with the heroin. He was convicted of trafficking and was arrested at the same time. He said, 'I was told three times about the gun planting before, during and after it happened. The first time, Bennett told me while we were in prison that they were going to buy up guns from all over Britain and plant them in Liverpool to make Customs think that they were informants. He told me he'd help get me free using phoney plants.'

Following the *Sunday Mirror* article, Kilfoyle urged Home Secretary David Blunkett to act. A week later, on 5 July 2004, Home Office minister Paul Goggins responded. A bombshell dropped – he instigated a police inquiry. In a letter to Peter Kilfoyle, Goggins said, 'If you have evidence that you believe would establish a conspiracy to pervert the course of justice, then it should be brought to the attention of the police.'

The only question now was who would carry it out: Merseyside Police, the Met in London or some other body. Kilfoyle was unhappy that Goggins had suggested Merseyside Police; he stated that it was one of the 'organisations that were compromised' by Haase's and Bennett's release, and would therefore be an inappropriate choice. He said that a force investigating itself would open 'a can of worms'. On 31 August 2004, Goggins put the matter in the hands of the chief inspector of constabulary, who would in turn appoint a Metropolitan Police superintendent to undertake the investigation, if warranted. The chief inspector of constabulary, Sir Keith Povey, was one of the country's top policemen, based at the Home Office's HQ in London. It was his job to decide whether there was enough evidence to warrant a full-blown police investigation into the scandal. Over the next few weeks, Sir Keith Povey sifted through the prima facie material.

On 10 October, the *Sunday Mirror* ran the story that the Home Office inquiry was in full swing, and that witnesses had come stating that they had been involved in bribe payments.

The article stated:

The Home Office has launched a new top-level probe into a £3.5-million bribery scandal involving Tory leader Michael Howard.

The investigation into a Royal Pardon granted by Howard when he was Home Secretary to free two of Britain's biggest drug barons is considered so important it is being led by Britain's top anti-sleaze cop.

News of the inquiry, to be headed by chief inspector of constabulary Sir Keith Povey, is likely to be a huge embarrassment to Mr Howard – who at last week's Tory conference delivered a hardline attack on soft punishment for offenders.

The *Sunday Mirror* has obtained vital evidence alleged to show how drug-traffickers John Haase and Paul Bennett used agents to deliver millions of pounds in bribes to high-level officials and plant guns for Customs to find, to dupe them, the trial judge and Howard into arranging the pardon.

Six months later – just ten months into eighteen-year sentences for heroin trafficking – the pair sensationally walked free from jail.

The 1996 Royal Prerogatives were authorised personally by Mr Howard as Home Secretary.

The decision to free two big-time drug barons after serving such a short period of their sentence – unheard of in British legal history – sent shockwaves through the judicial system.

Mr Howard's cousin, a convicted drug-dealer and fraudster called Simon Bakerman, will be investigated by police over his alleged role in the scandal. His name repeatedly crops up in connection with the claims that Haase and Bennett bribed officials to secure their freedom.

Today for the first time the *Sunday Mirror* can reveal the amount of the bribes – and that they were allegedly paid on four occasions to senior officials.

EPILOGUE: LIFE IN HIDING   275

£1 MILLION was taken by a drug-money courier called John 'Paddy' Scanlon from Haase's main lieutenant in Liverpool to a Turkish café in Paddington, West London.

A second bribe of £920,000 was handed over at room 133 of the former Forte Crest Regent's Park Hotel in North London.

A bribe of just under £1 MILLION was handed over at another location in the south-east.

A fourth, smaller, bribe was handed over in the north of England.

Scanlon told our investigators how he had received a call from a man codenamed 'The Bank Manager' while the drug barons were on remand awaiting trial. He used a kid called 'The Bank Clerk' to move money.

'I got a call to pick up the dough from a shop in Utting Avenue, Liverpool,' said Scanlon. 'The person in the shop handed over the bag and said, "Here's the bangers." [Slang for money.] I was told it was a million. I got a phone call the morning of the drop telling me I had to be at the café in London by teatime. The drop-off was a café in West London. The man I handed it to was a fella I'd met there before. I just passed it to him and said "here you are". I was paid £2,000 for it.

'I've always thought since, that for what I done for them, I was going to get a pull.' (Be arrested.)

The second bribe, of about £920,000, was taken to a London hotel from a flat in Liverpool owned by Haase.

The drop was planned with military precision by a female associate of Haase and his main lieutenant – known as 'The Supervisor' – who told our investigators the cash was split into four loads of £250,000. He took one bag and three couriers took the rest. All four were to pay themselves £20,000 from the cash.

In winter of 1995–6, each courier was told to go to

the Forte Crest Regent's Park Hotel (now a Holiday Inn) at different times and take the bag to room 133.

The Supervisor said, 'The detailed instructions were given to me by a female who was visiting Haase frequently in prison. The hotel room opposite was being watched by Haase's men and they were also outside the main entrance. There was a tray of food left outside the room.

'Just before each delivery, a keycard was left under a cup on the tray. I went in, left the money and then left.

'I was told the people we would be paying the bribe to would come and collect it in the same fashion, when all drops had been done. I was told that Bakerman was the link.'

The third bribe of a similar amount of money was arranged in much the same way. A fourth bribe of much less than £1 million was paid to two individuals.

Further corroboration of the bribe allegations has come from one of Haase's partners in crime. Suleyman Ergun has told *Sunday Mirror* investigators that £1 million of his money was used to fund the bribes. Ergun's gang – called the Turkish Connection – supplied Haase with so much heroin that at one time they single-handedly caused the price to drop from £25,000 a kilo to £22,000. They were all jailed in a series of trials in 1995.

In prison, Ergun later demanded £1 million that he claimed was still owed to him by Haase and Bennett for 50 kilos of heroin. He was told the money was going to be used to get them all out.

Ergun explained, 'Bennett said the money was getting switched to big people that would help us all get out. Bennett was so happy he was clapping about it. So I put the debt on hold.'

The bribes, it is claimed, were just part of a huge web

of deceit orchestrated by Haase and Bennett to win their freedom. The first move came immediately after their arrest for possessing 50 kilos of heroin in 1993.

The duo struck a deal with Customs officers to turn supergrasses. In return for a lesser sentence, they agreed to inform on organised criminals and IRA terrorists. Between October 1993 and June 1995, they led police to 26 gun and drug caches containing 150 firearms and explosives. The haul included 80 shotguns, AK-47 assault weapons, Armalite rifles, Thompson sub-machine guns, Uzis and 1,500 rounds of ammunition – which they claimed were destined for the IRA.

But it was all a scam. No arrests were ever made in connection with the caches because Haase and Bennett arranged to have the guns planted there while remanded in custody charged with heroin trafficking. They organised the operation from their cells using 19 stolen mobile phones . . . and their profits from drug-dealing. They even smuggled a gun into Strangeways Prison, Manchester, so they could say they had prevented a potential hostage situation. The weapon, hidden in a toaster, was wrongly blamed on another prisoner, Thomas Bourke.

It is alleged they had to pay the bribes to 'buy off' suspicions about the phoney arms caches.

A report to trial judge David Lynch praised Haase and Bennett for, 'The prevention of a possible hostage situation. A prisoner convicted of two double murders was planning to escape by use of a gun. A loaded gun was recovered and the prison officer responsible for smuggling the weapon into the prison was identified.'

Though he sentenced each of the pair to 18 years in jail in August 1995, Judge Lynch sent a letter and the report praising them to the then Home Secretary Michael Howard – who granted the Royal Pardons in

278

June 1996. A month later, they were released after serving just 10 months. The *Sunday Mirror* investigation has revealed that Howard's official reason for granting pardons was based almost entirely on their bogus supergrass claims.

One area of study for the new probe is the exact role of Mr Howard's cousin. Bakerman, originally a market trader, picked up his first conviction for deception in 1985. After problems with drink and gambling, he joined the Israeli Army as a tank gunner and saw combat in the Lebanon.

He returned to London and made a fortune as a financier and jewellery dealer. But he was jailed for three years for his role in a £20 million amphetamine gang.

The new probe into events leading up to the granting of the Royal Pardons follows a lengthy investigation by the *Sunday Mirror* and Liverpool Walton MP Peter Kilfoyle. In a letter to Mr Kilfoyle, Home Office undersecretary of state Paul Goggins confirmed that Sir Keith and his chief of staff chief superintendent Ian Quinton will head the team studying the claims in order to decide whether to hand the file over to the police.

He said, 'The decision whether to investigate will, of course, depend upon the seriousness and credibility of the allegations.'

Bakerman has always denied any involvement but he says his life is under threat.

A spokesman for the Tory leader said, 'Michael Howard acted entirely in line with procedure.'

For the first time, investigators tracked the source of the money for the bribes.

A breakout in the article stated:

ON TRAIL OF £1m IN HEROIN

Haase and Bennett raised the cash for the bribes by selling a stash of heroin that slipped through the Customs and Excise net when they were arrested.

Using official Customs and Excise surveillance logs, we tracked the missing heroin haul, which weighed 25–30 kilograms.

1. 17 May–2 June 1993: Haase buys heroin in Turkey.

2. 8–13 July: Heroin arrives in UK on Calais–Dover ferry. Stored in Purchase Street, Camden Town, London.

3. 14 July: Turkish Connection meets Bennett in Upper Street, Islington.

4. 16 July: Turkish Connection brings heroin to Backhouse Pub in Prescott Road, Liverpool.

5. 21 July: Gloves and bags to cut up heroin collected from Cherry Lane, Liverpool. Heroin picked up by Eddie Croker from Chaser Pub, Liverpool. Heroin taken to 26 Dane Street in heavy canvas bag to be cut.

6. Shortly afterwards, heroin taken to 31 Evesham Road in blue Honda Previa.

7. Customs officers lose car in traffic after it was driven away by Haase's right-hand man. Later sold for over £1 million in cash. Haase arrested days later.

The pressure was piling on the authorities to move the inquiry out of the Home Office into the hands of a proper police force. A week after the bombshell *Sunday Mirror* article, Kilfoyle and Johnson met staff officer Ian Quinton at the Home Office to press for a police inquiry. Information, including taped transcript evidential material, was handed over on 5 November.

On 19 January 2005, Kilfoyle received the news that he had been waiting for – written confirmation that the Metropolitan Police had taken over the inquiry. The chief inspector of constabulary had concluded that there was enough evidence to proceed and the Metropolitan Police were given the job of probing the case further. Led by one of the most senior officers in Scotland Yard, Assistant Commissioner Tarique Ghaffur, the investigation aimed to prove that the fake gun caches amounted to a massive perversion of the course of justice.

But shortly afterwards, the Conservatives accused Labour of dirty tricks by digging into the scandal. An article in the *Evening Standard* was headlined 'Labour's dirty tricks exposed'. It accused Labour of 'using the new Freedom of Information Act to mount a pre-election campaign against Michael Howard'.

It went on:

> An internal party document shows Labour is trawling Whitehall records to try to discredit the Tory leader.
>
> The 'dirt digging' operation is attempting to revive old claims that the opposition leader, when he was Home Secretary, might have helped a relative who was a drug-dealer.
>
> The confidential document shows Labour is organising a campaign in which gay activists, MPs and the anti-gun lobby are mobilised to request private papers relating to Mr Howard's time in government.
>
> Former Labour minister Peter Kilfoyle is being asked to demand the release of files about a relative of Mr Howard who was accused of drug offences.
>
> Questions have been submitted on whether Mr Howard abused his position to fast-track a replacement passport for journalist Petronella Wyatt, an allegation repeatedly denied by him.
>
> A Tory source said, 'It is obvious Labour is launching a very spiteful smear campaign. Tony Blair has gone back to his old ways of spin and personal abuse.
>
> 'Instead of focusing on issues that really matter, he appears determined to fight this election with dirty tricks.'
>
> A Labour source said, 'These are not the only questions we will be asking about Michael Howard. His

record as a minister of a government which gave us the poll tax and 15 per cent interest rates is going to be absolutely central to Labour's campaign.'

Election smear or not, Howard was concerned that his personal papers might be released. In an extraordinary move, he went into the Home Office himself to find out exactly what was in them.

An article in *The Observer*, again citing *Powder Wars* as a source, stated:

To the older generation of mandarins, the man sifting through ministerial papers with studious concentration was a familiar sight. As Michael Howard sat in a room at the Home Office in Queen Anne's Gate, London, surrounded by official correspondence last week, it must have seemed like old times. Almost.

Eight years on from the last time he discussed ministerial business, civil servants must have wondered why the Tory leader was taking vital time out from the election campaign to wade through documents from his time in office. In fact, Howard knows that what he was reading will have a vital effect on his political future.

The timing of the investigation could not be worse for Howard, but his aides will find it difficult to explain away the Met's decision as a Downing Street plot. Allegations in a dossier compiled over eight years by Kilfoyle, the former defence minister who is no friend to New Labour, were passed first to HM chief inspector of constabulary Sir Keith Povey last year. After consultation with Bernard Hogan-Howe, the chief constable of Merseyside, in early December 2004, the case was transferred to the Met because of the sensitivity of the case to the Liverpool force.

Scotland Yard has confirmed that Ghaffur, who has

responsibility for the Met's crack specialist crime directorate, will lead any investigation. The terms of the inquiry, as outlined by Povey, could not be more embarrassing for Howard as the general election campaign begins because they refer directly to his decision to grant the Royal Pardon.

Kilfoyle, whose eight-year campaign has finally led to a police investigation, said, 'It is important for the public to understand the consequences of the decision to release these gangsters, when the man who made it is asking them to vote him into the highest political office. It showed gross incompetence. I welcome the police investigation into this matter, but it will be difficult for the people of Liverpool to forgive Michael Howard or his disastrous decision that led to the city being further swamped with drugs and guns.'

A spokesman for Howard confirmed that he had returned to the Home Office last week: 'He did go and consult documents and has done on a number of occasions in the past to refresh his memory.'

He said that Howard had wanted to show he was an 'open and honest politician' and for this reason had authorised the disclosures.

Commenting on the police inquiry, he said: 'This is a matter for the Metropolitan Police. But all the procedures were followed. He has nothing to hide and the papers will show that.'

In a separate article, Nick Cohen made another blistering attack on the media for under-reporting the scandal, and he followed it up with an attack in the *New Statesman*. Quoting from *Powder Wars*, he said that if this had happened in America, Haase and Bennett would be household names.

A week later, the *Daily Record* in Scotland joined in with a two-page article:

Michael Howard's political leadership is under threat from a multi-millionaire drug baron contact of former Scots gangland enforcer Paul Ferris. The Tory leader faces new questions over why he freed John Haase – a vicious gangster who poured drugs and guns onto the streets of Scotland as well as his native Liverpool.

A fresh inquiry has been launched into the scandal which saw Haase and his nephew Paul Bennett serve just ten months of an eighteen-year sentence.

Today, the *Daily Record* can shed fresh light on the murky deals that led to the release of Haase – and tell for the first time of how Ferris played a major role as a fixer.

Ferris spent time in Manchester after being found not guilty of the murder of gangster Arthur Thompson's son, Fatboy, in 1992.

There, he hooked up with exiled Glasgow gangster Rab Carruthers, then a powerful criminal in the north-west of England.

In 1993, while Haase was in jail waiting for his trial on drug-trafficking, he sent a delegation to see Ferris and Carruthers.

Ferris said, 'These guys said Haase and Bennett had been offered a deal. If they gave information on the whereabouts of illegal arms, they would receive a lighter sentence for the drugs.

'They wanted to know if they should go ahead with this deal. Could they trust the cops?

'Tam McGraw, The Licensee, had been playing this game in Glasgow for years. I knew for a fact the cops simply forgot about one guy's serious RTA [Road Traffic Act] offences. Another bloke wanted on a murder charge was allowed home from exile in Spain for one last free Christmas with his family before being lifted.

'Both deals were secured by trading arms.

'I told Haase's men that McGraw's trick was to buy these arms from dealers. These were guns that never had been, or would ever be, used in crime.

'It was a kind of double con but nobody cared. The dealers got paid, the accused got a deal and the cops looked good. Everyone won.

'During one gun amnesty, a senior Strathclyde police officer was on TV proudly presenting all the arms they had taken off the street.

'Pride of place was a Kalashnikov. When have you heard of a Kalashnikov being used in Scotland? Apart from that guy Noel Ruddle taking a maddie and shooting folk a few years ago.

'That gun and a stack of others had simply been traded and the players kept their shooters.'

A well-known Liverpool gangster said of that time, 'Haase had just had the luckiest of breaks and escaped going to jail till he was an OAP. You'd think he would have kept a low profile.

'Yet the day after he got out of the nick, he was peddling smack openly. It was as if he thought he was immune to prosecution, licensed to commit crime.

'When the cops didn't lift him, I started to believe his boasts that he had bribed a lot of powerful people.'

Local MP Peter Kilfoyle, in whose Liverpool Walton constituency the drugs had been found, was outraged by Haase's and Bennett's release and immediately started asking questions.

The night before he was due to raise the matter in the House of Commons for the first time, he received a phone call from Howard.

Kilfoyle said, 'Howard asked me not to raise the issue because lives were at stake. We might have been in opposition but he was the Home Secretary. Thinking he meant our police or Customs officers were at risk,

I withdrew the question. Now I'm wondering if it was
Haase and Bennett he meant were at risk.'

The police investigation is still ongoing, but sources close to the
probe insist that charges against the main alleged conspirators are
likely to follow. A file has been shown to the Crown Prosecution
Service. Their lawyers are reportedly satisfied that the
investigation is on course and going well. On 26 June 2005, two
officers from the Met's Specialist Crime Unit came to see me to
discuss the evidence first aired in this book and how it might be
used to prosecute Haase. On Monday, 25 July, they applied for a
court order to gain possession of the statement given by John
Haase over a year earlier. It is expected that they will get more
court orders to get all the remaining taped evidence from me
and the *Sunday Mirror*.

Powder Wars has also helped in the pursuit of justice in two
other important cases, involving Joseph Kassar and Thomas
Bourke. The men had been jailed in unrelated cases. Evidence
from the book lead to the immediate release of prisoner Joseph
Kassar after 11 years behind bars. Kassar, now 54, was the only
man convicted of drug-smuggling following the 1993 Curtis
Warren cocaine trial. During that trial, Paul Grimes gave
evidence for the prosecution, but Customs and Excise never
revealed that he was a secret informant on the case – an alleged
serious breach of procedure.

Eleven years later, Paul finally let the secret out in *Powder Wars*
and Kassar, who was halfway through a 24-year prison sentence,
used it as a basis for an appeal against his conviction. It worked!
A source on Kassar's legal team said, 'We had been preparing
Kassar's appeal for a long time. But by a miracle, just before the
case was heard, *Powder Wars* was published. The evidence in there,
for us, was sensational. It said that Paul Grimes had been the
secret informant on Kassar's original case but this had not been
disclosed to the court at the trial in Newcastle.

'We rushed into court with a copy of the book. The Customs

and Excise threw the towel in straight away. They didn't even bother trying to contest the appeal. Kassar was released immediately.'

In a shock stand-down, the Crown Prosecution did not oppose the appeal after they conceded the failure to disclose crucial information at the trial meant Kassar's conviction was unsafe. The Appeal Court did not give full details for its decision and said it might not be able to because of the sensitivity of some of the information. Kassar's victorious Manchester-based solicitor, Keith Dyson, later praised *Powder Wars* for helping to right a miscarriage of justice.

The case of former Manchester garage owner Thomas Bourke is totally unconnected but his goal is the same – freedom. Bourke was jailed for life in December 1994 for the double murder of two MOT inspectors who had visited his business. His family – including his heroic sister Josephine Holt – have always claimed his innocence based on two points: mistaken identity and an unfair trial. *Powder Wars* may be able to help on the second point. Bourke's appeal is being prepared by his lawyers at the time of going to press.

As for Paul Grimes, life goes on as usual. Unfortunately, there is no escape for him, no freedom from the confines of a life in hiding. There will never be a way out from the personal prison he made for himself on the day he signed up for the witness protection programme. The ever-present fear of assassination is still there – in fact, since going public and raising his profile, the risks have increased. Before *Powder Wars* came out, Paul's employers – a security firm who supply guards to shops – did not know about his secret past as a gangster or a supergrass. They were even more alarmed to find out that there was a £100,000 contract on his head – and that there had been at least six attempts on his life to date. The company became worried that assassins might attempt to gun down Paul when he was at his most vulnerable: while he was at work standing in a shop surrounded by staff and members of the public. Bosses were concerned that shoppers were at risk of being shot in the crossfire during an attempt to kill him. He was summoned down to the company HQ in Croydon, South London, and sacked for being a security risk. Paul considered his sacking to be a great injustice and symptomatic of a society where criminals seem to have more rights than ordinary working people. He felt he was being punished for taking a stand against the drug-dealers.

But, on the positive side, Paul Grimes has had thousands of messages of support from people all over the country impressed by what he did after reading about it in *Powder Wars*. As the book got more and more publicity, the police feared that he would be recognised in the street. In response, they offered him the chance to move from his current safehouse in an old peoples' home to a secure flat in Hampstead, North London. Bravely, Paul refused, arguing that a move would be an act of fear and that he didn't want to hand that final victory to the gangsters he had helped put away. 'If I die, I die. If I live, I live. I don't really care. But I'm not giving in to any of them.'